MODERNIST RADICALISM AND ITS AFTERMATH

At the end of the nineteenth century social theories such as Marxism and Durkheimian sociology could lay claim to a critical role in public affairs. They promised a unique knowledge of modern society which would fulfil the radical potential of modernity. A century later these claims are no longer credible and the prospects for radical social theory are uncertain. *Modernist Radicalism and its Aftermath* investigates the ways in which Marx, Durkheim, Althusser and Habermas were all caught up in a paradoxical and fatal quest for foundational guarantees of knowledge.

Stephen Crook proposes a framework for the analysis of foundationalism in social theory and suggests a way forward from the impasse of postmodernism. He identifies important themes in the work of Simmel, Weber and Adorno, and in some postmodernist theory, but points out that these are at constant risk of regression into metaphysics or nihilism. The book concludes with a plea for an alternative 'post foundational' radicalism which can maintain the accountability of enquiry while facing up to the contingency of value.

Modernist Radicalism and its Aftermath is both an interpretation of classical social theory and an important contribution to contemporary debates on modernity and postmodernity. It will be of special interest to students of sociology, philosophy and other disciplines concerned with social theory.

Stephen Crook is Lecturer in Sociology at the University of Tasmania, Australia.

MODERNIST RADICALISM AND ITS AFTERMATH

Foundationalism and anti-foundationalism in radical social theory

Stephen Crook

London and New York

First published in 1991
by Routledge
11 New Fetter Lane, London EC4P 4EE

Simultaneously published in the USA and Canada
by Routledge
a division of Routledge, Chapman and Hall, Inc.
29 West 35th Street, New York, NY 10001
© 1991 Stephen Crook
Laserprinted from Author's disks by Jean Cussons
Printed and bound in Great Britain by
Biddles Ltd, Guildford and King's Lynn

British Library Cataloguing in Publication Data
Crook, Stephen, 1950–
Modernist radicalism and its aftermath: foundationalism and
anti-foundationalism in radical social theory.
1. Radicalism, History. I. Title. 320.9

Library of Congress Cataloging in Publication Data
Crook, Stephen, 1950–
Modernist radicalism and its aftermath: foundationalism and
anti-foundationalism in radical social theory/Stephen Crook.
p. cm.
Includes bibliographical references (p.).
1. Sociology–Philosophy. 2. Radicalism. 3. Postmodernism–Social
aspects. I. Title. II. Title: Foundationalism and anti-foundationalism in
radical social theory.
HM24.C78 1991 90–9149
301'.01–dc20 CIP
ISBN 0–415–02860–4
ISBN 0–415–06081–8 (pbk)

For Rosemary

CONTENTS

FIGURES

ACKNOWLEDGEMENTS

I first became interested in the issues discussed here as a graduate student in the Department of Sociology, University of York, in the late 1970s. I owe a debt of gratitude to Barry Sandywell, who supervised my thesis and who has continued to be a valued source of ideas and encouragement. I cannot refer to my time at York without acknowledging the stimulation I received from my fellow graduate students Peter Cressey, Peter McGavin, Shule Pojon and Andrew Webster.

During the years I spent at the College of St Mark and St John, Plymouth, I benefited from many discussions with my colleagues David Harris and Frank Gillies. The bulk of work on the book has been undertaken in the University of Tasmania, and I am grateful to my colleagues who have cheerfully tolerated my pre-occupations. In particular, I owe more than they may think to conversations with Jan Pakulski and Malcolm Waters. I completed the book on study leave in York. I am grateful to the Department of Sociology for their hospitality and to my parents for putting me up for long periods and giving me the use of a word processor.

Three other debts must be acknowledged. First, generations of students in Plymouth and Hobart have actively helped to shape my view of the nature and tasks of radical social theory. Second, Routledge have been model publishers. Chris Rojek has used the ideal editorial blend of patience, encouragement and gentle pressure to bring the book to completion, while comments from anonymous readers have been helpful. Third, and most important of all, Rosemary Crumpton-Crook accepted the role of book-widow, providing constant support and encouragement.

Chapters 1.3, 3, 4.2, 5.2 and 6 are revisions of material from my 1984 Doctoral thesis. Chapter 5.3 is drawn from my 'The End of Radical Social Theory', published in Roy Boyne and Ali Rattansi (eds), *Postmodernism and Society*, Macmillan Education 1990. I am grateful to the publisher and editors for their permission to use the material.

Stephen Crook
Hobart, May 1990

INTRODUCTION: THE DECLINE OF RADICAL SOCIAL THEORY

RADICAL SOCIAL THEORY AND THE CRISIS OF MODERNITY

The 1980s witnessed a growing sense among social theorists and cultural critics that the complex phenomenon of social and cultural modernity had entered a period of crisis, that decisive thresholds were about to be crossed. In this atmosphere, the terms 'postmodernism' and 'postmodernity' became the rather de-based coin of a wide range of overlapping debates about the causes, character and consequences of social and cultural change. A remark of Whitebook's captures something of the spirit of the decade. 'While the announcement that Minerva's owl is about to depart may be premature, one is increasingly struck by the sense of living in the closing of an epoch' (Whitebook, 1982: 53). The thematisation of a transition from modernity to postmodernity can be traced in substantive social theory, in aesthetic theory and in philosophy.

Sociological debates about the possibility of an imminent structural transformation of advanced industrial societies pre-date the 1980s, and claims by Bell (1973) and Touraine (1971) that a 'post-industrial' society was in the making formed a basis for many later reflections on 'postmodernity'. Bell's gloomy reflections (1976) on the pathological character of contemporary culture and its mis-match with advanced economic processes helped to shape a debate about the 'crises' of advanced societies which still continues (e.g. Habermas, 1985b). More recent studies have attempted to draw together elements of the post-industrialism thesis with theories of postmodern culture to produce models of the post-

3

modern order. In this spirit Lash and Urry (1987) plot the emergence of 'disorganised capitalism', while Harvey (1989) also draws together cultural, economic and political processes in his juxtaposition of 'Fordist modernity' and 'flexible postmodernity'.

While these issues are of the first importance for substantive social theory, on the face of it they induce no crisis in the idea and practice of social theory as such. After all, the differentiation of types of social structure and the investigation of the causes and consequences of social change have been the tasks of social theory since the classical projects of Marx, Durkheim and Weber. Why should not those forms of enquiry which successfully explained the transition from premodernity to modernity also be adequate to the alleged transition from modernity to postmodernity? The sources of uncertainty on this score, of the crisis in social theory itself, can more easily be discerned in aesthetic and philosophical conceptions of postmodernity.

The term 'postmodernism' first gained currency in aesthetic debates, and has been used to designate a bewildering range of artistic projects. Its use implies that a particular work of art, or artist, stands identifiably 'after' and 'against' the thematic and stylistic conventions which defined the modern art, music and literature of the first half of the century. However, the transition from modernism to postmodernism is more than a matter of style. One of the most typical phenomena of aesthetic modernity has been the *avant garde*, the group of radicals who force the pace of innovation in art, music or literature, and who typically insist that aesthetic radicalism be coupled with political radicalism. As Peter Bürger (1984) has argued, this quintessentially modernist idea of the radical *avant garde* now faces a crisis. In a way which suggests that the 'logic' of aesthetic modernity has played itself out, contemporary would-be *avant gardes* find that they can do nothing other than recapitulate the radical gestures of the 1910s or 1920s. The idea of the *avant garde* itself has become a cliché. If this is so, the arrival of aesthetic postmodernity involves more than the replacement of one set of stylistic and thematic conventions with another. It implies the exhaustion of the dynamic principles of modern art, music and literature, and heralds major transformations in the very idea of 'art' and in its relation to other social practices.

Caricature as it may be, this brief account of the crisis of aesthetic modernity prompts a disturbing analogy with social

4

theory. It requires only a minimal degree of sociological reflexivity to recognise that social theory is as much a part of the culture within which it is practised as is art, literature or music. Might not the idea of social theory articulated by Marx, Weber or Durkheim, and refined by subsequent generations, itself be a product of cultural modernity? Further, if social theory is inherently 'modernist', might it not also be subject to the 'exhaustion' which afflicts other modernisms? The suspicion that this might be so is intensified by a number of arguments associated with postmodernist (post-)philosophy.

The most direct challenge to social theory comes from the assertion that its object, 'the social', has no independent existence. Baudrillard (1983a, 1983b) offers an extreme formulation in which the social has collapsed, or 'imploded', and become invisible through a process analogous to that which produces the 'black holes' of astro-physics. More subtle challenges come from a variety of sources. Foucault (1977, 1980), for example, has argued that the human sciences should be understood as an integral part of the process through which power/knowledge re-shaped the 'social body' as a mechanism of discipline. Lyotard (1988) can stand for a more general 'linguistic turn' when he asserts that the 'universe' of the social is constituted and modulated by the 'phrase regimes' of the sociologist.

In Foucault, Lyotard and much other postmodernist 'theory', the challenge to the object of social theory is coupled with a challenge to social theory as a form of discourse. Its general form is that while modernist social theory represents itself as con-stituted in a radical break with outdated philosophical accounts of the social, in fact it stands in direct and discrediting continuity with such accounts. For Lyotard (1984a), social theory retains an anachronistic attachment to some 'grand narrative' as a legi-timating meta-discourse (most notably to narratives of 'enlighten-ment' and 'emancipation'). Foucault's essays in the 'archaeology' of knowledge (1970, 1972) have the effect of displacing the innately significant ruptures upon which social theory founds itself (ruptures between ideology and science, or philosophy and science, for example). His focus is the pre-conceptual deter-mination of a 'field' of discursive possibilities. Foucault's later 'genealogies' (e.g. 1977, 1981) subvert the self-understanding of social theory by displacing its history into that of the mutations of forms of power/knowledge. Although he rarely discusses social theory, Derrida's (e.g. 1976) analyses of the 'logocentrism' of a Western culture dominated by the 'metaphysics of presence' have beeen influential in shaping a view that generalising social theory is a symptom of, rather than an alternative to, metaphysical entanglements.

When the themes of social, aesthetic and philosophical postmodernity are drawn together, the contours of the crisis facing social theory begin to emerge. It is not simply that it is faced with new phenomena for analysis: social theory is itself caught up in the process of the transformation of modernity into postmodernity, and is equipped only with anachronistic and discredited models of enquiry and explanation. The crisis is particularly acute for projects in social theory which are 'radical' in a sense to be discussed below. The idea of a radical social theory, as it came to be understood in the late nineteenth century, claimed a central place in the cultures and societies of the emerging modern order. Marx, Durkheim and their successors offered theoretical systems which could comprehend the social totality, diagnose its pathologies, and determine its future. At the end of the twentieth century, in the face of the difficulties outlined above, such systems have little credibility. Indeed, it can now seem as if any reflection on the reasonableness of social processes is an impossible metaphysical regression or mere nostalgia. The very meaning of 'radical social theory' threatens to dissolve as each term in the conjunction becomes problematic.

The discovery of an autonomous social reality lay at the heart of the claims of radicalisms such as Marxism and Durkheimian sociology. Social reality was the site of specifically social pathologies, and the scientifically prescribed cure for these would enable the radical promise of modernity to be fulfilled. But, as has been seen, the idea of an autonomous social reality is now under challenge, and not simply as the result of analytic considerations. During the late 1980s the view has gained currency that the really big problems are not 'social', but involve the inter-penetration of natural, technical, signifying and psychic processes, the 'social' risks being left in the cold. To compound this down-grading, the 'theory' in radical social theory has been subject to a process of 'elitist splitting off' from day-to-day debates about society, politics and culture. Social theory is increasingly taken up with academic and meta-theoretical issues generated by its own practices: debates about 'realism', attempts to reconcile 'structure and action', or exegeses of 'classic' texts. The 'radicalism' of radical social theory cannot but come under question, given these displacements of its field of operations and mode of discourse. Indeed, the concept of a broad progressive, intellectual left, whose struggles for justice articulate the forward march of history, now has the feel of a period piece. In the advanced societies, the 'radicals' are now either to the right (if that term retains any meaning), or aligned with 'new social movements' which do not fit neatly into a left–right spectrum.

The claims of radical social theory to be a significant voice in the 'conversations' of the advanced societies are under challenge, and nowhere is this more so than in sociology.[1] Serious consideration is given to this state of affairs by the editors of, and many of the contributors to, *Sociological Theory in Transition* (Wardell and Turner (eds), 1986). Wardell and Turner argue that sociology has failed to come to grips with 'the dissolution of the classical project', with the loss of the sense of immediacy and relevance which characterised the work of Comte, Marx, Durkheim and the rest. The inevitable failure of the 'Parsons-Merton project' to reconstitute post-classical sociology as a mature and professionalised science has only accelerated the decline of the discipline. Stehr is among the contributors who argue that sociology's concern to purge itself of moral and political 'values' lies at the heart of its loss of relevance. For 'conventional historiographies' of social science, a purge of moral and political (as well as philosophical and epistemological) questions is the way to ensure 'the objective (scientific), effective (useful) and consensual (truthful) character of sociological discourse' (Stehr 1986: 39).

The editors regard this purge as an admission of failure which can be linked to the more obvious pragmatic concerns of institutionalised sociology.

> The apprehensiveness with which sociologists currently struggle to construct a new relationship with the state, as well as a 'market' of employers, an audience of materially motivated students, and hearers of other kinds who are not 'opinion leaders' but clients, program administrators and policy makers, is a sign that the core of sociological thought is failing in its relations with audiences that are outside the walls of disciplinary sociology. (Wardell and Turner, 1986: 163)

The relevance of sociology is lost as the discipline bifurcates into a self-absorbed academicism and, in a caricature of relevance, a research technology at the service of established interests. But what is to be done? A difficulty with the diagnoses offered by Wardell and Turner and by Stehr is that they can foster a 'golden age' myth, a nostalgia for the hopes and certainties of the past. This nostalgia, in turn, can encourage a belief that the future for sociology, and social theory more generally, lies in a revival of the 'classical project'.

The most notable example of such a strategy is Habermas's eclectic 'reconstruction' of historical materialism. In effect, Habermas reverses the 'purges' which Stehr objects to, restoring both values and philosophical reflection to an honoured place in a theoretical system. The possibility which 'reconstructive' strategies of this type do not quite face is that the 'classical project' was inherently pathological, that its certainties were always myths and its hopes always illusions. Were this the case, then nostalgia for the relevance of a Marx or a Durkheim would be quite misplaced and attempts to recapture it would pitch sociology and social theory from one kind of disaster to another. Just such a diagnosis underpins the reflections on the fate of radical social theory which make up this book. The seeds of the decline of radical social theory must be traced back to the period of its pomp, to the 'classical project' itself. The ills of radical social theory will not be cured by any 'reconstruction' of that project.

A FORMAT FOR ANALYSIS: INCLUSIONS AND EXCLUSIONS

The crisis of radical social theory, as sketched above, invites a wide range of responses. It may be useful to the reader if some of the limitations which shape the response offered here are spelled out. It is argued in the later chapters of the book, particularly, that it is unhelpful to imagine radical social theory as a privileged site of 'the unity of theory and practice'. The 'interests' which shape theoretical enquiry are not those which shape social and political practice. The first limitation to be noted, then, is that the argument here is oriented by a theoretical, rather than a practical, interest. Its focus is meta-theoretical, shaped by a concern to trace the possibilities and limitations of different conceptions of social theory.

This first limitation still leaves open a wide range of possible strategies. So, an author might strive for a complete and systematic treatment of the topic, whether in the form of an exhaustive history or an exhaustive typology of social theory. A second limitation here is that such completeness is not to be attempted. In part, this limitation reflects constraints on the length of the book and the capacities of its author. Beyond this, it acknowledges the argument that such claims to systematicity and completeness cannot, in principle, be redeemed. It follows that the format which frames the argument of the book cannot be other than selective and polemical, or rhetorical.

A major organising device is the rather unfashionable one of the critical analysis of the projects of specific social theorists. The first four and a half chapters use such analyses as exemplars of the emergence of opposing tendencies in radical social theory. They make possible the identification of themes which might find a place in a renewed radicalism, and themes which should be abandoned. Debate about the inclusion of some theorists and the exclusion of others could be as endless as that about the selection of the all-time Earth cricket team to play Mars, but one or two remarks may be useful. It is unlikely that the inclusion of Marx, Durkheim, Simmel, Weber or Habermas will questioned. Horkheimer, Adorno and Althusser might be controversial inclusions, while (simply for example) Nietzsche, Lukács, Benjamin, Marcuse and Parsons might seem unjustly excluded.

Lukács and Marcuse have been excluded simply because the full-blown modernist radicalism they represent is amply discussed in relation to other writers. Parsons has been excluded by the fiat that he does not seriously engage with the radical tradition in social theory. To take the book into a discussion of 'professional' sociology in North America would stretch its scope too far. Equally, to consider the seminal work of Nietzsche in detail would be to move outside the sphere of soi-disant radical social theory, and into a different kind of project. Rather similar considerations apply to the exclusion of the currently fashionable Benjamin and the inclusion of the less fashionable Horkheimer and Adorno. The latter are of interest here because, unlike Benjamin, they retain an attachment, however ambiguous, to the idea of methodically regulated social analysis. Even more unfashionable is Althusser, who shares with Spinoza the fate of the 'dead dog' (and much else besides). It is not so long ago that

Althusser was celebrated by many, perhaps most, British academic radicals as *the* radical theorist of the age. He is considered here because he requires to be understood as a critical liminal figure, standing both historically and analytically on the boundary between radical social theory and its postmodernist inversions.

The two final chapters offer a more general diagnosis and treatment of the pathologies of radical social theory. Given the direction taken by the argument, it is important to stress the contingency of this arrangement. Similar arguments could be built out of quite different materials, and different arguments out of the same materials. The test of such coherence as the book may possess lies in its capacity, or otherwise, to persuade readers that 'something needs to be done' about radical social theory. However, the reader should not expect the book to end with a systematic manifesto for a renewed radicalism. If the argument of the book is correct, it is not the task of a meta-analytic essay to pre-empt the findings of substantive enquiry, or to prescribe a programme for social–political practice.

THE ARGUMENT: A PRE-SUMMARY

The book begins by trying to give a sense of what 'the classical project' in radical social theory amounted to. The term 'modernist radicalism' is coined in chapter one as a label for that project, and it is exemplified in discussions of versions elaborated by the young Marx and by Durkheim. The first part of the conjunction, 'modernist', indicates the definitive claim that a new form of knowledge, a new science, is required to comprehend the contemporary emergence of a new and specifically modern form of social order. The second term, 'radicalism', designates two corollaries of this claim. First, the new form of knowledge emerges in the radical overthrow of pre-modern forms of reflection, notably in philosophy and in common sense. Second, the new form of knowledge will animate a radically new and transformative social practice which can complete modernity. The accounts of Marx and Durkheim lend support to a suggestion that modernist radicalism can be defined with reference to three themes. An 'ideology' theme articulates the generic superiority of the new knowledge over metaphysics and common sense. The perennial theme of the 'end of philosophy' overlaps with the ideology theme, but adds a doubly legitimating twist. The claim that modernist radicalism can extract the rational kernel from philosophy, and thereby redeem its promise, makes it heir to the dignity of philosophy and also warrants its break from philosophy. Finally, the power of new knowledge and new practice, in combination, to bring about the completion of modernity is articulated in the theme of a unique and privileged 'unity of theory and practice'. These three themes combined in projects of modernist radicalism have exercised an enormous influence on radical social theory in this century. Indeed, their combination has become virtually synonymous with the idea of radical social theory as such. But the discussions of Marx and Durkheim also try to convey a sense of unease about the pretensions of modernist radicalism. Both Marx and Durkheim advance strongly 'foundationalist' arguments to establish guarantees of the truth and effectiveness of their programmes of enquiry in advance of enquiry itself. But this foundationalism, which is necessary to the defining themes of modernist radicalism, also subverts them. Modernist radicalism is caught in a series of discrediting continuities with forms of ideological and metaphysical analysis which it claims to have superseded. So, for example, Durkheimian sociology can be understood as an attempt to solve the problems of Kantian philosophy by other means: it is the embodiment of 'rational will' and the site of a unity of pure and practical Reason.

Chapter two considers the sociologies of Simmel and Weber as early challenges to modernist radicalism. In the case of Simmel, four factors set him against the pretensions of modernist radicalism: the peculiar 'formality' of his analyses, his 'aestheti-cisation' of social reality, the limits he places on the scope of historical knowledge, and his continuing commitment to philo-sophy. These factors produce a sociological relationalism which subverts the claims for privilege of the defining themes of modernist radicalism. For Simmel, the 'ideology' theme is too crude to grasp the relations between social actors and analysts' syntheses of social reality, the specialised science of sociology cannot pre-empt the tasks of philosophy, and society is com-posed of countless unities of theory and practice, none of which can claim an a priori privilege.

Simmel's concerns can seem both remote from and subversive of the classical concerns of radical social theory. However, two important lessons can be drawn from his analyses to be put to work in the task of rethinking radicalism. First, radical social theory cannot evade the need for a judgement of value. There is no available version of 'social reality' which can compel assent to radical values with the force of logical necessity. Radical values are not immanent in a reality which is independent of judgement. Second, Simmel's distinction between a specialised science of sociology and other, more generalising, social studies sows a seed of doubt about the modernist radical project for a single unified social theory which integrates scientific knowledge with judgements about a desirable social practice.

Where Simmel directs sociological attention away from the 'great organs and systems' of society, Weber shares the classical concern to comprehend their place in the emergence of a specifically modern order. While there are a number of parallels between the diagnoses of Simmel and Weber, Weber confronts the claims of modernist radicalism all the more directly because they are closer to his own concerns. The alternative which Weber offers is an ironic conception of modernity. At the substantive level, this conception is summed up in the idea of a 'paradox of consequences', whereby the historical consequences of projects of action subvert their intentions. Weberian irony has proved to be a useful weapon in the critique of radical programmes, and through repetition and vulgarisation (sometimes by Weber himself) it has become something of a cliché. When taken up by radicals such as Adorno and Horkheimer (1979), it can seem to negate an optimistic historicism ('history will fulfil human purposes') with a negative one ('history will subvert and frustrate human purposes').

Weberian irony is of most interest at the methodological level. It turns on a relationalism which is itself ironic: the irony of a paradox of consequences emerges only in a complex juxtaposition of the 'points of view' of historical actors and of analysts. Two of the instruments of Weberian irony are of potential importance in the search for a radical alternative to modernist radicalism. The first is precisely an insistence on the cognitive and evaluative primacy of the 'point of view', which generates a telling account of the constitution of objects of analysis. It is perhaps here that Weberian irony offers its most substantial challenge to modernist radicalism. Second, the relationalism of the paradox of consequences generates a conception

12

of causality in history and society which allows analysis to move beyond the solipsistic elaboration of a given point of view, while also evading the myth of a presuppositionless knowledge.

However, the promise of Weber's account of the constitution of objects of analysis by points of view or 'interests' is subverted by the way it is pegged to a theory of values as the basis of interests. In Weber, values become pre-rational and given presuppositions of action and enquiry. Weber's relationalism degenerates into a foundationalism which parallels Durkheim's sociological theory of knowledge. While Durkheim founds knowledge on the given *unity* of social reality, expressed in collective representations, Weber founds knowledge on an equally given *plurality* of values. Weber's critique of modernist radicalism pulls up short because it, too, is complicit in foundationalism.

To different degrees, and for different reasons, Simmel and Weber work outside the presuppositions of modernist radicalism. Horkheimer and Adorno are of interest because they work towards a critique of modernist radicalism while maintaining a traceable connection with its Marxist variants. This 'auto-critique' of modernist radicalism is examined in chapter three. Horkheimer's vision of a 'critical theory of society' is caught in a three-way tension between two types of foundationalism and an incipient anti-foundationalism. Adorno moves much further in the direction of a post-foundational radicalism, but even he evinces an ambiguity about a thoroughgoing anti-foundationalism. The modernist radical theme which is the pivot of ambiguity in each case is the 'end of philosophy'. Horkheimer sometimes appears to align the project of the Institute for Social Research with modernist radicalism. Marxism (usually referred to by Horkheimer under some coy *nom de guerre*) can re-formulate the old philosophical problems in a way which admits of empirical investigation and solution. However, Horkheimer is reluctant to make a final end of philosophy: the archive of the classical and critical traditions in philosophy remains the definitive site at which radical demands for reason and justice have been formulated, and Horkheimer does not want to see that site finally superseded. But he is unwilling completely to identify critical theory with philosophy. Part of the difficulty here is the state of uncritical degeneracy which Horkheimer diagnoses in what passes for contemporary philosophy. The other complication which leads him to dither between social science and philosophy is the under-developed anti-foundationalism which is a counterpoint to his other concerns.

Some of Horkheimer's earliest work gives voice to a suspicion of the integrating power of language, of its capacity to create 'the illusion of a community', and to offer the appearance of a reconciliation of contradictions. Neither philosophy nor social science are well equipped to resist such integration. Horkheimer's anti-foundationalist suspicion of language points in the direction of a critical theory practised as a 'critical rhetorics', the artful use of the resources of language itself to resist the foundationalist temptations inherent in language. However, Horkheimer does not develop these insights. Instead, social scientific and philosophical foundationalisms are used to undermine each other until, in the end, Horkheimer reconciles himself to philosophy as the last faint hope for a humane discourse.

The way in which Adorno took up and developed the practice of critical theory as a critical rhetorics remains exemplary for the development of a post-foundational radicalism. His critical practice is directed against the temptations of 'identity thinking' in aesthetics, philosophy, and social theory. 'Negative dialectic' (or, in an expression which may better convey the intention, the 'dialectic of non-identity') defies easy summary. In chapter three a general account is exemplified by Adorno's critiques of Heidegger and Wagner. Although Adorno develops the idea of a critical rhetorics well beyond Horkheimer's rather general intimations, he does not entirely evade the ambiguities which trapped Hork-heimer. The critiques of Heidegger and Wagner testify to a reluctance to press the dialectic of non-identity beyond a certain point: having demonstrated that the claims of each, one in philosophy and the other in art, to have transcended classical antinomies are bogus, Adorno is tempted, at least, towards a nostalgic endorsement of classicism. His attitude towards social science is also ambiguous, and is one of the few of his concerns which fluctuates markedly over the years. In the early 1930s Adorno conceived of a division of labour between sociology and philosophy which has some points of contact with Simmel. Adorno is quite sympathetic to 'empiricist' programmes, arguing that empirical social research can inform a philosophy which has mutated into a 'materialist hermeneutic'. Adorno became involved with programmes of social research during his exile in the United

States, but after his return to Germany he became sharply critical of an allegedly positivistic sociology. The latter is contrasted unfavourably with a 'critical theory' of society which maintains a grasp on 'totality'. Adorno's late essays on social science do scant service to the attempt to rethink radicalism. Their failure to develop his earlier sense of the potential of an empirical moment in critical analysis leaves 'critical rhetorics' as the grin on the Cheshire cat of philosophical critique.

It would be possible to construct a history of social theory in which Simmel, Weber, Horkheimer and Adorno were presented as key figures in the triumphal march of a tradition of post foundational analysis opposed to, and contemporary with, the tradition of modernist radicalism. However, the real import of chapters two and three lies in the ambiguity, even failure, of the anti-foundational strands in the work of those figures. The matrix which modernist radicalism provides for understanding the origins and tasks of social theory proves to be extraordinarily difficult to break with. It is small wonder that Simmel and Adorno, who perhaps come the closest to making the break, both have reputations as brilliant but flawed eccentrics at the margins of 'serious' sociology and social theory.

Chapter four is given to a consideration of Habermas's developing programme for the 'reconstruction' of radical social theory. Habermas sets out, quite explicitly, to produce a systematic yet critical social theory which synthesises resources from both the 'modernist radical' and 'anti-foundational' traditions, and other traditions besides (interactionist and Parsonsian sociology, for example). If the synthesis holds together it solves the problem of the decline of social theory, as posed above, and absorbs the idea of a post-foundational radicalism as a moment in a more wide-ranging theoretical system.

Habermas's early concerns with the 'public sphere' locate the problem of a critical, social theory within a 'topology' of social institutions. The site of (critical) self-formation and self-reflection is specified as an institutional 'mediation' between civil society and state. This account of the public sphere links Habermas to the early Marx and to the Enlightenment project for the universal rule of Morality and Reason. By the same token, it is susceptible to aspects of the conservative critique of Enlightenment. A little later, Habermas comes to be absorbed in the problem of how to mediate between the 'ordinary language of practice' and the specialised languages of science, technology and policy-making. The need for a specifically critical theory arises because of the growing gulf between these types of communication. Habermas's differentiation between 'knowledge constituting interests' attempts to solve these problems in a typology of complexes of theory and practice, differentiated at the level of their specific 'rationalities'. Each complex gives rise to a specific type of science (empirico–analytic, historical–hermeneutic and critically oriented).

This second order formulation of critical theory replicates and amplifies many of the difficulties of modernist radicalism. The claim that the three interests enjoy a 'quasi-transcendental' status converges with a frank foundationalism in which epistemological and ontological foundations are fused. Habermas's defining problem of rationality, and his definitive solution in which the rational is demonstrated to be immanent-but-obscured in the structures of the real, add to the sense that the overall project is a continuation of critical philosophy. Habermas has shifted from this formulation in three main respects, and the question is whether his 'new' critical theory evades the metaphysical entanglements of the old.

The first shift is away from an epistemology of interests and towards a typology of communication. Habermas later glosses this shift as a break with 'subject centred reason', which he takes to be responsible for the metaphysical regressions of previous formulations of critical theory. The typology distinguishes between different modes of communication and the 'validity claims' which they invoke. The second shift is away from Habermas's long-standing concerns with 'self-reflection' as the ground and task of critical theory, and towards a conception of critical theory as a 'reconstructive' science. The third shift amounts to a return to Habermas's early 'topological' concerns. His account of the pathologies of modernity as the result of imbalances between 'systems' and 'lifeworlds' generalises his earlier concerns with the public sphere and the spread of technical rationality.

Habermas claims to have moved beyond the infelicities of both modernist radicalism and its merely negative critique. In practice, he has moved towards, rather than away from, modernist radicalism. His conception of 'communicative rationality' remains caught within the familiar figure of 'immanence-realisation', the idea of a reconstructive science remains 'quasi-transcendental', and the model of 'systems' and 'lifeworlds' revives problems of 'balance' and 'mediation'. In making 'subject centred reason' a scapegoat for the metaphysical temptations of social theory, Habermas has regressed behind the critical insights of Horkheimer and Adorno into the *linguistic* basis of metaphysics. As a result, he offers a foundationalist metaphysics of language in the guise of a critical social science. Habermas's project is presented in chapter four as the swan song of modernist radicalism, as a final and systematic attempt to transcend the limitations of the genre in a synthesis which also makes room for its more important critiques. Like Althusser, whose project is considered in chapter five, Habermas offers a minimalist modernist radicalism. He pares his metaphysical commitments to the bone but cannot, finally, break with them.

For some two decades the sharpest diagnoses of the metaphysical lapses of radical, particularly Marxist, social theory have come from French theorists associated with the tendencies which have been labelled (successively) 'structuralist', 'post-structuralist' and 'postmodernist'. Chapter five assesses this postmodernist critique, arguing that it offers only a monistic and nihilistic reversal of modernist radicalism. In this context Althusser's once influential but now disregarded attempt to re-found orthodox Marxism is important as a nexus between modernist radicalism and its postmodern critique. While offering versions of the 'ideology', 'end of philosophy' and 'unity of theory and practice' themes, Althusser is alive to the metaphysical temptations which they offer. His essays are replete with denunciations of 'humanism', 'historicism', 'empiricism' and other philosophical errors.

Althusser might be understood as attempting to construct the thinnest possible modernist radicalism. The significance, and the irony, of his project for the argument here is that his critique of metaphysical contaminations in Marxism is founded on the wholesale appropriation of a metaphysical system. Althusser's rejection of the 'ideological' problem of knowledge, and its replacement by an account of the 'knowledge effect', is pivotal to his claims to have advanced beyond metaphysics. However, the doctrine of the 'knowledge effect' recapitulates, point for point, the theory of knowledge from the *Ethics* of Spinoza.

Althusser is no longer fashionable, and it may be tempting to regard his Spinozism as an historical curiosity, the idiosyncrasy of a forgotten author. There is more to it than this, however. The metaphysical traces which hold such a continuing fascination for modernist radicalisms are generally dualistic. Modernist radicals worry about versions of the defining antinomies of the critical tradition: subject and object, spirit and nature, freedom and necessity. These oppositions are 'materialised' in some way, so that 'subject and object' might become 'individual and society', or 'freedom and necessity' mutate into 'agency and structure'. The task of social theory, like the task of philosophy, is then to reconcile the oppositions. Monisms such as Spinoza's are the time-honoured philosophical alternative to dualism: when postmodernist critiques of modernist radicalism follow Althusser into monism they follow a well-trodden path. The critical difference is that while Althusser's is a rationalist monism, enabling him to remain (just) within modernist radicalism, postmodernisms turn on *irrationalist* monisms.

The monisms of postmodernism fall into two basic types: physicalist monisms such as Baudrillard's or Deleuze's, and monisms of discourse, such as Lyotard's, or the 'discourse theory' of Hindess, Hirst and their associates. In each case, postmodernisms contrive to be both metaphysical and nihilistic. Their metaphysical character derives from the speculative designation of some single principle of world-production (see Rose, 1984).[2] Postmodernisms slip from metaphysics into nihilism because the world-producing principles, or substances, which they specify are quantitative phenomena only, admitting of no qualitative distinctions. The over-stretched term 'nihilism' is used here to designate a failure in the accountability of social theory. Postmodernist social theories lose any capacity to specify why change might be desirable or how it might be possible, a capacity which might be taken to be the *sine qua non* of radicalism. Nihilism in this sense can be seen at work in Guattari's 'micro politics', and it threatens Lyotard's opposition to the principle of 'performativity'.

The postmodern critique of modernist radicalism has not gone unanswered, of course. Habermas's *The Philosophical Discourse of Modernity* is conceived as a refutation of the Nietzsche-inspired critique of modernity. Postmodernism is held to be complicit in the same closures of 'subject centred reason' which trap metaphysical modernisms, and which Habermas's concept of communicative rationality allows him to evade. More orthodox Marxists than Habermas have attempted either to refute postmodernism and its forbears (e.g. Anderson, Callinicos) or to tame and appropriate some of its themes (e.g. Jameson, Poulantzas). These responses tend to be deficient in one of two ways. The more vigorous critiques simply re-assert the principles of a preferred modernist radicalism, while synthetic efforts fail to appreciate just how corrosive postmodernism is of the ambitions of modernist radicalism.

As the argument stands at the end of chapter five, the prospects for radical social theory are not good. It seems to be faced with a choice between the equally unappealing options of a 'meta-physical' modernist radicalism and a 'nihilistic' postmodernism. If there is to be any third way, it must lie in a development of the anti-foundational themes traced in Simmel, Weber, Horkheimer and Adorno. But radical social theory as it is traditionally conceived is not to be rescued, and suggestions for an alternative to it cannot take the form of a detailed programme. The incapacity of the author apart, there are good reasons for ending a book of this kind on a cautious note.

First, ambitious plans for imaginary sciences and practices have been among the main vehicles of traditional radical social theory. The programmatic impulse has been as responsible as anything for the drift into speculative and foundational syntheses. Second, if premature synthesis is a persistent flaw in traditional radicalisms, it may well be that there is no single alternative to it. A post-foundational radicalism is more usefully conceived as a constellation of loosely related research programmes than as a single 'theory'. Third, if the pre-emptive temptations of foundationalist social theory are to be evaded, greater priority requires to be given to processes of substantive or, in a term often regarded with suspicion, empirical enquiry. When these points are taken together, it is clear that it would be inappropriate to end a meta-theoretical essay of this kind with a programme for a post-foundational radicalism articulated around a single theory and setting an agenda of 'radical issues' to be addressed.

Chapters six and seven try to remain within this self-denying ordinance while taking the argument beyond the rather gloomy close of chapter five. It has been argued that 'foundationalism' is implicated in the failings of both modernist radicalism and post-modernism. Chapter six examines the syndrome of foundationalism and the ways in which it comes to dominate social theory. The claim that foundationalism is a 'syndrome' rather than a 'doctrine' indicates that the temptation to guarantee the status of knowledge prior to its actual production is 'protean and persistent', in Margolis's words (1986: 166). But foundationalist anxieties about knowledge are also odd: the routine production of knowledge in science and in everyday life proceeds without reference to the foundational efforts of philosophers and social theorists.

The foundationalist temptation is at its strongest in reflection on two 'instances' of enquiry: an instance of 'origin' in which the appropriate beginnings of enquiry become problematic, and an instance of 'autonomy' arising out of a concern to keep enquiry free of contaminating associations. Both of these instances are paradoxical. Brief examinations of the accounts of the origin of enquiry offered by Descartes and Dawe suggest that assertions of an originary moment in one discursive register must simultaneously invoke their denial in other registers. Similarly, attempts to assert the 'autonomy' of enquiry from contamination by interests, values and the like can only provoke just the sceptical and debunking critique they are designed to resist.

The two foundational instances are secured in a wide range of different ways. In chapter six, four such foundational 'modes' are identified in the relations which enquiry bears to 'method', 'goal', 'ground' and 'tradition'. In each case a paradoxical and aporetic foundational conception of the relations between foundational mode and substantive enquiry can be opposed by a more open and anti-foundational approach. The argument can be summed up in a distinction between two different types of strategy with respect to foundational issues. Strategies of *closure* insist that foundation is prior to enquiry, that foundational questions admit of definitive answers, that foundation and enquiry move in different discursive registers, and that the 'possibility' of enquiry depends on successful foundation. By contrast, strategies of *disclosure* deny each of these assumptions and point towards a post-foundational conception of enquiry.

Chapter seven ends the book by drawing together resources for a post-foundational radicalism, bearing in mind the self-denying ordinance noted above. Three major resources can be identified from earlier chapters: a 'relational' account of the constitution of analytic objects, an 'ironic' conception of causality, and the idea of a 'critical rhetorics'. These issues are rehearsed in relation to a distinction between two broad strategies which each have a place within post-foundational radicalism, but which are not to be pressed into a unity. Radical enquiry into the 'great organs and systems' of society is best conceived as a 'mundane' enquiry (to twist a concept of Pollner's) conducted under the auspices of a pragmatic relation to the interests of social members. Here, social theorists' and social members' 'syntheses' of society intersect. The second strategy is to approach the synthetic, or constitutive, activities of social members orthogonally, as it were, taking those activities as a topic of enquiry. Such enquiries are not usefully conceived as bearing any direct and pragmatic relation to members' interests. Neither of these strategies requires to be invented from nothing, of course. Many of the techniques and topics of orthodox sociological research can find a place in a mundane radicalism, while the extensive and vital research traditions of ethnomethodology and conversation analysis are major resources for an 'orthogonal' radicalism.

The radicalism of post-foundational enquiry does not consist in the production of a special kind of knowledge which can be guaranteed to be emancipatory. It lies, rather, in the ways in which knowledges are appropriated and put to work. One requirement which can be imposed on any radical production, or appropriation, of knowledge is that of maintaining the accountability whose absence leads to nihilism. Two aspects can be distinguished: the maintenance of 'reflexivity' and the maintenance of a 'relation to value'. Projects of enquiry vary according to the type of reflexivity, or self-reference, they engender. Some may have only a minimal reflexivity centred on 'relation to method', while others may explicitly aim for a high degree of reflexivity about all their auspices. It would not be appropriate to insist on a uniform type and intensity of reflexivity for post-foundational radicalism. A minimal demand might be that any project be able to account for the particular balance of reflexivity and non-reflexivity it entails. Such accounts can lay projects open to an always corrigible judgement about the costs and benefits of a particular balance.

A post-foundational radicalism must re-formulate the problem of value in a way which will evade the covert foundationalism and incipient nihilism of the Weberian version. Recent discussions of 'value' in a variety of different traditions converge on a theme which might be said to define a 'phase two' postmodernism which is much more congenial to post-foundationalism than the 'phase one' versions considered in chapter five. The defining

21

theme is that of the 'contingency' of value. If the impossible attempt to provide foundations for value is abandoned, then a recognition of the contingency of value does not have the force of a 'debunking' critique. Chapter seven traces this theme in a number of writers, notably MacIntyre and Smith, offering an account of the different 'relations to value' of mundane and orthogonal radicalisms. If post-foundationalism ditches the second order question of 'the value of value', as Fekete terms it, the way is open for a constructive and radical engagement with urgent first order value problems.

The final issue to be addressed is how a post-foundational radicalism is to understand its relation to transformations and thresholds in knowledge and in history. This has implications for the way in which 'the fate of the times' is to be conceived and faced. Modernist radicalism and postmodernism both place themselves in relation to a 'great divide' in which theoretical and historical thresholds are intertwined. Arguments derived from Blumenberg's defence of modernity can show how both versions of the great divide depend on discrediting continuities, and thus become caught in foundational paradoxes which open them to sceptical critique. A post-foundational radicalism which gives up the illusion of a 'new beginning' is in a position to face up to the contingencies of history.

Post-foundationalism disassembles and redefines 'radical', 'social' and 'theory'. The terms and their conjunction do not have the same meanings in mundane and orthogonal enquiries. 'The social' is no longer the privileged and given reality which is the site of the unities and ruptures of modernist radicalism. For mundane enquiries, the terrain of the social is constituted in a pragmatic convergence with the interests of social members. For orthogonal enquiries, the critical social relation is the process of constitution itself. 'Radicalism' is not defined in a new unity of theory and practice. From a mundane perspective, radicalism lies in the production of new insights into processes which are pragmatically defined as problematic. In orthogonal enquiry, radicalism lies in problematising the boundaries of the mundane idiom itself. 'Theory', considered as speculative and program matic synthesis, yields its privilege in both strategies to specific programmes of substantive enquiry, whether into mundane problems and processes or into the production of mundaneity itself.

There is no future for radical social theory in attempts to recover the kind of salience it purported to enjoy in a classical golden age. The classical project has left only the wreckage of its great theoretical systems, the pathos of attempts to recover their greatness, and the corrosive effects of their postmodern critique. A wide-ranging post-foundational radicalism, conceived as a constellation of diverse enquiries, has some capacity to break with the self-absorption of social theory. In rejecting the privilege of 'the social', the unities of 'radicalism' and the pre-emptions of 'theory', it might begin to look outward and forward, rather than inward and back.

1

THE IDEA OF MODERNIST RADICALISM

1.1 PRELIMINARIES

The project-form[1] of 'modernist radicalism' has defined the paradigmatic sense of what is to count as a radical theoretical response to social modernity from (at least) the middle of the nineteenth century until the present day. The present chapter attempts to define modernist radicalism and to show how its assumptions saturate the projects of Marx and Durkheim. It is largely through later appropriations of these projects that the pattern of modernist radicalism has been transmitted to twentieth-century social theory. Before moving on to these examples, however, a number of more general orienting remarks on radicalism and modernism in social theory may be helpful.

The Republic of Plato has a number of claims to be the first text of radical social theory. Indeed, such a claim on its behalf underlies Popper's celebrated denunciation (1962) of the fatal thread of holism which links Plato, Hegel and Marx together as enemies of the 'open society'. Two particular Platonic themes resonate with the argument about radicalism which is to be developed here. First, Plato juxtaposes his account of the measures necessary to the realisation of Justice within the state with a classification of known imperfect forms of organisation (Plato, 1974: part nine). Second, the possibility of attaining, or even conceiving of, Justice is shown to depend on a mode of knowing (*epistēmē*) which is radically distinct from the mere opinion (*doxa*) which prevails in the imperfect world as it is (ibid.: part seven, section 6).

A comparison of *The Republic* with the foundational texts of nineteenth-century social science on these matters might show, first, a shift in the way the relations between 'imperfect and 'just' societies are conceived. Plato's simple juxtaposition gives way, most commonly, to a placing of the just society on the horizon of evolving forms of imperfection. The just society will crown the last of Comte's 'three stages' of social evolution or will mark the end of the cycle of modes of production in Marx. However, the comparison would also reveal that the second Platonic theme had retained its centrality. Comte, Marx, Durkheim and others offer a knowledge of society which they take to be qualitatively distinct both from the knowledges which are current among social members, and from other soi-disant expert knowledges such as political economy or philosophy. One final twist can be added to the comparison. For the radicals of the nineteenth century, the two Platonic themes converge in a non-Platonic synthesis. A scientific knowledge of the laws of motion of imperfect societies will furnish the basis for an actual social transformation which will realise justice. According to which element of the synthesis is taken to be decisive, the radical projects of the nineteenth century stand in a relation of either continuity or discontinuity with the classical tradition. On the one hand, such projects can be portrayed as re-cyclings of the classical *epistēmē/doxa* distinction on the terrain of the social. On the other hand, the translation of *epistēmē* from a philosophy of perfection into a science of imperfection can be presented as a rupture of epochal significance.

The present essay cannot undertake the task of tracing the history through which Platonic radicalism mutates into the radicalism of a Marx or a Durkheim. Indeed, the latter two projects are to form the beginning of an account of modernist radicalism. However, precisely because this starting point is so conventional, it is all the more important to avoid complicity with what Giddens has termed the 'myth of the great divide'. In this 'myth'

> a fundamental watershed separates the pre-history of social theory, when it was not yet disentangled from speculative philosophy or the philosophy of history, from its foundation as a distinct and novel science of society.
>
> (Giddens, 1982: 40)

Different versions of this myth animate the autobiographies of Marxist and non-Marxist social theory. For the latter, Parsons' claim that the generation of Durkheim and Weber wrought 'a major movement in the structure of theoretical thinking' (Parsons, 1968: viii) still exerts a powerful attraction (despite the subsequent marginalisation of Marshall and Pareto). For the former, the critical watershed is placed earlier, at some point in the corpus of Marx. It is perhaps ironic that the success of Giddens' own text (1971) on the founders has served in practice, if not in intent, as a pedagogic resource for a renewed 'great divide' myth centred on the trinity of Marx, Durkheim and Weber.

Evidence with which to challenge any given version of the myth is almost embarrassingly easy to obtain from the most cursory dip into the history of ideas. Marx's concerns can be placed in a context which displays them as a salad of Jacobin, Hegelian and political–economic themes.[2] Durkheim can equally easily be portrayed as an academic entrepreneur whose doctrine did little more than re-shuffle insights from Rousseau, Comte and Renouvier.[3] But evidence of this type is question-begging in at least two respects. First, it may be that the fortuitous synthesis attained by Marx or Durkheim actually does entirely recast the significance of its borrowed materials, so as to re-draw the line between *doxa* and *epistēmē*. Second, and perhaps more important here, however hubristic such claims may seem with the benefit of hindsight, there can be no doubt that Marx and Durkheim themselves believed that they, and they alone, had crossed a 'great divide'. This belief is central to each of their projects. Giddens' account of the 'myth' can usefully be given something of a twist. The critical issue is not whether and where contemporary historians of sociology might wish to locate a 'real' break between pre-science and science in the development of the discipline. It is, rather, that of the place which the *idea* of such a break played in projects such as Marx's and Durkheim's. Consideration of this issue leads, in turn, to the question of the extent to which the idea continues to animate contemporary projects. When posed in this way, the question of the great divide is of more than antiquarian interest. The way it is answered will, for example, be consequential for debates between modernism and postmodernism in social theory. One point of contention in these debates has been, precisely, the ways in which social theory may or may not 'end' its connections with critical and classical philosophy.

With these preliminary and cautionary notes accomplished, it is possible to turn more directly to the question of 'modernist radicalism'. The expression conjoins two characteristics of the range of projects it is held to designate: 'modernism' and 'radicalism'. The term 'modernism' is more at home in aesthetic and literary contexts than in sociology and social theory. In those contexts, the modernist work is one which exemplifies a particular type of formal and thematic response to the experience of specifically modern life, or 'modernity'. Just how that experience is to be defined, and just which responses to it are to count as 'modernist', is the stuff of literary and aesthetic debate. A prominent model is one in which the experience is of isolation, fragmentation and flux, so that the appropriate response offers a critique of stable forms and stable selfhood. The idea of 'modernity' is more familiar to sociology and social theory than 'modernism'. Indeed, much of the significance of the 'great divide' concept lies in its contribution to the claim that crossing the divide enables social theory to produce compelling accounts of modernity which are beyond the resources of those disciplines stranded on the other side. That is, the divide is created by the discovery of some principle which unlocks the secret of specifically modern forms of social organisation. Marx and Durkheim advance similar claims to have made such a discovery. The new sciences of historical materialism and sociology both combine a methodological discovery ('dialectic' or 'rules of sociological method') with an ontological discovery (the 'forces and relations of production' or the *sui generis* 'reality' of the social). Thus founded, the new sciences can comprehend the other 'great divide' which separates pre-modernity ('pre-capitalist modes of production' or 'segmented societies') from modernity (the 'capitalist mode of production' or 'organised societies'). Also, and crucially, these sciences comprehend the laws by which the former come to be transformed into the latter.

There is an important sense, then, in which Marx and Durkheim might be said to be modernists, although it is a sense which diverges from more common usages. For both writers, the peculiarity of social modernity can be captured only in the figures of a new social scientific discourse. The term 'modernism' seems tailor-made for such claims. The divergence from common usage lies in the rather abstract analogy implied here between modernism in aesthetics and modernism in social theory. This analogy is some distance from claims that there are clear formal and thematic continuities between certain strands in social theory and notable tendencies in aesthetic modernism. It is in this latter sense that Frisby (1981, 1984, 1985) advances the claim of Simmel to be the 'first sociologist of modernity', or that Berman claims Marx for modernism on the grounds that he sometimes offers a 'melting vision' of modernity as constant flux (Berman, 1982: ch. II).[4] To the extent that the two usages do not conflict, the only problem is that of avoiding confusion as to which usage is in play on a given occasion. There is, however, a point of substance in dispute. Marx and Durkheim do not take the experience of fragmentation and flux as given, but seek to explain it as the phenomenon of a deeper process which can be subjected to analysis. This point has the corollary that Simmel's significance lies not in his discovery of modernity *per se*, but in his inauguration of a revisionist and ironic modernism which begins to challenge the foundations of radical modernism. This part of the argument is pursued in the next chapter.

The 'radicalism' of modernist radicalism has two closely integrated dimensions which the rehearsal of Platonic themes above has already identified. First, the new *epistēmē* of modernity will discipline both the prejudices of popular opinion and the pretensions of traditional philosophy. Historical materialism is the transcendence of both the mystified consciousness of the proletariat and the mystical shell of Hegelian philosophy. Second, this radically new knowledge of the social is the means through which the conduct of social life is to be revolutionised. The transcendence of opinion and metaphysics is also the transcendence of the practices in which they are embedded. Enlightened by historical materialism, 'men' (particularly proletarian 'men') can proceed to make history 'consciously' rather than 'behind their own backs'.

This very brief and preliminary sketch suggests that three themes are definitive of modernist radicalism: they delineate the contours of the 'great divide' which modernist radicalism situates between its predecessors and itself. It is clear, first of all, that modernist radicalism requires a 'theory of ideology' which will articulate its generic superiority to mere opinion or common sense. Second, the demands of modernism (in the abstract sense outlined above) require that a clear distinction be made between the claims of modernist science and those of pre-modernist philosophy. The definitive theme of the 'end of philosophy' warrants separate consideration, although it has clear overlaps with the 'ideology' theme. Finally, modernist radicalism claims to achieve a uniquely powerful 'unity of theory and practice'. This combination of themes is complicit with foundationalist' claims to have secured guarantees which grant a unique discursive privilege. These three themes can set an agenda for this chapter, which will exemplify the ways in which they weave together to constitute two specific projects. A brief note on the modernist radicalism of Marx's early critique of Hegel is followed by a rather longer attempt to show how Durkheim's project must be understood as an example of the same genre.

1.2 MODERNIST RADICALISM IN THE YOUNG MARX

The massive presence of Marx presents a dilemma for this essay. On one side, there would be something inherently otiose about an elaborate attempt to demonstrate that Marx is a radical thinker, or that his radicalism is developed in an attempt to grapple with social, economic and political modernity. If anyone is a modernist radical, Marx is. On the other side, no account of the development of radical social theory can ignore Marx's pivotal position. Here, two early Marxian texts are argued to establish a theme which is crucial to the development of modernist radicalism. The point is commonly made that nineteenth-century social science draws on the earlier delineation in philosophy and political economy of the space of a 'civil society', distinct from the family and the state.[6] Marx's radicalisation of the idea of civil society in the course of his *Critique of Hegel's 'Philosophy of Right'* (Marx, 1975b)[7] provides an early and condensed example of the way in which modernist radicalism transforms that concept through a combination of its three definitive themes. It links Marx with the earlier Enlightenment critique of the state in the name of reason and morality, and suggests that modernist radicalism inherits some of the paradoxes of Enlightenment political programmes.

Hegel's threefold distinction between family, civil society and state in *The Philosophy of Right* works in two ways. The three sets of institutions[8] are both elements within the structures of modern 'society' (to use an anachronism), and different principles of totality on which different phases of social development are based. The rationale for these two usages lies, of course, in Hegel's philosophy of history. History is to be understood as the process through which *Geist* re-creates at a higher level the lost unities of classical Greek civilisation. Each of the family, civil society and the state represents a stage in that re-creation. The principle embodied by the family is that of 'the immediate substantiality of mind' (Hegel, 1952: 110). Hegel maintains that the immediate unity of the family is bound (both in logic and in nature) to dissolve into a plurality of persons and families. This plurality becomes the basis of the institutions of civil society, where the units are 'private persons whose end is their own interest' (ibid.: 124). For the members of civil society the principle of unity, or universality, appears initially only as a means to self-interest. Although civil society becomes the arena for the development of law, public authority and the corporation (or guild), its ethical content can be realised only through its development into the state. For Hegel, 'the state is the actuality of the ethical Idea' in which individual self-consciousness finds 'as its essence and the end and product of its activity, its substantive freedom' (ibid.: 155).

The principle of Marx's objection to Hegel's attempt to show how the state realises the potential of civil society is stated early in the piece: 'Hegel everywhere makes the idea into the subject, while the generic, real subject, such as 'political sentiment' is turned into the predicate' (Marx, 1975b: 65). A little later on Marx explains this peculiarity by noting that 'Hegel's true interest is not the philosophy of right but logic' (ibid.: 73). In the 1843 text this methodological critique is developed in a painstaking attempt to show how Hegel falls into error on the substantive relations between civil society and state.[9] He is particularly scornful of the claim that a legislature based on the Estates[10] can mediate between civil society and state, thus enabling the latter to realise the former. Marx constantly asserts that Hegel's 'mediations' or 'syntheses' are rhetorical tricks which disguise, but do not resolve, contradictions. If the classes of civil society are not political entities, no amount of mediation can make them so. If they are political entities, they require no mediation: 'the middle term is the wooden sword, the concealed antithesis between the particular and the universal' (ibid.: 151). Hegel's basic trick is to define some element of the state in terms of its basis in civil society, then to define that element of civil society in terms of its role in the state, and finally to present this circularity as a synthesis, or mediation. So, Marx argues that the 'apparent identity' between the political Estates and the classes of civil society is

> artificially upheld by the supposition that, on the one hand, the class distinctions in civil society are defined by citizens rooted in the public sphere and, conversely, the class distinctions in the public sphere are defined by criteria rooted not in itself but in civil society. (ibid.: 149)

This type of 'uncritical mysticism' can only produce contradiction at the level of Hegel's account of the constitution of the state:

> Hegel would like to retain the medieval system of Estates, but in the form of the modern legislature, and he would like to retain the modern legislature, but in the shape of the medieval system of Estates! It is syncretism of the very worst sort. (ibid.: 163)

It transpires, then, that Hegel's error is of a subtly different order than a cursory reading of Marx's remark about 'subject' and 'predicate' might indicate. It is not so much that Hegel directly absorbs civil society into the state, in some single inversion of their proper relations, but that the figures though which he seeks to relate the one to the other can only produce a hopeless confusion about the order of priorities between them. In a series of inversions

> the most simple thing becomes the most complicated and the most complicated becomes the most simple. What should be a starting point becomes a mystical result and what should be a rational result becomes a mystical starting point. (ibid.: 99–100)

It is this self-induced confusion which Hegel's doctrine of the state as concrete universal can then appear to resolve idealistically. Marx proposes to cut through the Gordian knot of Hegelian confusion, first of all, by posing clearly alternative starting points and orders of priority. So, the Hegelian view of 'man as the subjectivised state' must be counterposed to the democratic view of 'the state as objectified man' (ibid.: 87). Again, either there is an unbridgeable gulf between civil society and state, or 'alternatively, civil society is the *real* political society' (ibid.: 189). Marx is in no doubt that when alternatives of this kind are posed clearly, the correct choice between them is quite clear. The starting point for the analysis of the relations between civil society and state can only be an understanding of civil society as it is. These arguments of Marx's articulate the basic defining themes of a project of modernist radicalism, and illustrate their foundationalist character.

Perhaps the theme which is least obviously present is that of 'ideology'. Indeed, Hegel gives more prominence to the limita-

tions of *doxa* than does Marx:[11] individuals in civil society are tied
to their private interest, capable of conceiving and achieving only
an 'abstract' unity, or universality. Only in the state can the individual transcend particularity. 'Since the state is mind objectified, it
is only as one of its members that the individual himself has
objectivity, genuine individuality and an ethical life' (Hegel, 1952:
156). If it is allowed that this Hegelian problem of the transcendence of particularity and abstract universality pre-figures the
problem of ideology, then Marx's critique of the Hegelian solution
might be seen as taking a step closer to a sociological conception
of ideology. The issue turns on the role of the Estates in giving
substance to the 'will which wills the universal' in the 'thinking
consciousness' of the member of the state (ibid.: 200). Marx insists
that Estates cannot embody a 'real' universality: they merely insti-
tutionalise the shared 'particular' interests of members of classes
in civil society. In the Estate or corporation 'instead of the individual function being made the function of society, the individual
function is made into a society for itself' (Marx, 1975b: 148). This
may work well enough as an account of the basis of a 'false consciousness' of universality, but it leaves Marx with a problem. All
he can oppose to Hegel's insistence that 'thinking consciousness'
becomes substantial in Estates are Feuerbachian claims about 'the
species belonging to the *universal generic essence* (which is) *its*
particularity' (ibid.: 192). In a radicalised civil society, species
essence will be expressed in a 'true' universality.

What Marx clearly lacks in the 1843 text is a specific peg on
which to hang the prospects for 'true' consciousness and universality. In the slightly later *'Introduction' to the Critique of Hegel's
Philosophy of Right*, this problem is directly tackled and resolved
in the manner which comes to define Marxism. Radical change
requires that 'one particular class undertakes from its *particular
situation* the universal emancipation of society' (Marx, 1975c:
254). The only class which can undertake this task without producing a merely partial, self-serving, revolution is 'a class of civil
society which is not a class of civil society, a class which is the
dissolution of all classes, a sphere which has a universal character
because of its universal suffering' (ibid.: 256). That class is, of
course, the proletariat. The proletariat as 'universal' class is not
only a solution to the practical problem of revolution, but also to
that of ideology. The universal class is the 'bearer' of universal
consciousness, the vehicle through which the truth of philosophy

32

can be realised in the world: 'Philosophy cannot realise itself without the transcendence of the proletariat, and the proletariat cannot transcend itself without the realization of philosophy' (ibid.: 257).

The second theme to be addressed is that of the 'end of philosophy', and although Marx continues to refer to his own enterprise as 'philosophy' in the 1843 text, his critique of Hegel articulates a version of the theme. Hegel purports to offer an account of the reality of family, civil society and state. As Marx allows, in Hegel 'empirical reality is accepted as it is, it is even declared to be rational' (Marx, 1975b: 63). But Hegel's methodological confusions can only obfuscate that reality by predicating it on his idealist account of the state, so that empirical reality 'is not rational by virtue of its own reason', it always 'has a meaning other than itself' (ibid.). Marx's critique establishes a 'great divide' between an un-critical Hegelian philosophy of the state which resolves into mysticism, and his own alternative of a critical philosophy of civil society as it really is. The key to the understanding of the structures and problems of civil society is to be found in the analysis of civil society itself. As the brief discussion of the mediating role of Estates above has made clear, Marx's claims to cross the divide rest on a series of propositions about the appropriate starting points of enquiry, and about the real relations of priority and dependence between the various objects of enquiry. These propositions index Marx's foundationalism: the superior power of his analyses is to be guaranteed in advance by a series of discoveries in the realms of general methodology and ontology. If enquiry *begins* from these discoveries, they can act as supports for its procedures and can secure its *autonomy* from other, potentially discrediting, dependencies. So, if enquiry into the state begins from the assumption that 'civil society is the *real* political society', a warrant is provided for the investigation of the political activities of the classes of civil society, and the enquiry is released from complicity in doctrines such as that of the state as a 'higher' form of unity. These foundational 'instances' of origin and autonomy will be discussed further in chapter six.

The third theme which defines modernist radicalism is that of the 'unity of theory and practice'. At the heart of Marx's critique of Hegel is an insistence that the effect of Hegel's conceptual labour is to leave the world just as it is: the real contradictions of civil society are massaged to produce an apparent resolution only.

Indeed, on the critical question of the Estates Marx inclines to the view that Hegelian doctrine is more actively regressive:

> The *constitution based on the Estates*, when not a tradition of the middle ages, is the attempt, partly within the political sphere itself, to plunge man back into the limitations of his private sphere ... and to use the existence of political class distinctions to re-introduce corresponding distinctions of social class. (Marx, 1975b: 147)

If for no other reason, critical philosophy must attain a unity of theory and practice precisely because the uncritical philosophy which it confronts articulates a 'bad' unity of the two. But the uncritical and critical unities are not quite equivalent. For reasons which have already been considered, the former is condemned to theoretical, and therefore to practical, confusion and (in the last instance) impotence.

Critical philosophy, however, enjoys a privileged foundational relationship to the real ground of the unity of theory and practice. 'Democracy' enjoys a privilege over all other political programmes and doctrines, because in democracy alone 'we find the constitution founded on its true ground: *real human beings* and the *real people*, not merely *implicitly* and in essence, but in *existence* and in reality' (ibid.: 87). Further, the realisation of a true political constitution, of democracy, requires real, and not merely conceptual, change in civil society. Only unrestricted suffrage can bring a political existence to civil society, but such a realisation must also be an abolition since in it 'civil society ensures that its civil existence, in so far as it is distinct from its political existence, is *inessential*' (ibid.: 191). The demand for electoral reform, argues Marx, is a demand for the 'dissolution' of the 'abstract political state', 'and this in turn implies the *dissolution of civil society*' (ibid.: 191). A radical theory of civil society and the radical transformation of civil society are held to require each other, and to attain their unity at the foundational level of the 'true ground' of human existence. As has been noted in the discussion of the 'ideology' theme, the 1843 text does not resolve the question of the 'agent' of the unity of theory and practice. This resolution is announced in the later *Introduction*. There is, however, a well-known passage in the earlier text which intimates where the resolution might lie, and which underlines the foundationalism of Marx's conception of civil society:

The *absence of property* and the *class of immediate labour*, of concrete labour, do not so much constitute a class of civil society as provide the ground on which the circles of civil society move and have their being. (ibid.: 146–7)

To sum up, Marx's 1843 critique of Hegel already articulates the basic figures of a project of modernist radicalism.[12] Marx deploys the themes of 'ideology', the 'end of philosophy' and the 'unity of theory and practice' to display the 'great divide' which separates him from Hegel. In doing so, he puts into play a series of foundational claims to ontological and methodological privilege. These claims turn on the discovery of civil society as the 'true ground' of modernity, and therefore of the possibility of its radical transformation.

The issue was raised earlier of Marx's complicity in the paradoxes of Enlightenment politics. Koselleck has traced the emergence in eighteenth-century Europe of a broad social stratum which 'shared the fate of being unable to find an adequate place within the absolutist state's existing institutions' (Koselleck, 1988: 66). The bourgeois 'public sphere' has its roots in the *sociétés de pensée* and masonic lodges within which this stratum begins to articulate a moral critique of absolutism. In the institutions of the Enlightenment 'bourgeois ethics, essentially tacit and secret, moves into the public domain' (ibid.: 55).

Viewed in this way, the Enlightenment turns on a series of paradoxes which amount, for Koselleck, to hypocrisy. In proclaiming their commitment to reason and morality alone, the institutions of Enlightenment deny that they offer a political challenge to the state. The 'secret', the 'other side of the Enlightenment' (ibid.: 95), is that the antithesis between state and civil society on which this denial hinges masks a challenge which is at once political and apolitical. The Enlightenment is secretly political to the extent that it does, indeed, challenge the authority of the state. It is apolitical to the extent that it does so in the name of a universal reason and morality rooted in civil society. The goal, as Koselleck writes of the masonic lodges, 'was as far as possible to make the state superfluous' (ibid.: 88).

Koselleck's is a provocative re-formulation of themes of the conservative counter-Enlightenment. He echoes Hegel's critique of the 'abstraction' of Enlightenment and its proximity to terror (see Hegel, 1949: 599–610) in the claim that the error and 'historical hypocrisy' of Enlightenment was to mistake its mere negation of the authority of the State for a political programme (Koselleck, 1988: 122). To the extent that Enlightenment criticism fails to engage with political issues of rule and sovereignty it becomes utopian. Alternatively, when Rousseau fuses the political problem of 'sovereign will' with the Enlightenment assertion of the 'moral autonomy of society', the result can only be 'permanent revolution', 'permanent dictatorship' (ibid.: 163–4).

Hegel's theory of the state is an attempt to overcome the opposition between Enlightenment and counter-Enlightenment. Marx's riposte is able to expose the inversions, mystifications and anachronisms of Hegel's reconciliation of state and civil society. But in doing so it re-capitulates the paradoxes, or hypocrisies, of Enlightenment in a reversion to civil society as the true ground of a rational universality. Marx sharpens, but does not move far beyond, the Enlightenment critique of the state in the claim that a realisation of the rationality immanent-but-obscured in civil society will abolish the distinction between civil society and state and restore to civil society its 'political existence'. In these early texts of Marx's the Enlightenment programme for a paradoxically apolitical politics is translated into the defining themes of modernist radicalism and bequeathed to social theory, where its problematic consequences continue to haunt radical projects such as Habermas's (see chapter four).

1.3 SOCIOLOGY AS MODERNIST RADICALISM: EMILE DURKHEIM

To suggest that Durkheim's work constitutes a project of modernist radicalism is to run counter to a once widely-maintained view that Durkheim is a 'conservative' thinker. It also implies that the most popular alternative view of Durkheim as a political 'liberal' cannot capture his peculiar blend of sociological and political themes.[15] Durkheim's vision of the role of sociology is extraordinarily ambitious. Sociological discourse enjoys a unique relation with the domain of the social, its privilege being secured in foundational claims of both a methodological and an ontological character. The privilege which sociology enjoys extends from 'theory' into 'practice': sociology is the basis on which alone the problems of specifically modern societies can be understood and resolved.

The three defining themes of modernist radicalism can again serve to organise the discussion. The 'ideology' theme plays a crucial role in establishing the 'privilege' of sociology throughout Durkheim's work, and in doing so invokes a privileged 'unity of theory and practice'. Durkheim's theory of morality serves as a case study in the scope of his pretensions in this area, and has direct connections with the 'end of philosophy' theme in which Durkheim represents sociology as both 'beyond' philosophy, and a continuation of it. The ambiguities of this position are important because they point to a chronic vulnerability in the project-form of modernist radicalism. The 'great divide' which separates and insulates modernist science from pre-modern philosophy can seem to shrink, becoming one small topographical irregularity among others, so that separation is transformed into discrediting continuity.

Durkheim's theory of ideology occupies a strategic position in *The Rules of the Sociological Method*, supporting a series of demonstrations that sociology is the science of a specific object, 'society'. The doctrine of the objectivity of 'the social' is a connecting thread running between the three definitive themes of Durkheim's modernist radicalism. The doctrine first appears in *The Rules* through the well-known, and much criticised,[14] definition of 'social facts' as external to, and constraining of, individuals (Durkheim, 1964a: 13). Once social facts are defined in this way, the injunction to 'consider social facts as things' (ibid.: 14) follows naturally, since 'the most important characteristic of a 'thing' is the impossibility of its modification by a simple act of the will' (ibid.: 28). In the second chapter of *The Rules*, the objectivity of the social is established in a linked series of oppositions between two chains of terms: individuality–teleology/will–ideology versus objectivity–causality–science. 'The social' moves independently of the teleological grid through which individual will and consciousness try to appropriate it. In common sense, and other pre-scientific conceptions of the world, social relations are thought in close connection with models of desirable states of affairs. These goal-directed conceptions of things are then 'mistaken for the things themselves', and individual consciousness 'gives itself up to boundless ambition and comes to believe in the possibility of constructing, or rather reconstructing, the world, by virtue of its own resources and at the whim of its desires' (ibid.: 17).

To forget the objective, refractory, nature of the social is to suc-
cumb to the ideological temptation to see it as the product of
(intentional) consciousness, and vice versa. Durkheimian
sociology stakes its claim for privilege and autonomy on its
capacity to offer an alternative to such individualistic, ideological
conceptions of the social. In one way, the shift from ideology to
science is easily accomplished: 'in considering social phenomena
as things we merely adjust our conceptions in conformity with
their nature' (ibid.: 29). To accept that the social is a domain of
external, observable processes is to have made the major part of
this adjustment:

> Social phenomena are things and ought to be treated as
> things … it is unnecessary to philosophize on their nature
> …. It is sufficient to note that they are the unique data of
> the sociologist. All that is given, all that is subject to
> observation has thereby the character of a thing. (ibid.: 27)

But the simple recognition and observation of an 'external'
domain cannot be that simple. The whole point of Durkheim's
ideology theme is to show that for most of the time, for most
people, the objectivity of the social is not immediately available precisely because it is obfuscated in the chain individuality–teleology/will-ideology. What Durkheim terms the 'natural
bent of the human mind' (*la pente naturelle de notre esprit*) (ibid.:
16) which lures it towards ideology is not merely a psychological 'given', but is rooted in the exigencies of practical
life.[15]

These exigencies haunt the emergence of science itself,
threatening to hobble its flight from ideology:

> Since [science] comes into being only for the purpose of
> satisfying vital necessities, it finds itself quite naturally
> oriented towards the attainment of practical results. The
> needs which it is called on to relieve are always urgent, and
> consequently hasten it to a conclusion; they demand
> remedies, not explanations'. (ibid.)

Unrestrained by scientific method, the practical needs which
motivate science will produce ideology. It follows that Durkheimian science presents two 'faces', one in its relations with its
object, the other in relations with (human) subjects. In its relation
to the object, science is the simplest procedure in the world, a

receptivity to its 'nature'. But in its relations with the subject, science requires considerable artifice to achieve this simplicity. It must police a consciousness whose nature and circumstances tend it towards ideological misrepresentation. *The Rules* oscillate between these two faces. On the one side, sociology requires us 'simply' to seek external characteristics of things, 'merely' to adjust our conceptions to the nature of the object, 'all that it asks' is that the principle of causality be applied (ibid.: 55, 26, 141). On the other side, avoidance of error in sociology requires 'long and special training', or 'distinctively sociological training', and scientific method is seen as 'a complex apparatus of precautions' (ibid.: xxxvii, 145, 146).

These two faces of Durkheimian sociology correspond to two aspects of its cognitive privilege. Most importantly, sociology enjoys a privileged relation to the social object, the full dimensions of which will become clear later. In addition, sociological method attains a privileged relation to human subjectivity, as a secular version of the spiritual exercises. These privileges also have a practical dimension. The roots of science lie in the requirements of practice, and it is incumbent on Durkheim to show that the abandonment of ideology in favour of science can produce useful results. In his discussion of the intertwining of ideology and the roots of science, Durkheim remarks that the ideological point of view characterises 'alchemy rather than chemistry, astrology rather than astronomy' (ibid.: 16).[16] Not only do alchemy and astrology misrepresent their objects, they don't work. Motivated by the desire to achieve immediate practical results, they fall into errors of a magnitude which renders them practically, as well as theoretically, void.

The first step to a practically useful science is a rigorous distinction between 'cause' and 'function', and Durkheim is scathing about what he takes to be Spencer's relapse into metaphysics through a failure to make that distinction.[17] Once the distinction is made, sociology can be useful in at least two ways. First, Durkheim appeals to the structural isomorphism between explanation and prediction:

> It can be shown that behaviour of the past, when analysed, can be reduced to relationships of cause and effect. Those relationships can then be transformed, by an equally logical operation, into rules of action for the future. (ibid.: xxxix–xl)

Scientific knowledge of the social object yields means adequate to its control. Second, and more radically, the combination of causal with functional analysis suggests a more than instrumental role for sociology. Durkheim states his claim modestly to begin with:

> If ... we can find an objective criterion, inherent in the facts themselves, which enables us to distinguish between health and morbidity in the various orders of social phenomena, science will be in a position to throw light on practical problems, and still remain faithful to its own method. (ibid.: 49)

Durkheim's first criterion for determining the 'health' (or normality) of a social phenomenon is that of generality. This can be ascertained by observation, conditioned only by the necessity (which Durkheim discusses at length) of ensuring that like is compared with like. The generality of a phenomenon may well 'throw light' on practical issues, but it is unlikely to be decisive.

However, Durkheim cites a second criterion of normality, that of a normality 'grounded in the nature of things' (ibid.: 59), or as it might be, a 'normality-as-functional-necessity'. Such a criterion could be deployed only in a mature sociology which could provide 'an almost complete explanation of the phenomena concerned' (ibid.: 63). Should such conditions hold, however, Durkheim will be less modest about the efficacy of sociology. Through the scientific identification of functionally necessary social phenomena, and their differentiation from the pathological, 'should be settled all controversial questions such as those concerning the normality of the decline in religious beliefs, or of the development of state powers' (ibid.: 62). It is clear, then, that Durkheim's 'ideology' theme also addresses the issue of theory and practice. The scientific alternative to ideology comes as a package of the two dimensions: the 'great divide' which separates science from ideology is between different ways of organising social affairs, as well as between different ways of thinking about them.

Durkheim's version of the great divide is refined in later texts which focus more clearly on the 'representational' character of social reality. 'The Dualism of Human Nature' of 1914 aligns three familiar Durkheimian oppositions between subject–object, individual–collective and profane–sacred. These oppositions are concentrated in the duality which human beings 'feel', and which all civilisations recognise in variants of body–soul dualism. They correspond 'to the double existence that we lead concurrently, the one purely individual and rooted in our organisms, the other social and nothing but an extension of society' (Durkheim, 1960: 337). This text offers a neo-Kantian equation of 'individual representations' with sensations and of 'collective representations' with concepts.[18] All generalising, conceptual thought is ascribed to the collectivity, a view which Durkheim clearly expects to be contested: 'We do not mean to deny the individual the capacity to form concepts. He learns to form representations of this kind from the collectivity ... they are constructed in such a way that they can be universalised' (ibid.: 339n.).

Durkheim's emphasis on collective representations does not require that the equation of ideology with subjectivity be abandoned.[19] In *Pragmatism and Sociology* Durkheim draws a distinction between 'mythological' and 'scientific' truth which clearly re-introduces the subject–object dichotomy. Both types of truth have a collective character, but are otherwise distinct. First, science but not myth is subject to the authority of method, to 'testing and demonstration' (Durkheim, 1983: 86). Second, and critically, science but not myth is conditioned by the nature of the object. Individual minds communicate 'either by unifying to form a single collective mind, or by communicating with one object which is the same for all'. The first unity is myth, the second science (ibid.: 88). Third, myth provides instant solutions to problems which require extended scientific consideration; 'society cannot wait for its problems to be solved scientifically' (ibid.: 90). Finally, myth is a continuing obstacle to science. There is within society 'a tendency towards objective scientific truth and a tendency towards subjectively received truth, towards mythological truth. This is also one of the great obstacles which obstruct the development of sociology' (ibid.: 91). Here, the subjectivity–objectivity opposition is re-inscribed within the realm of the collective: the collectivity of myth aggregates, but does not transcend, the limitations of individuality.

Durkheim's 'ideology' theme provides him with a set of arguments for the formal superiority of sociology as a form of theory and a form of practice. It does not in itself give a content to that form, however. Substantive diagnosis of the ills of modernity begins in *The Division of Labour in Society* with the differentiation of mechanical and organic solidarity. This familiar distinction enables Durkheim to demonstrate that social modernity is a new kind of social order, not just a degenerate old one, and *ipso facto* to demonstrate the explanatory power of sociology as the privileged discourse of modernity. Once Durkheim has established the link between the new society and the new science at the level of theory, he can do so at the level of practice. The discussion of the 'abnormal forms' of the division of labour in Book 3 is an early case study in the diagnostic powers of the new science.

'When we know the circumstances in which the division of labour ceases to bring forth solidarity, we shall better understand what is necessary for it to have that effect. Pathology, here as elsewhere, is a valuable aid of physiology'. (Durkheim, 1964b: 353)

In a series of later texts, notably *Suicide*, Durkheim refines a model of anomie and egoism as twin threats to the regulation and integration of specifically modern societies.[20] The two major solutions which he proposes are, first, the establishment of occupational groups and their insertion into a new political structure and, second, the development of a new morality fitted to the demands and constraints of modernity.

It is in this area that Durkheim most clearly inherits and refines the Enlightenment utopia of an apolitical rational politics. Durkheimian sociology exemplifies what Bauman (1987: 4) has termed the 'typically modern strategy of intellectual work ... [which is] ... best characterized by the metaphor of the "legislator" role'. The sociologist is able to transform the ideological problems of politics into scientific problems susceptible to expert analysis and solution. The solutions which Durkheim proposes are only superficially 'political': they blur the boundaries between state and society and subordinate the former to the immanent rationality of the latter. In this, of course, Durkheim is at one with the Enlightenment as Koselleck understands it. Durkheim's programme found powerful allies and sponsors among radical republicans and established an institutional basis in the reformed 'new Sorbonne'. It also made enemies, however. Lepenies (1988: chs 1 and 2) has shown how the rift between Durkheimians and anti-Durkheimians aligns with a rift between social scientific and literary intellectuals over the legislative pretensions of the former, a rift which echoes that between Enlightenment and counter-Enlightenment.[21]

Durkheim's account of the relations between sociology and morality is of particular interest given the centrality of the demands of morality to the legislative programmes of the Enlightenment. For Durkheim, sociology is as much a solution to a practico-moral problem as morality is a solution to a sociological problem. Sociology is to be the modern solution to the Kantian problem of the projected unity of 'pure' and 'practical' reason.[22] The 'rational kernel' of Kant's moral theory is his insistence on the *impersonality* of morality, for Durkheim (e.g. see Durkheim, 1976: 445). Moral rules stand over and above the individual, transcending individual interest: 'Morality begins with disinterest, with attachment to something other than ourselves' (Durkheim, 1960: 327). Of course, the 'something other' can only be society, or the collectivity, for Durkheim.[23] He 'materialises' Kant's treatment of the impersonality of morality, rejecting any claim that the source of value lies beyond the phenomenal world: 'If the ideal does not depend on the real it would be impossible to find in the real the conditions and causes which would make it intelligible' (Durkheim, 1974: 88). However, this materialisation does not reduce the theory of morality to an empirical sociology of morality. *Moral Education* insists on a distinction between morality 'as it is' empirically and the 'idea' of morality. The former 'consists in an infinity of special rules, fixed and specific, which order men's conduct in ... different situations' (Durkheim, 1961: 25). But the latter is inseparable from the idea of authority itself, which is 'what there is in the conception of rules beyond the notion of regularity' (ibid.: 29). There follows the strikingly Kantian claim that 'One must obey a moral precept out of respect for it, and for this reason alone' (ibid.: 30).

The Elementary Forms of the Religious Life makes a similar case about 'society'. Durkheim asks whether it is the 'real' or 'ideal' society which is the basis of religion: the 'real' society seems too imperfect while the 'ideal' seems too fanciful (Durkheim, 1976: 420). The dilemma is resolved in an account of the 'collective life' in which society can 'assemble and concentrate itself' (ibid.: 422). In the cases of both 'morality' and 'society' Durkheim offers concepts which purport to go beyond the empirical 'given', while refusing appeals to transcendental principles. This strategy leads him to a further, and consequential, departure from Kant's position. *Moral Education* notes Kant's 'keen sense' that morality contains two apparently opposed principles of 'obligation' and

43

'autonomy'. Kant fuses the two elements in a concept of the 'rational will': an individual will in perfect harmony with the dictates of reason would autonomously pursue only those ends which morality renders obligatory for lesser spirits.

This doctrine would seem to be tailor-made for a Durkheimian 'sociologisation'. He could portray the properly moralised and integrated individual as wholly in tune with the collective life of society. Indeed, this is sometimes taken to be Durkheim's view.[24] But the possibility is explicitly rejected, as Durkheim insists that 'the moral law is invested with an authority that imposes deference even upon reason' (Durkheim, 1961: 110), and later that 'we are finite beings; and, in a sense, we are still passive with respect to the law that commands us' (ibid.: 118). While Durkheim's views on the individual as *homo duplex* are implicated in this doctrine,[25] it cannot entirely be explained by appeals to the 'animality' inherent in the human constitution. A fuller answer requires attention to the connections between Durkheim's theories of morality and of knowledge. In turn, this issue points to the heart of the 'end of philosophy' theme and to a sense of the scope of Durkheim's radicalism.

A critical piece of the puzzle lies in the historicist dimension to Durkheim's late theory of knowledge. Conceptual thought gains its peculiar power because its categories are a distillation of a collective human history, 'a complete section of the history of humanity is resumed therein' (Durkheim, 1976: 19). No individual consciousness could ever grasp the richness of this history. 'In relation to ... collective thought, we stand in the same relation as Plato's *nous* to the world of ideas. We never manage to see it in its entirety or in its reality' (Durkheim, 1983: 105). Since knowledge and morality share a foundation in the collective life of society, the limitations of the individual will be the same with respect to both. If the laws of both theory (knowledge) and practice (morality) are beyond the apprehension of individuals, individuals cannot be the site of the 'unity' of the two. Any Durkheimian analogue to the Kantian 'rational will' which unites obligation with autonomy, and points to a unity of pure and practical reason, must lie elsewhere. There is, of course, only one candidate for this role. The power of any science derives from its collective character, which allows it to transcend the limitations of individual consciousness, and from its subordination to method, which provides regulated access to objectivity. Among the sciences, sociology enjoys a uniquely privileged position: its object is the ground of all objectivity and authority, the collective life of society itself. Sociology alone has the capacity to function as the 'rational will' of society and to secure a rational unity of theory and practice.

The doctrine of 'moral individualism' illustrates Durkheim's belief in the function of sociology as the unity of theory and practice. The value of individualism is doubly conditioned for Durkheim. First, the moral value of the individual depends on attachment to the collectivity as 'the highest reality in the intellectual and moral order' (Durkheim, 1976: 16). It follows that from a sociological perspective 'true' individualism cannot be equated with egoism.[26] Second, in *The Division of Labour* increasing heterogeneity and individualism are identified as inescapable elements in the emergence of organic solidarity. By a Durkheimian 'cunning of reason' the development of society itself has provided the material basis for a specifically modern morality. It falls to sociology to give a theoretical account of the relations between individual and society under conditions of modernity, and to draw out its practical implications. Sociology can demonstrate that a modern morality must be individualistic because individualism reflects the character of collective life in modern society, and that moral individualism is the appropriate corrective to anomie and egoism.

It will be clear by now that Durkheim places his sociology in a complex relation of continuity and discontinuity to philosophy. A version of the 'end of philosophy' theme appears in *The Division of Labour*, where the process of scientific specialisation is held to make the traditional integrating role of philosophy impossible, for a familiar reason.

> As long as the same mind could, at once, cultivate different sciences, it was possible to acquire the competency necessary for their unification. But, as they become specialised ... it becomes more and more impossible for one human intelligence to gain a sufficiently exact knowledge of this great multitude of phenomena, of laws, of hypotheses which must be summed up. (Durkheim, 1964b: 362)

In scientific, as in social development a 'mechanical' solidarity based on sameness gives way to an 'organic' solidarity based on specialisation of function. This process is consequential for philosophy which 'is the collective conscience of science, and, here as elsewhere, the role of the collective conscience becomes smaller as labour is divided' (ibid.: 364). If this argument is projected on to the later doctrines discussed above, it appears that sociology acquires a privilege in relation to science which differs from that once enjoyed by philosophy in the same way that its privilege in relation to morality differs from that once enjoyed by religion. The privileges of philosophy and religion are appropriate to 'mechanical' solidarity, that of sociology to 'organic' solidarity and modernity. However, Durkheim is keen that sociology should be recognised as the legitimate heir of rationalist philosophy, and his enthusiasm leads to a plethora of not always consistent claims about the relations between sociology and philosophy.[27]

The title and form of *The Rules*, for example, echoes the tradition of rationalist texts on method reaching back to Descartes' *Discours*. A more nearly contemporary example, which influenced Durkheim particularly, was Renouvier's *Essais de critique générale*. This text places philosophy on the side of science rather than theology: 'so-called rationalism, in France at least, borrowing its tenets from theological traditions, becomes highly conventionalised: it is frightened of logic' (Renouvier, 1875: xi). Durkheim's project has clear connections with this scientific turn in rationalist philosophy. Renouvier's claims for philosophy as a strict science turn on the doctrine of representations: ' The method of *science* or *general criticism* consists in the analysis of what is given in representations, considered at the highest possible level of generality' (ibid.: 179). Durkheim is therefore well able to present the prospect of a sociological resolution of philosophical problems as a continuation of Renouvier's project. He cites as his authority for the treatment of categories as representations 'recent disciples of Kant' (Durkheim, 1982a: 239). *Moral Education* equates the 'rationalist postulate' with 'the postulate which is the basis of science', that is, 'there is nothing in reality that one is justified in considering fundamentally beyond the scope of human reason' (Durkheim, 1961: 4).

At the roots of the shift from Kantian 'categories' to Durkheimian 'representations' is a relativisation of knowledge which Renouvier sets in train. 'Kant set himself an impossible task in wishing to prove that his categories were the real ones, and that there were neither more nor less than he had enumerated'

(Renouvier, 1875: 208). Relativism in these matters is for Renouvier, the key to the door between philosophy and science.

> *Everything is relative*, this great saying of scepticism, this last word of the philosophy of pure reason in antiquity, must become the first word of the modern method, and in consequence of science, because it points the way out of the realm of illusion'. (ibid.: 123)

Relativism is something of a double-edged sword for Durkheim, however. He requires enough of it to allow him to impute a social origin to the categories, but too much would prejudice the authority and objectivity of truth, thereby undermining sociology as an embodiment of the rationalist project. This dilemma is resolved in a neo-Kantian *coup de main*. The threat which excessive relativism poses to the authority of truth as universal and unconditioned is to be met by rendering the authority of truth as a *moral* authority, so that 'truth is a norm for thought in the same way that the moral idea is a norm for conduct' (Durkheim, 1983: 98). Durkheim regards pragmatism as a relativism which goes too far, and forgets that truth 'cannot be separated from a certain moral character ... in truth, there is something which commands respect, and a moral power to which the mind feels properly *bound* to assent (ibid.: 73). Truth and morality are simply two faces of the authority of the collective, which finds its articulate form in sociology: it is the *existence* of sociology, rather than any of its specific findings, which solves the problems of rationalist philosophy.

Sociology is conceived by Durkheim as a project of modernist radicalism which yields nothing to Marx in its audacity. No less than Marx, Durkheim wishes to inaugurate an *epistémē* which will not only uniquely comprehend modernity, but will also serve as a vehicle for the realisation of its as yet unrealised potential. The evident differences between the specific programmes which Marx and Durkheim endorse[28] should not be allowed to obscure this fundamental continuity. Marx's (re)discovery of civil society as the ground of universality and Durkheim's theory of morality can both be understood as re-inscriptions of the Enlightenment project into social theory by way of the defining themes of modernist radicalism. Given the paradoxes of Enlightenment, it is not surprising that a series of pervasive ambiguities, or paradoxes, appear in the foundational claims of modernist radicalism. The new *epistēmē* will 'end' philosophy, but will also 'complete' it; it will be the simple and direct expression of objective reality, but it will also be a complex and inaccessible expert discourse; it will be qualitatively different to the practical discourse of *doxa*, but it will be able to solve practical problems. Paradoxes of this kind must be related to the inherent limitations of the foundationalist conceptions of enquiry which modernist radicalism puts into play. The question of 'foundationalism' is taken up in chapter six. The intermediate chapters consider exemplars of modernist radicalism and its developing critique, beginning with the emergence of a sociological critique in the work of Simmel and Weber.

2

THE SOCIOLOGICAL
CRITIQUE OF MODERNIST
RADICALISM

2.1 PRELIMINARIES

Durkheim and Weber are conventionally linked together as cautious and reformist members of a generation which moved beyond the over-simplifications of Marx's radicalism.[1] On the present argument, however, a line must be drawn which separates Weber from Marx and Durkheim. The two latter writers are 'modernist radicals' while Weber offers a forceful critique of modernist radicalism. The subsequent development, or dissolution, of social theory makes of Weber a liminal figure, poised on a number of thresholds and feeding into a variety of otherwise opposed traditions. Here, Weber's critique is placed in relation to Simmel's. In many respects, Simmel offers the more radical alternative to modernist radicalism, one which pitches him well beyond the boundaries of the 'classical project'. The tasks of this chapter are to identify those cruces at which Weber and Simmel break from modernist radicalism, to assess the implications of these breaks, and to reach a preliminary judgement about the capacity of each break to inform a post-foundational radicalism in sociology.

2.2 SIMMEL AND THE EXPERIENCE OF MODERNITY

That Simmel does not fit easily into the pattern of classical sociology is the source of the fascination of his work and the difficulty of interpreting it. Indeed, ritual references to Simmel's singularity, brilliance and marginality have become a cliché. It may be because he moves so far outside the orbit of modernist radicalism that Simmel seems so odd. Four aspects of Simmel's work can index his distance from modernist radicalism: the particular type of 'formality', or abstraction, which Simmel puts into play, the centrality to his work of the category of 'experience', the strict limits which he places on the possibility of historical knowledge, and his continuing commitment to philosophy. Taken together, these factors lead Simmel to negate each of the defining themes of modernist radicalism, that is, the ideology theme, the end of philosophy theme, and the unity of theory and practice.

(a) Formalism

It is instructive to contrast the ways in which Simmel and Durkheim try to establish the basis of sociology as a 'special science'. Durkheim states the problem in the opening paragraph of *The Rules*:

> the designation 'social' ... is currently employed for practically all phenomena generally diffused within society, however small their social interest. But on that basis there are, as it were, no human events that may not be called social ... [so that] ... sociology would have no subject matter exclusively its own, and its domain would be confused with that of biology and psychology. (Durkheim, 1964a: 1)

Durkheim's well-known solution turns on the 'discovery' of the social as a reality *sui generis*, which establishes the study of social facts as the defining task of sociology.

Simmel's point of departure recalls Durkheim's. In 'The Problem of Sociology' he argues against a 'conception of sociology as the science of everything human', a conception which becomes 'the El Dorado of the homeless and rootless' in the world of socio-historical studies (Simmel, 1959a: 311). However, the object of Simmelian sociology is not a more discretely bounded region of reality. To begin with, sociology must be defined as a 'new *method*, an instrument of investigation, a new way of getting at the subject matter [of other human sciences]' (ibid.: 312). The 'method' consists in analysing socio-historical phenomena 'in terms of interaction and co-action' (ibid.). But as Simmel recognises, using the parallel of induction, a method is not in itself a science. Sociology does, indeed, require a subject matter but one which is to be found, as in the case of linguistics, 'by drawing a new line through facts which are quite well known' (ibid.: 313). The 'line' which is to define sociology is 'a concept of society which subjects socio-historical data to a new mode of abstraction and coordination' (ibid.). It is here that the question of formalism emerges, because the discipline-defining 'mode of abstraction' is to be specified as the identification of 'forms of sociation'.

Simmel's debt to Kant is the key to his elusive concept of 'form' and its relation to that of 'content'. In Kant's famous slogan, 'thoughts without content are empty, intuitions without concepts are blind' (Kant, 1970: 93). Knowledge is produced only in the 'synthesis' of concepts and intuitions. In enquiries into the possibility of knowledge, the specific content of intuition is not to the point: the synthetic regularities which ensure the unity of nature are to be discovered through the analysis of the forms, or concepts and categories, under which contents/intuitions are brought. Simmel draws the lesson that sociological enquiry into the 'synthetic unity' of society must be equally indifferent to the variable contents of social life. These latter 'materials which fill life' and 'motivations which propel it' are not, in themselves, social (see Simmel, 1959a: 314–15). However, and as Frisby notes, there seems to be an important difference between Kant's formalism and Simmel's: Simmel does not ask 'how is knowledge of society possible?', but rather (in the title of Simmel's essay) 'how is society possible?' (see Frisby, 1981: 64). The consequential nuance which divides Simmel from Kant has its rationale in a version of the contemporary neo-Kantian distinction between the natural and cultural sciences.[2]

Simmel gives an orthodox account of natural science, arguing that for Kant the unity of nature 'emerges in the observing subject exclusively' (Simmel, 1959b: 338). For the cultural sciences, however, matters are different: 'The unity of society needs no observer. It is directly realised by its own elements because these elements are themselves conscious and synthesising units' (ibid.). Sociology is to investigate social processes in their aspect as 'part of the synthesis to which we give the inclusive name of "society"'(ibid.: 340). The condition of sociology must always be shaped by what might be termed a 'double synthesis' (to adapt Giddens's 'double hermeneutic'): the 'contents' which sociology synthesises are already the 'forms' of a first-order synthesis. Because the synthetic unity of society is accomplished independently of the sociological observer, its investigation cannot be an epistemological reflection. Sociology is to be a special science, rather than an enquiry into the possibility of science,[3] and its formalism is to be the product of scientific abstraction: 'Abstractions alone produce science out of the complexity or the unity of reality' (Simmel, 1959a: 316). The specific type of abstraction which sociology requires is, of course, the abstraction of the forms from the contents of sociation. Simmel is most insistent that forms are not 'things': forms and contents are not two kinds of entity which compose the world. As he puts it, 'in any given social phenomenon, content and societal form constitute one reality' (ibid: 315). The process of abstraction through which the analyst identifies societal forms is just that, a process of abstraction and not the direct observation of a type of entity. It follows that the way in which the form–content distinction is applied must be, to a degree, a function of the scope of the analyst's concerns: what may quite legitimately be abstracted out as 'form' in a small-scale study may itself be absorbed as 'content' in the sweep of a broader analysis.[4]

Durkheim was familiar with Simmel's work,[5] and while he sympathised with the attempt to establish sociology as a specialised science, he saw that Simmel's version ran in a direction other than his own. Durkheim takes Simmel's view to be that 'the association is the only expressly social thing, and sociology is the science of association *in abstracto*' (Durkheim, 1982b: 190). Durkheim has no objection to 'abstraction' as such, but 'things must be divided up according to the way they fit together naturally', so that abstraction is 'in conformity with the nature of things' (ibid.: 190, 191). On this criterion, Durkheim objects to the way in which the form–content opposition excludes from analysis 'the various phenomena which constitute the very stuff of social life' (ibid.: 191); 'contents', too, may have an origin in collective life and can count as social. In Simmel's hands, sociology can become only 'a formal, vague philosophy' (ibid.: 193). On the other side, Simmel claims that 'naive naturalism errs in assuming that the given itself contains the analytic or synthetic arrangements through which it becomes the content of science' (Simmel, 1959a: 316). To a sociology conditioned by a 'double synthesis', Durkheim's social realism could only appear as a 'naive naturalism'.

Simmel's sociology of form (a more appropriate label than 'formal sociology') challenges the model of sociology as a modernist radicalism on at least two fronts. First, the topography of society which emerges from Simmel's analyses closes off the prospect of any privileged 'unity of theory and practice'. The institutions and processes which fill the space of Marx's social formations, or Durkheim's societies, are also the focus for various schemes of social and political change. Simmel (1959a: 326) terms them 'official' social formations. Capitalist enterprises, social classes, forms of state organisation, suicide rates, solidary groups and the rest are matters about which policies can be formulated and pursued with some prospect of recognition as salient. These 'great organs and systems' 'seem to constitute society, and therefore appear to be the subject matter of the science of society' (Simmel, 1959a: 326). But they cannot be the objects of sociology for two related reasons.

First, they are too large, they obscure the 'microscopic-molecular processes within human material ... [which are] ... the actual occurrences that are hypostatized into those macroscopic, solid units and systems' (ibid.: 327). Second, hypostatized macro-units are detatched from interaction, or sociation, between individuals. One arm of Simmel's challenge to the 'unity of theory and practice', then, is that the institutions which are the focus of practice cannot be the focus of science. Conversely, the focus of Simmelian sociology is unlikely to be a focus for practice: 'smash the dyad' is not a slogan which would lead many to the barricades.

The second way in which Simmel's formalism undermines modernist radicalism is slightly less obvious but no less consequential. The 'ideology' theme serves at least two functions for modernist radicalisms. First, it articulates a claim that the favoured project can produce founded Knowledge, while both other projects and common sense are doomed to re-capitulate variously defective knowledges. This claim can be linked, second, to the 'unity of theory and practice' theme: a new kind of Knowledge of the social can guide a new kind of Practice which will displace inferior practices. Simmel occupies only a small corner of this terrain in his claim that the analysis of forms of sociation is the sole basis for scientific sociology. Critically excluded is any sense that sociology is in competition with 'common sense' accounts of society. The point can be taken further. The subject matter of sociology is, in an important sense, accomplished by actors pursuing the concerns of everyday life: the first order 'synthesis' of society is produced in a multitude of social interactions.

This precisely does not mean that sociology simply re-capitulates actors' models of the social world. As Simmel puts it, the actor 'is absorbed in innumerable, specific relations and in the feeling and knowledge of determining others and of being determined by them' (Simmel: 1959b: 338). Actors will not be conscious of the 'abstract notion of unity' (ibid.) which is the concern of sociology. Sociological accounts of society bear a complex relation to actors' accounts which cannot be trimmed to fit the 'ideology' theme, since sociology abstracts from reality to constitute its subject matter on quite different principles from those employed by the actors absorbed in social life. This relationship allows sociology to be be 'expert' about its concerns in a way that actors do not attain, but without the necessity of construing actors as defective sociologists.

(b) Experience

Simmel's category of 'experience' can be connected to both his Kantian and vitalist engagements: for the Kantian, experience is the site (and product) of synthesis, while for the vitalist experience taps into the flow of 'life' itself. Simmel's account of experience in terms of the form–content distinction draws together these two strands, and issues in an account of 'modernity' in which modernity itself becomes a category of experience, rather than a condition of a *sui generis* social 'reality' in the manner of Durkheim. It is in this sense, most directly, that Simmel's emphasis on experience contradicts the tenets of modernist radicalism. The point can be illustrated with reference to *The Philosophy of Money*, which comes closest of all Simmel's texts to inviting a reading which aligns it to modernist radicalism.

The case that *The Philosophy of Money* should be read in this way has been pressed forcefully by Turner. The text not only prefigures the Weberian rationalisation theme (Turner, 1986: 99), but also offers a 'definite perspective on the three dimensions of estrangement: reification, alienation and objectification' (ibid.: 100). For Turner it was Simmel, rather than his epigone Lukács, who '"rediscovered" the alienation theme in Marx's treatment of money in the capitalist economy' (ibid.: 102). There is textual support for this reading. Within a few pages Simmel claims that in modernity there is a 'preponderance of objective over subjective culture' (e.g. Simmel, 1978: 449), and reflects on the relations between this (putative) 'reification' and the modern division of labour (ibid.: 453). He further notes how money, along with intellectuality and law, 'are defined by their complete indifference to individual qualities' (ibid.: 442) and connects this indifference to the 'feeling of secret self-contradiction' which characterises modern life (ibid.: 443). It seems plausible to assimilate these concerns into a generalised 'lament over reification' (to borrow Rose's phrase),[6] joining Simmel with Marx, Weber, Lukács, Adorno and others.

To leave matters there would be to blur important distinctions, however. Simmel departs from Marx's 1844 treatment of the alienation theme in two crucial respects. First, for Marx, alienation is primarily a structural condition of capitalist production, distribution and exchange. It is only secondarily a category of experience. He refers to 'private property, greed, the separation of labour, capital and landed property, exchange and competition, value and the devaluation of man, monopoly and competition etc.' as 'this entire system of estrangement' (Marx, 1975d: 323). The manifestation of alienation in the experience of the worker is to be explained by reference to the structures of the 'system of estrangement'. Because Marx's account of alienation turns on the relations between experience and its extra-experiential roots, he is able to argue that there is a solution to the problem of alienation in the transformation of material conditions.

It is tempting to impose this pattern on the Simmelian theme of the dominance of 'objective' over 'subjective' culture, so that 'subjectivity' is seen to be crushed by the material structures of modern society. But the heart of Simmel's distance from Marx lies in his effective rejection of the distinction between experience and its extra-experiential foundation. The distinction between objective and subjective culture is not one between material and spiritual/mental realities. Objective culture is the empirical realisation of 'objective mind' which has become independent of any particular individual. Adapting Simmel's own illustration (1978: 452), one might say that scientific practices are part of objective culture, while the truth of science is part of objective mind. Two implications can be drawn from this. First, Simmel's thesis of the dominance of objective over subjective culture concerns the relations between different constellations of experience, not the relations between experience and its non-experiential foundation. Simmel is not a Marxist materialist.[7] Second, as the inclusion of science within it makes clear, the category of objective culture does not designate a wholly pathological reification.

A further problem with Turner's reading of Simmel, in which money is taken to be 'the classic illustration of [the] congealing of content into reified form' (Turner, 1986: 96) is that form as such is not a reification of content. Content can only be experienced as *formed* content, and subjective as well as objective culture is form-dependent. The processes through which particular forms become part of objective mind and culture, and which Simmel sees as an integral part of any advanced culture, are not usefully labelled as 'reification'.

This oddity can be related to the second major difference between Simmel and Marx on alienation, which turns on Marx's conception of 'species being'. Marx's 1844 text is a 'critique' of alienation not only in the technical sense that it delineates the foundations and limits of a phenomenon, but also in the more colloquial sense of a 'criticism' of something undesirable. The doctrine of species being allows Marx to draw together these two senses. Alienated labour is possible because it shares with labour 'as such' that capacity for conscious productive activity which is human 'species being'. Alienated labour puts into play this capacity for labour, but crucially distorts it:

> 'In relation to the worker who *appropriates* nature through his labour, appropriation appears as estrangement, self activity as activity of another and for another, vitality as a sacrifice of life, production of an object as loss of that object to an alien power, to an *alien* man'. (Marx, 1975d: 334)

The idea of species being furnishes Marx with a model of what human beings are in their essence which can unify his account of how capitalist production is possible with an account of why it is unacceptable. It helps to establish versions of the 'unity of theory and practice' and 'end of philosophy'.[8]

Simmel has no conceptual equivalent to 'species being' which can form the basis for evaluations of supposedly universal validity. The absence is not an oversight. Simmel is both a Kantian and a relativist: as a Kantian, he knows that evaluation cannot evade the necessity for a judgement of value, and as a relativist he knows that the standards for such judgements are not fixed. Further, *The Philosophy of Money* is a reflection on the dynamics of value, where value is a fundamental form, or category of experience. Given these commitments, it would be a *petitio principii* to found the enquiry on a claim about the superiority of some particular value.

To summarise, there are two infelicities in reading Simmel as a quasi-Marxist theorist of alienation–reification. First, for Simmel, one may judge some consequences of the objectification of culture to be 'good' and others to be 'bad'. But the judgement remains just that, goodness and badness does not inhere in the process itself. Second, the elements which are judged to be good and bad come as a package, as faces of the same process: among the varied forms of modernity one must take the rough (impersonality and commercialisation, perhaps) with the smooth (scientific knowledge, material prosperity and individual autonomy, perhaps). Further, the same form, or phenomenon of material culture, may embody divergent tendencies, one of which may be judged good and the other bad. The typewriter, for example, destroys the individuality and style of handwriting. But it also preserves individuality: first, by obviating the need to reveal the 'personal element' of handwriting in routine communications and, second, by facilitating the direct expression of intended meaning (see Simmel, 1978: 469). It is difficult to dissent from Rose's judgement that 'there is no justification for implying that Simmel was concerned with reification as such' (Rose, 1978: 35).

The close, if not always entirely clear, relations between Simmel's accounts of form, experience and objectification can help to explain what Frisby refers to as the 'aestheticization of reality' in Simmel. This category is central to Frisby's reading of Simmel, allowing him to align Simmel with the artistic *avant garde* and to portray him as a 'critical' theorist, albeit one who did not follow through the 'practical consequences of his critique. Simmel might shock the bourgeoisie ... but, at the same time, leave them undisturbed' (Frisby, 1985: 40). The first point to note is that Simmel is able to 'aestheticise' reality in the sense of taking an attitude like that of an artist because he is an 'aesthetic' theorist in an older philosophical sense. The term 'aesthetic' derives from the Greek concept of perception, and in a usage up to and including Kant it designates a concern with the structures and origins of the perceptual element in experience. Simmel's entire philosophy is 'aestheticised' to the degree that he takes experience as the site and principle of the unity of the perceptible world.

For anyone whose conceptions of 'the social' and of the tasks of criticism have been formed within the ambit of modernist radicalism, this fundamental 'aestheticisation' is very difficult to come to grips with. Even sympathetic commentators such as Turner and Frisby, in different degrees, cannot avoid the temptation of reading Simmel as if he was asking Marx-like questions. So, if Simmel offers a 'critique' of reification, it ought to have practical consequences; if he delineates shifts in the forms of experience, they should be explained in relation to real (extra-experiential) structural processes. Now, when Simmel is read in this way, he cannot but come off second-best: he is a 'formalist' while Marx is concerned with 'real economic processes' (see Turner, 1986: 109). It is no surprise that for Frisby (1985: 107) 'Marx is a better guide [than Simmel] out of the world of appearances generated by the exchange and circulation processes precisely because ... he did not regard them as the end point of his analysis'.

It may be more useful to follow Lepenies in relating Simmel's undoubted ambiguities to those cultural tensions which left him 'torn forth between science and art' (Lepenies: 1988: 244). The modernist radicalism of a Marx or a Durkheim is an unequivocal polemic in the struggle between a social scientific and a literary/aesthetic intelligentsia for the title to an authoritative critical discourse of modernity. Simmel's opposition to modernist radicalism, his 'failure' to generate Marx-like prescriptions, follows from his continuing attachment to the literary/aesthetic model even while he practices social science.

(c) 'Totality' in history and philosophy

Simmel's challenge to modernist radicalism is at its most explicit in his conceptions of the tasks of history and philosophy. In each case the argument turns on the extent to which analysis can lay hold of 'totality'. Here, again, Simmel's exegetes and critics understand Simmel as a defective modernist radical. For Frisby, Simmel replaces the idea of a 'real historical totality' with 'aesthetic connections', and his work lacks a 'genuine historical dimension' (Frisby, 1981: 130, 155). This response is adequate only on the assumption that a modernist radical conception of history is correct. It is just this assumption which Simmel questions in The Problems of the Philosophy of History, which presents a powerful challenge to 'historical materialism' and to the realist conception of history more generally.[9]

Historical knowledge, like knowledge of the natural world, is a 'synthesis' of elements rather than a reflection of reality. Like sociological knowledge it is a 'double' synthesis. What Simmel terms the 'threshold of historical consciousness' is defined by the intersection of an 'existential interest' in reality with 'an interest in the significance of content' (Simmel, 1977: 172). On the latter, we can be 'interested' in, or engaged by, meanings or emotions regardless of whether a particular instance 'really occurred' or not (see ibid.: 161). Hence the possibility of fiction. On the former, 'an interest in facticity that is independent of any metaphysical considerations, is the essential feature of all history' (ibid.: 169). Historical knowledge is a 'second-order' synthesis which selects and orders its content on the basis of the two 'interests'. History 'can only comprehend material which already falls under the category of direct experience' (ibid.: 86–7). This selectivity explains how and why 'history weaves a fabric from fragments of material that have been transformed by the process of emphasis and omission. Its threads and categories are very different from those exhibited by concrete reality' (ibid.: 80).

It should now be clear why Simmel is so opposed to the doctrines he collects under the label of 'historical realism'. Historical knowledge is possible, but only under the conditions of selection, emphasis and synthesis. The form of historical knowledge is precisely a knowledge, not a reflection, of 'what really happened'.[10] This argument is turned against claims that historical knowledge can reflect not only aspects of historical reality, but its 'totality'. He takes 'historical materialism' to be a claim that the totality of historical processes is a function of economic development. The economistic or psychologistic infelicities of Simmel's interpretation of Marx are not critical to his argument, which is that any conception of historical totality is a work of synthesis and not a reflection of reality. It follows that any alleged principle of totality is the product of interest-based selection and emphasis, so that 'the role of the ultimate *explanans* of the totality of history may be ascribed with equal legitimacy to every historical moment' (ibid.: 187).

Simmel's relativisation of the category of totality extends to his conception of philosophy, which he resolutely refuses to 'end'. The negative dimension of this refusal can be reconstructed from matters already considered. First, Simmel's sociology is the specialised science of a quite specific aspect of social relationships and processes. It is too specialised to be the heir to philosophy. Second, Simmel is clear that the science of sociology is implicated with epistemological questions which remain philosophical. The insight that society itself is a synthesis must raise questions about the 'epistemology of society' (Simmel, 1959b: 342). It is a mark of Simmel's distance from modernist radicalism that 'How is Society Possible?' does not construe this epistemology of society as the secret whose discovery can stand philosophical epistemology the right way up. The 'epistemology of society' is an epistemology by analogy with other epistemological issues which it complements but does not supplant. Third, Simmel's insistence that *experience* is the site and principle of unity works against the projection of philosophical categories, from 'value' to 'totality', on to putatively more 'real' social processes.

More positively, Simmel retained a commitment to the irreducibility of philosophy, even during his most sociological period. 'The Problem of Sociology' insists that questions of meaning and purpose in social life are philosophical, rather than sociological. 'The philosophy of society certainly has no right to escape the advantages and disadvantages that result in its belonging to philosophy in general by constituting itself as a special science of society' (Simmel, 1959a: 334). Simmel conceives of philosophy as the attempt to think how things in general hang together, so that its task is unavoidably bound to the category of totality. He defines the philosopher as 'the man who has an organ which is receptive and reactive to the totality of being' (Simmel, 1959c: 285). The ambiguities in Simmel's treatment of 'totality' have been a rich vein for his exegetes and critics. Frisby's influential reading suggests that Simmel's analyses aim to grasp the totality in the study of the fragment: 'Every fragment, every social snapshot, contains within itself the possibility of revealing "the total meaning of the world as a whole"' (Frisby, 1985: 58).

A possible flaw in Frisby's otherwise acute interpretation is that 'totality' is read as if always prefixed by the definite article.[11] If this is done, Simmel's idiosyncratic approach to *the* totality can compared to, say, Marx's, and found wanting in a familiar way. If the prefix is dropped, Simmel's approach to totality appears to be much more consistent with the reading advanced here: one can move from the fragment to the reconstruction of *a* totality, but all versions of totality share the condition of selection, emphasis and synthesis. Totality, too, is inescapably a category of experience.

In Simmel's later work the categories of 'form' and 'content' become the key-terms in an explicit 'philosophy of life'.[12] Tenbruck's (1959: 62) reference to Simmel's 'unique combination of Kantianism and *Lebensphilosophie*' points in the right direction. As a good Kantian, Simmel knows that the 'thing in itself', the world as 'existence determined by itself' (Simmel, 1959c: 288) is beyond the possibility of apprehension 'in its immediacy'. This world-as-content is 'nevertheless apprehensible in that it is articulated in a variety of forms, each of which assumes in principle the totality of the world as its content' (ibid). That is, 'the totality of the world' cannot be known 'as it is', it can only be approached through 'forms', each of which presupposes a different version of totality. Further, Simmel's forms (unlike Kant's categories) are mutable (ibid.: 290), so that the world is a process in which the life-constituting tension between content and form is constantly re-enacted as forms are created and destroyed. Simmel summarises the unavoidable but endless task in a *chiasmus* which would do credit to Adorno.

> The world is given to us as a sum of fragments, and it is the effort of philosophy to substitute the whole for the part. It accomplishes this in substituting the part for the whole. (Simmel, 1959c: 299)

Two theses can be extracted from this account. First, radical enquiry cannot dispense with a moment of judgement. There is no privileged version of 'reality' or 'the totality' which can necessitate radical values with a force akin to that of logic. The world can, indeed, be apprehended under forms of value, but once again no particular form has an a priori privilege. Second, Simmel's distinctions between the special science of sociology and other, more generalising, social studies (in philosophy or the sciences of culture) points in a different direction to much radical social theory. It suggests that it may be actively counter-productive to work for a single social theory which can synthesise the results of a technically proficient science of social relations with wider concerns about a desirable social practice.

2.3 WEBER ON MODERNITY AND VALUES

Skirmishes with sociological realism or the materialist conception of history aside, Simmel is not directly concerned to rebut modernist radicalism. The force of his challenge derives precisely from the testimony he offers to what can be accomplished by a sociology which largely ignores the pretensions of modernist radicalism. Weber shares an intellectual context with Simmel in many respects. Their methodological concerns are shaped by the same debates about the 'logic' of the cultural and historical sciences, and they both attempt to specify the nature and tasks of a specific science of sociology within the framework of these debates. However, Weber's concerns lead him to a programme for sociology which confronts the claims of modernist radicalism more directly than does Simmel's.

Weber is concerned with the historical development of occidental modernity, with the structures of its 'great organs and systems', and with its consequences and prospects. These themes are related to a powerful account of the ways in which social scientific knowledge may and may not be brought to bear upon practical questions. Weber asks questions which lie in a clear continuity with those of Marx and Durkheim, but he answers them in ways which give a subversive ironic twist to the defining themes of modernist radicalism. In this sense, Weber poses a more immediate threat to modernist radicalism than does Simmel. One index of its force has been the history of attempts to tame Weberian themes and to integrate them within modernist radical projects, from Lukács to Habermas. By contrast, modernist radicalism has largely ignored Simmel's challenge.

The remarks which follow fall into two sections and attempt to show how Weber contests modernist radicalism at the level of world-outlook, and how this contestation links with technical issues at the level of methodology. The first section offers a brief and general sketch of Weber's ironic conception of modernity, while the second relates this conception to the theory of values. It is suggested that Weber's value theory severely limits the potential of his critique of modernist radicalism.

(a) The ironies of modernity

Simmel and Weber do not aestheticise reality and modernity to the same degree. Weber has a robust sense of the relations between the experience of modernity and the extra-experiential structures of 'modern western capitalism'[13] which seems to align him more closely with Marx. Weber itemises and analyses the 'great organs and systems' of modern western capitalism which include: the market economy, social strata based primarily on social class, bureaucratic forms of organisation, a highly developed legal system and a mass-state. The clearest point at which Weber departs from Marx is in his refusal to 'privilege' economic institutions as the core of modernity. Institutional modernity hangs together through a mesh of intersecting 'elective affinities', but it is not a bounded and systemic totality. Indeed, the exodus from models of social structure based on metaphors of 'base' and 'superstructure' is a prime case in which, as Turner puts it (1981: 25), 'Max Weber has been an unwanted and largely incognito guest in modern Marxist debates about the real nature of Marx's historical materialism'.[14]

Similar considerations hold for those questions about occidental development which dominated Weber's thinking. Weber's insights are not formulated in the context of a systematic theoretical exposition, unless that role is accorded to the very late lectures which comprise the *General Economic History* (Weber, 1961).[15] As Abrams (1982: 104) has remarked, Weber 'hardly offers an explanation of the rise of capitalism at all but only of the rise of capitalism in western Europe in a particular historical epoch and setting'. Weber's most important, and always partial, answers to the questions of why rational capitalism took root only where and when it did, and with what consequences, emerge in studies of specific and exemplary instances of that development. The best-known example is *The Protestant Ethic and the Spirit of Capitalism*, but others include the studies of 'Economy and Law' and 'The City' which are incorporated in Part Two of *Economy and Society*. Weber's reluctance to systematise and integrate the different instances he has studied has a clear rationale. Versions of the history of modernity, or of episodes within it, can be written which topicalise the impact of religious ideas and practices, the development of rational law, or changing forms of urban political and economic organisation. But these partial histories are not fragments of some vast, incomplete, 'real' history of modernity as such. Each projects a slightly different version of the historical totality, and the unity they achieve when taken together is one of articulation and juxtaposition, rather than of integration.[16]

It has been convincingly argued that the 'rationalisation' theme is the key to Weber's conception of the development, structure and likely fate of modernity (see Giddens, 1971, Brubaker, 1984). More questionable is Löwith's (1982) suggestion that the theme parallels Marx's concern with alienation, which can seem to imply that rationalisation is the essence of modernity, or that the tension between formal and substantive rationality is its core contradiction. Weber's conception of modernity is ironic in a sense in which Marx's is not, and it maintains its irony precisely by eschewing the figures of essence and contradiction. Brubaker gives a clue to one dimension of Weberian irony when he sets out what he terms the two 'axioms' of Weber's thinking on rationality. They establish a relationalism which ironises sociological or historical judgement by tying it to a 'point of view'.

> First, rationality does not inhere in things, but is ascribed to them. Secondly, rationality is a relational concept: a thing can be rational (or irrational) only from a particular point of view, never in and of itself. (Brubaker, 1984: 35)

Clearly, rationalisation cannot be the essence, nor its tensions the core contradiction, of modernity as it is 'in itself'. However, the significance of this limitation is rather less clear. Löwith is able to cite passages in which Weber reflects gloomily, and in the most sweeping terms, on the implications of rationalisation for the fate of western culture. To understand how Weber is able to reach such judgements without an appeal to 'essential' processes it is necessary to explore Weberian 'irony' a little further.

A critical figure here is 'the paradox of consequences'. The 'Protestant Ethic' thesis exemplifies this irony at two levels of intensity. First, those consequences of the economic activities of Weber's Calvinists which are of the most significance sociologically, or historically, are not those which would have been the most significant to the Calvinists themselves. Weber is interested in the organisation of labour, forms of commercial accounting, or class-formation, while the Calvinists are interested in salvation and the glory of God. The second, and more intense, level of irony is that at which the processes which the Calvinists help to set in train are, in the long term, subversive of their own objectives. The 'rationalisations' of ethical and economic life have two dismal and related consequences. First, the 'Protestant Ethic' itself is progressively secularised out of existence. Second, through a logic which prompts one of Weber's best-known gloomy generalisations, the mechanism of the 'modern economic order', freed from the need for ethical foundations, has become an 'iron cage' (Weber, 1976: 181). As Turner has observed, later attempts to tame Weberian irony in a sociology of 'unanticipated consequences' and 'latent functions' quite fail to capture the 'evil ambience' of Weber's formulations (Turner, 1981: 10).

The question of relationalism is intertwined with these issues in a way which constitutes a third level of irony. The ironies of the 'Protestant Ethic' argument emerge only in the juxtaposition of two different 'interests' or 'points of view': that of the historical actors and that of the historical sociology of western culture. Such reflexive ironies multiply rapidly: it is only from the point of view of historical sociology that the 'point of view' of the historical actors becomes visible, while the point of view of historical sociology is a part of that modern culture which is, in part, a product of the point of view of the historical actors, and so on. To summarise, three dimensions of Weberian irony have been identified: the irony of relationism, the irony of unintended consequences (at two degrees of intensity), and the reflexive ironies which result from the conjunction of these two.

Now, it might be accepted that Weber is an ironist in these senses, but then asserted that this does not divide him from Marx. After all, Marx's account of the dynamics of capitalism is replete with ironies. The bourgeois class creates the class of proletarians who will be their 'gravediggers', and capitalist relations of production which begin as 'forms of development' of productive forces turn into 'fetters'. Indeed, Marx provides what looks like a general formula for the irony of unintended consequences: 'men make their own history, but they do not make it just as they please' (Marx, 1968: 96). But the ironies to which Marx draws attention find their place in an historical totality which has an overall *telos*. The necessity for actors to address problems thrown up by their material environment generates a 'cunning of history' which underpins this directedness.

Weberian irony, by contrast, is tragic to the degree that specific 'causal chains' are identified which link the formulation and initial execution of a project of action to its eventual ironic fate. Weberian actors are responsible for the consequences of their action. Weber's relationalism stands in marked contrast to Marx's realism here. It is precisely because Weber does not admit history as a rational and objective totality that the causal chains which he reconstructs (always from a particular point of view) take on the quality of tragic irony. This distinction feeds into Weber's conception of a politically salient 'ethics of responsibility', which will be considered below.

It is clear to Weber that any attempt to identify and engage with the problems of modernity, whether in science or in practice, must confront the ironies of rationalisation. What is ruled out, however, is the 'unity of theory and practice' which partly defines modernist radicalism. That unity is to secure the completion of the project of modernity, an idea which can make no sense to Weber. His judgement on Marxism can make the point. Weber reads the *Communist Manifesto* as a 'prophetic document' which expresses 'the authentic and final hope: the proletariat cannot free itself from serfdom without making an end of *all* domination of man over man.' (Weber, 1978a: 256). It is a cornerstone of Weber's political and ethical theory that such prophetic hopes simply do not admit of possible realisation. The increasing contradictions which are supposed to realise the prophecy fail to develop, and the more acute Marxists replace the 'lofty hopes' of the *Manifesto* with 'much more prosaic expectations' of an evolutionary sort (ibid.: 259). Now, attempts can be made to realise such expectations, but they fall prey to the paradox of consequences. The reformist socialisation of economic relations does not complete modernity in the sense that modernist radicalism requires, but intensifies its pathological characteristics: 'What this form of socialisation means is a proliferation of officials' (ibid.).

Weber has at least three levels of objection to the project for a 'completion of modernity', then. First, the more chiliastic formulations of the project do not admit of a recognisable translation into a realistic practice. Second, more modest formulations which do translate into practice become caught in the irony that their consequences subvert their intentions. Third, this subversion intensifies, rather than reduces, what appear from Weber's point of view as the major pathologies of modernity.

That Weber rejects any notion of a unity of theory and practice which will complete modernity does not imply that he regards his own ironic conception of modernity as without political consequences. This question is perennially controversial within Weber scholarship. Those who wish to argue that Weber exemplifies the value-freedom of sociology, or that his overall position is fundamentally liberal, are faced with the problem of what to make of

Weber's far from value-free and far from liberal political writings, beginning with the ultra-nationalist 1895 inaugural lecture (Weber, 1978b). One solution is to insist on the widest sustainable gulf between Weber's 'sociology' and his 'politics'. However, a series of texts starting with Mommsen (1959) have demonstrated the limits of this approach.[17]

There is no space here to take up these debates. One major issue can illustrate the complex connections between Weber's ironisation of modernity and his view of the prospects for a political practice. In both methodological essays and more political writings Weber recurs to the distinction between an 'ethics of ultimate (or absolute) ends' and an 'ethics of responsibility'. Formulations appear in 'The Meaning of Ethical Neutrality' (Weber, 1949a: 16) and in 'Politics as a Vocation' (Weber, 1970a: 120). In the 'ethics of ultimate ends' moral judgements are made on the basis of the purity (or otherwise) of actors' intentions, while in the 'ethics of responsibility' the consequences of actions enter into the moral equation. This distinction is far from satisfactory on a number of grounds. Turner and Factor (1984: 32) suggest that it rests on 'a particular type of confusion between two kinds of choices, substantive moral choices and choices between ethical theories', for example. Weber's favourite, equally suspect, use of the distinction is to assert that disfavoured political programmes rest wholly on an 'ethic of ultimate ends'. 'All radical revolutionary political attitudes, particularly revolutionary "syndicalism" have this character' (Weber, 1949a: 16).[18] This is why the 'prophetic hopes' of Marxists cannot begin to be realised: they are not oriented to the realities of a modernity in which the best intentions lead to the worst consequences.

As Giddens (1972: 47) has noted, the paradox of consequences lies at the root of the 'two ethics' argument. It is precisely because modernity subverts and ironises 'ultimate ends' that an 'ethics of responsibility' is the only basis for political action. 'If …one chases after the ultimate goal in a war of beliefs, following a pure ethic of absolute ends, then the goals may be damaged or discredited for generations because responsibility for *consequences* is lacking' (Weber, 1970a: 126). Scientific analysis, then, has identified a preparedness to take account of consequences as one of the critical parameters of any feasible political programme. To over-simplify, Weber has two models of the relations between science and politics. In the better-known model, the doctrine of

67

'value neutrality' asserts that political value judgements have no place in scientific teaching and research (see, e.g., Weber, 1949a: 11 and 1970b: 145). But in the second model, the necessity in both science and politics to 'bear the fate of the times like a man' (Weber, 1970b: 155) establishes an affinity between them. Science, which demands that illusions be dispensed with, can teach to politics the necessity to face the realities of a disenchanted modernity. In Schluchter's roseate version, 'the sciences participate in spreading an ethic of responsibility' (Roth and Schluchter, 1979: 107).

(b) Value, value relevance and value neutrality

Weber's ironic conception of modernity subverts each of the three defining themes of modernist radicalism. First, and most obviously, the idea of a modernity-completing unity of theory and practice gives way to a grim stoicism in the face of disenchantment. Second, like Simmel, Weber has little interest in a 'theory of ideology' in the manner of Marx. The paradox of consequences suggests of actors that they know not what they do, but this irony is in turn conditioned by the relationalism which ties analysis to the analyst's point of view. Third, Weber rarely mentions the fate of philosophy, but it is a clear implication of the rationalisation theme that any notion of philosophy as an objective reflection on absolutes and ultimates must fall prey to disenchantment. Philosophy reaches a *finis* but not a *telos*: it is not transcended and completed in any new and rational practice. It will not do, however, to leave matters quite there. The rationale for Weber's sociological analysis of modernity, and his prescription for treating its ills, turn on different aspects of his conception of 'values' in relation to enquiry and practice. An understanding of the strengths and weaknesses of this conception can help to inform a judgement about whether Weber has anything to offer to a post-foundational radicalism.

In the outline of 'Basic Sociological Terms' which opens *Economy and Society*, Weber defines sociology as 'a science concerning itself with the interpretive understanding of social action and thereby with a causal explanation of its course and consequences' (Weber, 1968: 4). Sociology becomes implicated with the problem of values, first of all, because the demand for 'interpretive understanding' requires an engagement with the meanings which actors ascribe to their experience and behaviour. Weber offers no systematic phenomenology of the types of experiential items that can be meaningful. However, the typology of social action (Weber, 1968: 24–25) and the less well-known typology of action orientations (ibid: 29–31) suggest that a list would include: emotions and other 'affects', attachment to usage and custom, ultimate values, and self-interest. The distinction between 'value rationality' and 'instrumental rationality' suggests the kind of line that divides the latter two items. The line between values and emotions (and perhaps usage and custom, too) is neatly drawn in 'Knies and the Problem of Irrationality':

> In contrast to mere 'emotional contents', we ascribe 'value' to an item if and only if it can be the content of a commitment: that is, a consciously articulated positive or negative 'judgement', something that appears to us to 'demand validity'. The 'validity' of a judgement is a 'value' 'for' us. (Weber, 1975: 182)

Why, then, do 'values' thus defined come to occupy such a prominent place in Weber's sociology?

Two related answers suggest themselves. First, as Rose (1981: ch. 1) has argued, the problem of the relations between 'validity' and 'value' dominated the concerns of the tradition from which Weber took his bearings (see the quotation immediately above, for example).[19] Weber's predecessors in the cultural sciences could take for granted that in some way 'culture' was to be defined in terms of 'value', although they might argue about precisely which way. Turner and Factor (1984: 35) point out that in Weber's own time 'the word "value" had become, as it is now, a portmanteau term for any sort of moral, evaluative or aesthetic good or aim'. Nonetheless, the conviction that the problems of culture are problems of value lives on in Weber.

The second answer concerns the way in which Weber takes up and modifies the problematic of value at the level of his world-outlook and substantive sociology. The fate of modernity is one in which processes of disenchantment and rationalisation are fragmenting and weakening cultural values. Considered 'objectively', this fragmentation generates distinct 'value spheres', such as science, politics and religion, whose values are incommensurable. 'Subjectively', different individuals will generate specific 'value orientations' which are similarly incommensurable.[20] A strong individual attachment to some set of ultimate values (tempered by an ethic of responsibility), and the pursuit of a vocation within some value sphere become, for Weber, the only possible expressions of integrity and courage in the face of disenchantment (see, e.g. Weber, 1970a and b).

Weber is at pains throughout the 'Methodological Foundations' section of *Economy and Society,* chapter one, as elsewhere, to emphasise the critical role of the 'ideal type' in sociological explanation. From the outset, ideal type analysis privileges 'rational' (non-affectual, non-traditional) action: 'It is convenient to treat all irrational, affectually determined, elements of behaviour as factors of deviation from a conceptually pure type of rational action' (Weber, 1968: 6). On the other hand, 'irrational, affectually determined' behaviour may be related to its context empathetically, but empathy has little place in Weber's sociology. Later on, (ibid.: 20) Weber seems to qualify this point, implying that ideal types of 'affectual modes of action' are possible and useful. However, no examples are provided, in contrast to the plethora of examples of ideal types of 'rational' action, and the suggestion seems out of tune with the overall argument.

In practice, the ways in which Weber defines key terms such as 'meaning', 'understanding' and 'rational', lead to the conclusion that the major interpretive task of sociology in respect of meaning must be the ideal-typical analysis of values. Now, this view of the sociological task is quite congenial to that positive evaluation of the role of values sketched above. From time to time a metaphysics of the world-constitutive power of values, of 'the ultimate value-axioms which underlie practical activity' (Weber, 1949b: 60), finds its way into methodological discussions, where it sits uncomfortably with the recognition that 'in the great majority of cases actual action goes on in a state of inarticulate half-consciousness or actual unconsciousness of its subjective meaning' (Weber, 1968: 21). Weber goes on from this passage to argue the importance of ideal types of subjective meaning which both abstract and deviate from the 'concrete facts' (see ibid.: 22). The problem, perhaps, is that while the process of ideal-typical abstraction is not problematic in itself, Weber has a pre-disposition to abstract and deviate from the concrete so as to identify those meanings of which the actor is 'half-conscious' with alleged 'ultimate values'.

Weber's substantive theory of value also informs the twin

methodological principles of 'value relevance' and 'ethical neutrality'. The doctrine of 'value relevance' shapes Weber's relationalism, and its core is brought sharply into focus by a dispute between Parsons and Habermas. For Parsons (1971: 34), the doctrine says only that the problems taken up by social science have a pre-scientific paternity: 'Scientific explanation is never purely an occupation of the ivory tower, and its problems are not "immaculately conceived"'. He goes on to argue (ibid.: 39) that Weber has no real concern with questions about the grounds of the possibility of valid knowledge in social science. Habermas (1971b: 61) offers a stronger version, in which the doctrine 'is not related in the first place to the *choice* of scientific problems, but to the *constitution* of possible objects of cultural–scientific knowledge'.

There are passages, notably in the 'Ethical Neutrality' paper, which lend support to Parsons' reading:

> The problems of the social sciences are selected by the value relevance of the phenomena treated ... the expression 'relevance to values' refers simply to the philosophical interpretation of that specifically scientific 'interest' which determines the selection of a given subject matter and the problems of an empirical analysis. (Weber, 1949a: 21–2)

Even here, however, Weber explicitly links his own concept of 'value relevance' with Rickert's stronger version.[21] The weight of the evidence from other of Weber's texts supports Habermas's reading. Passages in 'Knies and the Problem of Irrationality' relate the specificity of the historical 'interest' to the conditions under which 'action' can become a topic of enquiry, for example (Weber, 1975: 102–3). The extended discussion of the possibility of economics in '"Objectivity" in Social Science' provides some of the clearest evidence of Weber's commitment to a strong doctrine of value relevance. He asserts that 'the quality of an event as a "social-economic" event is not something which it possesses objectively. It is rather conditioned by the orientation of our cognitive interest' (Weber, 1949b: 64). The point is amplified a few lines later: 'A phenomenon is economic only insofar as and *only* as long as our *interest* is exclusively focussed on its constitutive significance in the material struggle for existence' (ibid.: 65).

The core of the doctrine of value relevance is a theory of the constitution of scientific domains by cognitive interests. This theory underpins Weber's relationalism and the ironisation of modernity which flows from it. The theory is also built in to the 'ideal type' concept. In the 'Objectivity' paper, Weber ties the requirement for ideal-typical constructs in social science to a recognition that social science cannot be 'presuppositionless' (Weber, 1949b: 92). The definition of the ideal type he offers a little earlier emphasises that ideal types involve the 'one sided *accentuation*' of points of view, allowing diverse phenomena to be 'arranged according to those one-sidedly emphasised viewpoints into a unified *analytical* construct' (ibid.: 90). One might say that the ideal type is a doubly selective device. It selects, first, one cognitive interest from among a range of possible interests: it is implicated in the constitution of its object on the basis of value relevance. So, the concept of economic value selects, or constitutes, a specific problem within the scientific domain of economics. Second, on the basis of that interest, the ideal type selects, accentuates and orders those phenomena which are relevant to it.

It is, of course, just such a theory of cognitive interests which Habermas (1972) adapts as the foundation of his first systematic attempt to re-formulate the modernist radical project.[22] This rather tenuous connection begins to kindle a suspicion that all is not as it seems in Weber's ironic subversion of modernist radicalism. In a formal sense, Weber's argument follows Simmel's almost exactly, but it moves away in two important respects, one of which might be thought to be important and productive, the other of which again problematises Weber's reliance of the concept of 'value'.

Weber's productive divergence from Simmel concerns his insistence that the principles of a causal ordering of interpreted materials are not identical with those of interpretation as such. In the course of his critique of Eduard Meyer, Weber considers as a possible object of historical analysis 'the total modern culture, i.e. the present day Christian capitalistic constitutional ... culture which "radiates" from Europe and which is a phantastic tangle of "cultural values" which may be considered from the most diverse standpoints' (Weber, 1949c: 155). This general 'primary object' of analysis (the term is Rickert's) is constituted as such by our 'interest' in it, or some aspect of it. If we want a causal explanation of even such a general object, our analysis must proceed through the construction of a highly selective 'chain'. In this task, the interest which constitutes the 'primary object' cannot select the elements of the chain. We must omit 'a great wealth of objects which arouse to a high degree our "interest" "for their own sake"' (ibid.). The criterion of selection must be causal efficacy. For example, an historical analysis based upon an 'interest' in the modern market economy would overlook the causal efficacy of religious factors if the 'interest' in markets selected the elements of the chain, thereby identifying only market phenomena. It is this model of causal explanation, more than anything, which allows Weber to break with what Parsons (1971: 29) terms the 'socio-cultural solipsism' of the German cultural sciences, but without relapsing into a myth of presuppositionless knowledge.

The less helpful aspect of Weber's divergence from Simmel can be approached, slightly obliquely, through the doctrine of 'ethical neutrality' or 'value freedom'. To the extent that the doctrine is more than a weapon in academic power struggles, it is most usefully regarded as a clarification of the implications of the far more important doctrine of value relevance. In almost all Weber's accounts of value relevance, he is at pains to insist that the doctrine does not imply that 'value judgements' have a place in scientific analyses. Weber uses two arguments to make the point. The first asserts a version of the fact–value distinction, so that the 'establishment of empirical facts' and the making of 'practical evaluations' are 'logically different' and 'heterogeneous problems' (Weber, 1949a: 11). Weber adds nothing to the Humean and Kantian versions of this argument, and shows no interest in exploring its problems.[23] The second argument is more interesting and connects with both the substantive sociology of values and the doctrine of value relevance. Roughly, the prohibition against value judgements in science is itself a value, and one which is definitive of the 'specifically scientific "interest"' which is, in turn, constitutive of possible objects of science. The rather dense argument which concludes the 'Objectivity' paper (Weber, 1949b: 110–12) is best read as articulating this view. Viewed from a different angle, a commitment to value freedom is demanded as the central value of the scientific vocation, it is definitive of the value sphere of science and differentiates it from other spheres. This version of the argument is urged, most notably, in 'Science as a Vocation', where 'science is a "vocation" organised in special disciplines in the service of self-clarification and knowledge of interrelated facts'; it cannot dispense 'sacred values and revelations' (Weber, 1970b: 152). The value of the scientific vocation is a 'presupposition' of scientific activity (ibid.).

The doctrine of the value freedom of sociology, at least as it had established itself in the post-war USA, became controversial during the 1960s. The doctrine was attacked as a conservative attempt to prohibit radical, committed and critical sociological analysis.[24] The serious issue which the debate raised was that of the degree to which social scientific knowledge could be presuppositionless. That issue came to dominate a wide range of attempts to differentiate 'radical' from 'conservative' sociologies at the presuppositional, or foundational, level. Albrow can stand for a tradition when he asserts that 'sociologists have strategic choices to make about basic methodology [which are] moral and not merely technical' (Albrow, 1974: 183).[25]

Weber works hard to produce an answer to the presuppositions problem in which both the problem and the answer are framed by the more general problematic of value. But it is precisely this reliance on the concept of 'value' which renders Weber's approach dubious, a point largely overlooked in the heat of arguments about *freedom* from values. This question leads back to the matter of Weber's second, and less productive, distance from Simmel. In effect, Weber re-formulates Simmel's 'formal' accounts of the constitution of social experience and sociology in the more substantive vocabulary of 'value'. Two objections can be levelled against this re-formulation. First, it elides all presuppositional questions with the problem of value. So, as Runciman (1972: 15, 41) points out, Weber consistently confuses value judgements with 'theoretical presuppositions'. As Bauman (1978: 74) remarks, Weber's methodological vocabulary 'emerged as a transposition of concepts forged in the smithy of historical hermeneutics'. A wide range of later developments, notably in the post-Kuhnian theory of science and the post-Wittgensteinian theory of language, make the Weberian conceptual tool kit look anachronistic and inadequate.

One of the reasons why Simmel's approach does not suffer this fate to quite the same degree relates to the second objection to Weber's re-formulation. The attempt to think the problem of presupposition through the category of value substantialises the problem in a way which binds Weber to a form of foundationalism very similar to that of the modernist radicalisms he contests. A parallel with Durkheimian doctrines discussed in chapter one can make the point. It will be recalled that Durkheim more or less directly transposes Kant's conception of knowledge as a product of synthetic activity on to 'society'. The categories which bring order to experience are social in origin, and all generalising thought is a function of society. This theory of knowledge is joined with a moral theory, in which society is the source of all moral authority, to produce an account of sociology as the 'rational will' of society, able to secure the unity of pure and practical reason.

Weber, too, conceives knowledge as a synthetic activity, so that the problem of the presuppositions of science is a problem about the synthetic constitution of objects of science. In Weber's solution, as in Durkheim's, substantial features of the object of science enter a reflexive loop to become conditions of the possibility of knowledge of the object. For Durkheim the features in question are 'collective representations'; for Weber they are 'values' formed into 'cognitive interests'. What divides them is Durkheim's insistence on a foundational 'unity' and Weber's insistence on a foundational 'plurality'. For Durkheim it is the essential unity of the social object which loops back into its foundation, while for Weber it is the essential plurality of values.

The way in which Weber articulates his insights into the synthetic character of science and its reflexive relations with its object through the value doctrines sets limits to his critique of modernist radicalism. Baldly, Weber cannot offer a 'post-foundational' critique because he is himself committed to a view of values as the foundation of science. His subversive ironisation of modernity turns on a relationalism which the doctrine of value relevance underwrites. But that doctrine drifts towards a closed assertion of the determination of science by given values. On this view, the need for 'decisive choice' in the 'unceasing struggle of [the] gods', through which 'each finds and obeys the demon who holds the fibers of his very life' (Weber, 1970b: 152, 156) is the presupposition and foundation of science.

So, with these problems in mind, what do Simmel and Weber respectively have to offer to a possible post-foundational radicalism in sociology? A balance sheet with five entries can furnish the beginnings of an answer. First, both develop versions of sociology as a specific type of 'synthesis', reflexively related to its object. The burden of the argument here has been that Simmel's version is to be preferred, precisely by virtue of what is often seen as its major drawback, its 'formality'. It is Weber's attempt to substantialise the sociological synthesis through a theory of value which generates his convergence with Durkheim's foundationalism.

Second, both Simmel and Weber emphasise the need for choice in the evaluation of social processes: no evaluation can be logically derived from an insight into the rational principle of the social totality. But again, Simmel's version is to be preferred as the more open. Simmel calls for a judgement while Weber calls for a decision in the war between the gods.[26]

Third, both writers have a sense of the distinction between the tasks of science and the tasks of practice and of the perils which face attempts to unify the two. Neither version is entirely adequate as it stands. Weber's, of course, turns on the problematic value doctrines. Simmel's distinction between sociology and social philosophy is suggestive, but retains a rather anachronistic model of 'philosophy'.

Fourth, neither Simmel nor Weber conceives sociology as a solipsistic hermeneutic. For Simmel, sociology can be a science because social forms attain an objective status. But perhaps it is Weber's insistence on the peculiar logic of causal sequences in relation to cognitive interests which is the more powerful here. This judgement relates to the fifth, and final, item. Both Simmel and Weber are attuned to the 'paradox of consequences', but Weber's conception of causality gives a real analytic bite to his studies of the paradox in action, a bite which is perhaps lacking in Simmel's more abstract formulae.

3

THE AUTO-CRITIQUE OF MODERNIST RADICALISM

3.1 PRELIMINARIES

The sociological retreat from modernist radicalism, exemplified in the projects of Simmel and Weber, is echoed and re-worked in a number of sociological traditions during the 1930s. As Levine *et al.* have remarked (1976: 813), Simmel is 'the only European scholar who has had a palpable influence on sociology in the United States throughout the course of the twentieth century'. In the late 1930s Simmel figured in courses in many major centres, and had influenced the Chicago research tradition. Weber was perhaps the most important single influence on, and element in, Parsons' effort to synthesise a coherent 'theory of action' from the previous generation of European social theory. Fascinating as these continuities may be in their own right, they tend away from the central concerns of this essay. In the professionalisation of sociology in the United States questions about modernism, foundationalism and radicalism are not at the forefront of attention, and neither the Simmelian 'aestheticisation' of reality nor the Weberian war of the gods are quite at home.

In Europe during the same period, on the other hand, the critique of modernist radicalism was taken up with some energy, but largely outside the confines of disciplinary sociology. European debate about the future of radicalism turns on the claims of Marxism (and Freudianism) as putative 'successor disciplines' to philosophy. An uneasy juxtaposition of these European themes with North American developments came with the emigration of so many European intellectuals in the late 1930s. This is the first of two chapters concerned with the most significant tradition within European (and, later, North American) debate on the future of radicalism, that of the 'Frankfurt School' of critical theory.[1] A major source of the interest of this tradition for the present essay is its ambiguous relationship to modernist radicalism. Marcuse's trajectory, for example, can be read as a

77

series of attempts to 're-found' a programme of modernist radicalism.[2] Adorno's work, on the other hand, forms one of the most important archives for the development of a post-foundational radicalism, and is constituted as a thorough-going critique of the claims of modernist radicalism.

The next chapter will argue that the work of Jürgen Habermas, the most prominent heir to the Frankfurt tradition, is a dead end for radical social theory to the extent that it aligns itself with the foundationalist, rather than anti-foundationalist, strand of critical theory. The present chapter will trace the principles of the latter strand in the work of Horkheimer and Adorno. It will be argued that while Horkheimer remains poised between foundationalism and anti-foundationalism, Adorno comes very close to a consistent anti-foundationalism. The qualification here is important: while Adorno explores issues which must remain central for a post-foundational radicalism, his anti-foundationalism is pulled up short in a way which is itself instructive.

3.2 HORKHEIMER'S 'CRITICAL THEORY'

That there is a major line of fault running through critical theory has often been noted. Agger (1977: 16) suggests that 'critical theory has two broad cultural themes, the one tragic or Nietzschean, the other more optimistic or Hegelian–Marxist'. If this division draws a line between, say, Adorno and Marcuse, it also identifies an ambiguity within Horkheimer's *corpus*. Indeed, ambiguity might be Horkheimer's hallmark. Although he was the dominant figure in the development of the Frankfurt 'Institute for Social Research' his work has received less attention than that of his junior colleagues. Although he sometimes appears a more orthodox Marxist than his colleagues, in his later years he turned much further to the right than other Institute members.[3] The ambiguity which is of most interest here is that between foundationalism and anti-foundationalism, and it can be approached by way of an issue which lies at the heart of the concerns of modernist radicalism: the competing claims of philosophy and social science to form the template of radical theory.

Horkheimer's 1931 'Inaugural Address' as Director of the Institute for Social Research articulates the social scientific alternative for critical theory. Horkheimer urges a research programme which will investigate 'the question of the interrelations between the economic life of society, the psychic development of the individual and the change in the cultural sphere' (cited in Howard, 1977: 98). This programme represents

> a formulation adequate to the method at our disposal and the status of our knowledge of the old question of the interrelation of particular existence and universal reason, of reality and idea, life and spirit, now posed in terms of the new constellation of the problem. (ibid.)

The 'new constellation of the problem' is Marxism, and Horkheimer is advancing a straightforward modernist radical version of the 'end of philosophy' in which social science both ends and realises philosophy. Elsewhere, he asserts that the term 'critical' 'is used ... less in the sense it has in the idealist critique of pure reason than in the sense it has in the dialectical critique of political economy' (Horkheimer, 1972a: 206). But as Connerton (1980: 36) has noted, the 'less ... than' figure retains a certain ambiguity which reflects a deeper uncertainty about the fate of philosophy.

Kilminster, himself committed to an 'end of philosophy' argument, has a nice sense of Horkheimer's ambivalence. He judges that Horkheimer 'saw that social science had indeed historically overcome philosophy in the methodological sense' (Kilminster, 1979: 238). However, he tried to preserve, if only in a 'cancelled and negated state', the idea of *philosophy as wisdom* as the fulcrum between the conscious desires of men and the possibilities of their fulfilment' (ibid.). For Kilminster, this refusal to make a final 'end' of philosophy leaves Horkheimer in danger of 'veering towards irrationalism or mythology' (ibid.: 230). Horkheimer's conception of science remains philosophical, and serves as a foil against which the wisdom of philosophy can be displayed. This is not the whole story of Horkheimer's ambiguity about philosophy, however, and the way he uses the term requires a little attention.

Philosophy is not just a series of loosely connected enquiries for Horkheimer, but an historically rooted, developing and goal-directed project. The philosophical tradition is the highest manifestation of the self-formation of humanity. It is, of course, this elevated sense of philosophy which end-of-philosophy arguments want to end. First of all, Horkheimer interrogates the philosophical tradition to extract what is 'rational' within it. In 'The

Social Function of Philosophy' two kinds of slimmed-down defini-
tions emerge. In terms of its intrinsic programme, 'philosophy
insists that the actions and aims of men must not be the product
of blind necessity' (Horkheimer, 1972b: 257). When that demand
is placed in the context of existing social relations, it becomes
clear that 'the real social function of philosophy lies in its criticism
of what is prevalent' (ibid.: 264).

One problem which Horkheimer faces in identifying critical
theory straightforwardly with philosophy is the radical falling
away of contemporary philosophy from these twin benchmarks of
its value. In 'The Latest Attack on Metaphysics' he portrays a
philosophy split between two irrationalisms, one 'empiricist' and
the other 'neo-romantic'. Both are attempts to 'bring unity and
harmony into the inconsistencies of the modern consciousness
(Horkheimer, 1972c: 182). Although one does this by 'disparaging'
and the other by 'hypostasising' the sciences, they 'have a
common feature. Neither apprehends reality in conscious connection with a definite historical activity ... but takes it in the
immediate form in which it presents itself' (ibid.). Philosophy is
thus in danger of losing its most important insight, brought to it
by Kant, 'who proved that the world of our individual and
scientific consciousness is not given to us by God and unques-
tioningly accepted by us, but is partially the result of the workings
of our understanding' (ibid.: 158).

Horkheimer's dilemma, then, is that what passes for philosophy
is fast becoming a betrayal of the immanent demand and the
social function that gave it value. Why, then, does he not simply
embrace the alternative of a 'new constellation of the problem'
which can end and realise the rational kernel of philosophy? Part
of an answer can be found in Horkheimer's concern with
language, which opens into the anti-foundationalist dimension of
his thinking. Horkheimer's early work has a strong sense that
language is more than a transparent medium of thought, and a
suspicion of its integrating power. 'The very nature of language is
to create ties, to establish community, to be urbane ... language
must therefore be prevented from creating the illusion of a community that does not exist in class society' (Horkheimer, 1978a:
75). It is not clear that either philosophy, as traditionally conceived, or 'the new constellation of the problem' are equipped to
resist these subtle pressures towards affirmation. Specifically, a
critical social science may be capable of a 'critique of ideology'

which can trace the class-origins and functions of doctrines which are, as it were, foisted upon language from the outside, but it is not the appropriate tool for a reflexive monitoring of language as such.

Horkheimer returns to the problem of language during the 1940s, suggesting that a critical interrogation of language is not only a necessary prophylactic against the power of affirmation, but is itself a potential source for the critique of given, immediate, meaning.

> Philosophy must become more sensitive to the muted testimonies of language and plumb the layers of experience preserved in it. Each language carries a meaning embodying the thought forms and belief patterns rooted in the evolution of the people who speak it. (Horkheimer, 1974: 165–6)

On this view, an interrogation of 'the word, with its half forgotten layers of meaning' (ibid.) can form part of the alternative to the 'industrialised' formalism which leads philosophers 'to feel that concepts and categories should leave their workshops clean cut and looking brand new' (ibid.). This kind of enquiry does not seem to match either of the available patterns for critical theory. It does not look like Marxist social science, and although the interrogation of language is aligned with 'philosophy' here, it does not look much like the Great Tradition.

These passages convey the beginnings of a sense that critical theory might be constituted as an activity which is neither philosophy as traditionally conceived, nor Marxist social science conceived as the realisation of philosophy. Horkheimer's concerns with the movement and effects of language articulate an anti-foundationalism which points toward a 'critical hermeneutics', or 'critical rhetorics', and away from philosophy and modernist radicalism. A critical rhetorics might begin to come to terms with language considered neither as the 'foundation' of theory, nor as its transparent medium, but as its unavoidable topic and resource.

The problem which Kilminster identifies as 'irrationalism', and which he ascribes to Horkheimer's failure to complete the shift from a philosophical to a social scientific foundationalism, is better seen as a result of Horkheimer's failure to develop his anti-foundationalist insight in its own right. In the end, he tries to assimilate it to philosophy and even (towards the end of his life) theology, with curious results. The question of this three-way ambiguity between philosophy, social science and critical rhetorics in Horkheimer can be developed briefly in relation to four aspects of his attempts to pin down the specificity of critical theory: the 'validity' of the theory, its goals, its social location and (again) its relation to philosophy.[4] A brief final section will review the issue of anti-foundationalism.

(a) Validity

Horkheimer frequently concedes the subordination of critical theory to traditional canons of formal validity. He insists that 'the individual steps within the theory are, at least in intention, as rigorous as the deductions in a specialised scientific theory' (Horkheimer, 1972a: 227). Equally, he sets no very great store by the discriminating power of this requirement: 'What theoretical structure, however radically faulted, cannot fulfill the requirements of formal correctness?' (ibid.: 223). One way of glossing this tension is as a way of requiring that social scientific critique be oriented by philosophical reflection. Held, for example, comes close to this view.

> Conventional criteria specifying standards of adequacy for scientific theory and research ... are to be respected. This respect, however ... must not exclude systematic reflection – employing philosophical, theoretical and interdisciplinary perspectives – on the nature of the phenomenon under scrutiny. (Held, 1980: 188)

Two considerations militate against the immediate adoption of this nicely balanced view.

First, the kind of 'systematic reflection' which Horkheimer favours has implications at the level of formal validity, and from time to time points to a distinct 'logic' of enquiry as the key to the foundational specificity of critical theory. He argues that while 'specialised science' proceeds through 'hypothetical' judgements, critical theory 'is, in its totality, the unfolding of a single existential judgement' (Horkheimer, 1972a: 227). The point here is not simply that critical theory must work with a concept of totality which other forms of theory cannot attain. The cases of Carnap's *Aufbau* and Wittgenstein's *Tractatus* demonstrate that logical empiricism, which Horkheimer regards as one arm of irrationalist philosophy, can formulate sophisticated concepts of totality.[5] However, the totality which empiricism constructs is made up of singular 'elementary propositions'. Universal propositions are cast in hypothetical form, and make no existential claim.[6] Horkheimer's reference to a 'single existential judgement' can be read as a claim that critical theory must break the logical tie between universality and the hypothetical form in scientific theory. It points forward to the post-war 'positivism dispute' which engaged the attention of Adorno and Habermas. Critical theory must make judgements which combine existential claims with universal scope and normative force. When the unreasonableness of contemporary reality can be encompassed in a single judgement, the demand for reason cannot be evaded.

A second problem with the view that Horkheimer balances formal validity with philosophical reflection in critical theory is that he sometimes links the question of its validity directly to its goals. Critical theory has a definitive commitment to a qualitative social transformation which has yet to take place. It is framed within a future-orientation which limits the salience of traditional criteria of validity and truth: 'If the proof of the pudding is in the eating, the eating here is still in the future' (Horkheimer, 1972a: 221). Horkheimer is aware that this inescapable characteristic must render critical theory dubious in terms of those traditional criteria. It can only appear, by traditional standards, to be 'subjective and speculative, one sided and useless' (ibid.: 218). Horkheimer is uncertain, then, about the kind of validity which critical theory is to enjoy. Sometimes it can reach an accommodation with traditional criteria, sometimes it requires a specific re-working of those criteria, and sometimes it points quite away from them, to a transformed sense of validity over the horizon of present reality.

(b) Goals

Horkheimer's remarks on the goals of critical theory fall into two distinct variants, echoing the ambiguities of his conception of validity. In one variant he stresses the reasonableness of the theory's goals, and cites respectable philosophical authorities who have endorsed them. In the other type, the goals of critical theory disappear over the horizon of the present, and survive only in intimations of something which is wholly 'other'. The latter variant comes to predominate in the later work,[7] but both types can be found in the essays of the 1930s. In the spirit of the first variant, 'The Social Function of Philosophy' argues that the philosophical conception of 'Reason', from which critical theory can continue to draw credit, implies the goal of 'an equitable state of affairs' (Horkheimer, 1972b: 267). Again 'Traditional and Critical Theory' stresses the 'concern for reasonable conditions of life' (Horkheimer, 1972a: 199). This variant points towards a critical theory in which the demands of 'Reason' have been translated into 'materialist' demands for social transformation.

This strain in Horkheimer's thinking reaches its fullest, least cautious, expression in 'Egoism and the Freedom Movement', the main site of Horkheimer's attempt to recuperate hedonistic goals in critical theory.[8] Despite the inherent selfishness of capitalism, hedonism is condemned in bourgeois philosophy and political practice. 'What is expressed in philosophy as the contempt for all instinctual desires turns out in real life to be the practice of their repression' (Horkheimer, 1982: 16). Drawing on Freudian, Nietzschean and Weberian themes, Horkheimer argues that all bourgeois revolutions have turned upon the repression of egoistic and hedonistic demands, and that this has betrayed their commitment to 'liberty, equality and fraternity'. Against repression, Horkheimer insists that 'the badness of egoism lies not in itself but in the historical situation, if it is changed, then its concept transfers to that of the more rational society' (ibid.: 58–9). The critical goal of 'Reason' is translated here into two inter-dependent processes of material tranformation, the transformation of society and the emergence of a 'freer psychic constitution' (ibid.: 60).

The other variant of Horkheimer's reflection on goals seems at odds with the materialism of the first. In 'Traditional and Critical Theory' remarks on the reasonableness of critical theory are accompanied by a claim that its goals defy specification in the here and now. 'In regard to the essential kind of change at which the Critical Theory aims, there can be no corresponding concrete perception of it until it actually comes about' (Horkheimer, 1972a: 220). This circumspection can be connected with Horkheimer's suspicion of the affirmative power of language, noted above. In his early work, language has only a limited capacity to articulate that which is not 'given', so that 'we are still surrounded by a sea of darkness which cannot be illuminated by any language. Language has the choice of being a finite tool or an illusion'

(Horkheimer, 1978a: 31). In the late 1960s Horkheimer intensifies his suspicion of affirmation, drawing on both Jewish theology and the Kantian concept of a noumenal realm beyond experience to justify the assertion that while critical theory can articulate the nature of evil, it cannot do the same for good. In the most radical sense, the positive goal can only appear in the 'negation of the negative' (see ibid.: 237).

(c) History and practice

Modernist radicalisms, most notably Marxism, understand themselves as grounded in the historical process they seek to comprehend, and in the practice of the historical agent which is to 'complete' that process. Although essays such as 'Egoism and the Freedom Movement' do appeal to history as the guarantor of critical theory, Horkheimer's main thrust is away from the unities and guarantees of modernist radicalism. Even in Horkheimer's early discussions of Marxism, there is a caution about the question of grounding. The possibility of socialism is not ruled out, but there is scant evidence that progressive tendencies will prevail. There is no logic of history tending towards socialism, and the development of the German working class makes it an unlikely revolutionary subject (Horkheimer, 1978a: 35, 37, 61–4). The continuing possibility of socialism depends not on historical or class grounding, but on will and commitment. By the late 1930s the tie between critical theory and the working class is very loose, and Horkheimer denies that there is any 'social class by whose acceptance of the theory one could be guided (Horkheimer, 1972a: 242).

Horkheimer's anti-foundationalism is evident in his awareness that while critical theory remains radically contingent upon its socio-historical grounding, that grounding can no longer be seen as the source of foundational guarantees. 'On the Problem of Truth' asserts that any 'extra-historical, and hence exaggerated concept of truth ... is impossible' (Horkheimer, 1978b: 421). This opens the possibility that Marxism (referred to coyly as 'the theory which we regard as correct') 'may disappear because the practical and scientific interests which played a role in the formation of its concept, and above all the facts and circumstances to which it referred, have disappeared' (ibid.). In similar vein, 'Traditional and Critical Theory' argues that without 'men speaking and acting in such a way as to justify it' critical theory has no historical significance (Horkheimer, 1972a: 220).

Horkheimer's initial problem, then, is that the evaporation of the collective subject of critical thought and activity leaves critical theory exposed to historical contingency. By the 1940s, Horkheimer's re-working of Freudian themes has brought him to the view that the individual subject is suffering the same fate. Economic and cultural developments are 'in process of liquidating the individual' (Horkheimer, 1974: 157). Patterns of behaviour regress to a mimetic conformity to the norm, or to the empty clichés of self peddled by mass culture. Traditional processes of self-formation are undermined to the extent that 'the individual no longer has a personal history' (ibid: 159). The irony in which Horkheimer is caught, and of which he is well aware, is that the need for critical theory increases precisely as the sites on which it might be grounded are eroded.[9] The mysticism and irrationalism of Horkheimer's late work reflects an inability to escape this irony. To make the break would require a fire sale of traditional philosophical oppositions between subject and object, spirit and matter, idea and reality, etc. To adapt Horkheimer's own formula, it would require a form of analysis which embraced the finitude of language understood as both the source of illusion and the only resource for its critique. Unable to make the break, Horkheimer can only retreat to formulations which remain at a safe distance from the historical collapse of collective and individual subjectivity.

(d) The end of philosophy again

During the 1930s the Frankfurt Institute set about a systematic evaluation of the critical potential of classical and contemporary philosophy. This served both to re-interpret the tradition and to legitimate critical theory as its contemporary heir. This kind of legitimation converges with modernist radicalism, understanding the demand for the abolition of injustice as 'the materialist content of the idealist concept of reason' (Horkheimer, 1972a: 242). However, Horkheimer consistently resists any claim that critical theory can overcome all of the aporias and oppositions of philosophy in an identity of 'idea' and 'reality'. A 1933 essay insists that the materialist dialectic 'achieved an awareness of the ever-changing but irreducible tension between its own teaching and reality'

86

(Horkheimer, 1972d: 32). Horkheimer is never entirely a modernist radical.

As Horkheimer shifts to a more philosophical conception of critical theory, he insists more and more on the antinomical condition of all theory. Thus, in the 1940s he argues that the polarity between 'spirit' and 'nature' is an 'unavoidable aporia of all theory of knowledge': the distinction between the two is an abstraction, but their unity is never given (Horkheimer, 1974: 173). During the 1960s Kant increasingly figures as a model for critical theory and Horkheimer traces a Kantian authority for two of the defining themes of modernist radicalism. First, 'the *Critique of Pure Reason* tells us something about ideology, the analysis of necessary experience' (Horkheimer, 1978a: 187). Second, 'Marx's teaching concerning the unity of practice and theory is already present in Kantian philosophy' (ibid.: 215).

Although Horkheimer consistently legitimates critical theory by relating it to the philosophical tradition, the significance of that relation is mutable. In some of the more orthodox passages from the 1930s, philosophy is not the only, or even the most significant, emancipatory tradition. It deserves to be honoured but its project has passed, both theoretically and practically, into other hands. In Horkheimer's later work, however, philosophy (and now theology) are the only critical traditions left, and even their hold on critical values is tenuous and paradoxical. Philosophy has become 'the futile attempt to achieve recognition for a kind of knowledge which is more than merely instrumental' (Horkheimer, 1978a: 159).

(e) Foundationalism and anti-foundationalism

The crucial ambiguity in Horkheimer's conception of critical theory is not that between philosophy and social science, but a three-way contest between two types of foundationalism (philosophical and social scientific) and an incipient anti-foundationalism, or 'critical rhetorics'. Horkheimer is a cautious writer, and it is difficult to pin down clear-cut examples of each option, since an example no sooner appears than it is modulated into another register. So, the specification of the goals of critical theory in terms of materialist demands is required to challenge the idealist foundationalism of traditional philosophy. But the refusal of any complete specification in such terms, cast in an apparently idealist appeal to some wholly 'other', is also required to prevent critical theory from degenerating into a merely affirmative materialist foundationalism.

Horkheimer has a clear sense that critical theory must walk a thin line between the provision of metaphysical guarantees for critical values and the nihilistic abolition of such values. The dilemma is particularly acute for Horkheimer since he sees nihilistic degeneration not just as an abstract possibility facing theoretical work, but as the actual course of historical development. A wholly affirmative theory would amount to either a nihilistic endorsement of the status quo or the metaphysical endorsement of a philosophical system (which would turn out to be an endorsement of the status quo). An entirely negative critical theory, on the other hand, faces the problem of whether the 'negation of the negative' can preserve critical values if the 'negative' of present day society is simply a nullity.[10]

To argue that Horkheimer does not produce a coherent, systematic resolution to these difficulties may be to judge him by impossibly high standards. Nevertheless, there are problems with the solutions Horkheimer does produce which are both instructive and avoidable. First, and most generally, he rarely follows through the logic of his anti-foundational insights. Instead, he oscillates between philosophical and social scientific foundationalisms, using the one to mobilise anti-foundationalist arguments against the other. Second, while Horkheimer is unwilling to endorse the defining themes of modernist radicalism, he is almost equally unwilling to abandon them entirely. Critical theory is not unambiguously the 'science' which will overturn 'ideology', but the ideology theme inflates to convey a suspicion that all of language is 'affirmative'. The 'unity of theory and practice' and the 'end of philosophy' pose problems which Horkheimer never tries to resolve by a theoretical *coup de main*. Unities and realisations are never 'present', but neither are they simply illusions. They are projected over the horizon of the present, to serve as intimations of an otherness which remains the regulative idea of critical theory.

Critical theory is often charged by radicals of a more robust persuasion with being too 'thin' and aestheticised for any effective engagement with the real world. When Horkheimer's version is considered from the perspective of a search for anti-foundationalist alternatives to modernist radicalism the problem is rather the reverse. His critical theory remains too 'thick', he prefers to post-pone and virtualise metaphysical figures rather than to develop the anti-foundationalist critique whose possibility he intimates. Given this apparent failure of critical nerve and imagination, there is some justification, in Horkheimer's case at least, for the claim that critical theory risks degeneration into an 'attitude' (Howard, 1977: 109), a 'mythology' (Kilminster, 1979: 221) or a '*prise de position*' (Therborn, 1977: 68).

3.3 ADORNO'S CRITICAL RHETORICS

Horkheimer's foundational ambiguities leave two clear options open to critical theory. One is to return to a more straightforward foundationalism, and to search for a specifically 'critical' foundational principle. This option is developed, in different ways, by Marcuse and Habermas. The other option is to develop the idea of critical theory as an anti-foundationalist critical rhetorics. Adorno's essays (and, as with Simmel, even his big books are really sequences of essays) explore this option. They are constituted as critiques of all synthesising, unifying modes of thinking and writing. The style exemplifies the critique, and militates against a systematisation which would betray the inten-tion, a characteristic which creates difficulties for commentators. The sections which follow examine facets of Adorno's alternative to the foundationalist temptations facing critical theory. The first gives a pre-summary of the critique of 'identity'. The second relates this to the 'end of philosophy' theme through Adorno's engagement with Heidegger. The third follows the critique into aesthetics by way of Adorno's study of Wagner. A concluding section considers Adorno's views on sociology.

(a) Identity

In one sense, at least, Adorno presents fewer exegetical diffi-culties than do many of his contemporaries. His work is re-markably consistent thematically throughout his career, so that there is 'no significant young–old problem for Adorno scholar-ship' (Jay, 1984a: 57). However, Adorno's thematic consistency is the outcome of a complex interplay between many different lines of influence and development,[11] and it would be an impossible task to weigh up each of these lines here. Adorno's relations to substantive themes elaborated by Horkheimer and to Benjamin's method of cultural analysis loom large in what follows, but that implies no judgement about their weight relative to other possible influences.

Adorno's enemy is the syndrome of 'identity thinking' which he finds to be pervasive in aesthetics, philosophy and social theory. Rose (1978: 18–26) argues that Adorno's hostility to this syndrome can be understood only in the light of Nietzsche's critique of traditional logic as the imposition of identity and unity upon a non-identical, non-unified reality. Identity thinking insinuates that the work of art 'represents' its object and 'expresses' an emotion, that the philosophical concept 'determines' an aspect of reality, or that the sociological model 'displays' social processes. Against this pervasive 'will to identify' Adorno sets a 'negative dialectic' of non-identity thinking. Buck-Morss argues that Adorno drew two modes of opposition to identity thinking from Benjamin. The first is a refusal to subordinate the particular instance to a general category. For Adorno and Benjamin 'the general was contained *within* the particular. The smallest unit, the extreme, the detail – these were the sources of truth' (Buck-Morss, 1972: 138). The second is a sense of the critical gulf between subjective intention and objective meaning. Both sought 'objective reality within expressions which appeared despite subjective intent. The artwork, not the artist, the philosophy not the philosopher, was the object of theoretical enquiry' (ibid: 139).

These themes resonate with the under-developed 'anti-foundational' strain in Horkheimer, and Adorno often takes them up on a terrain which is more Horkheimer's than Benjamin's: that of the significance of philosophical antinomies. Two such are particularly important, concept–object and subject–object. *Negative Dialectics* defines non-identity thinking, or dialectic, in terms of the former: 'dialectics says no more, to begin with, than that objects do not go into their concepts without remainder … it indicates the untruth of identity, the fact that the concept does not exhaust the thing conceived' (Adorno, 1973a: 5). If this provides a general formula for the irreducibility of the particular, Adorno's suspicion of subjectivism is articulated through a critique of the subject–object dichotomy. The two terms are 'resultant categories of reflection, formulae for an irreconcilability; they are not positive, primary states of fact but negative throughout, expressing nothing but non-identity' (ibid.: 174). To assert either the 'ultimate unity' or the 'ultimate duality' of subject and object is to relapse into identity thinking.

The importance of the subject–object dichotomy for Adorno's critique of identity has often been noted. Jay (1984a: ch. 2), for example, constructs an account of Adorno's entire philosophy around it. Adorno's sense of the dilemma which the dichotomy poses for his project is of the first importance to the search for a post-foundational radicalism. It has clear implications for the pretensions of much postmodernist theory, for example. On the one hand, Adorno insists that his dialectic of non-identity is materialist in its rejection of the claims of a constitutive subjectivity: 'It is by passing to the object's preponderance that dialectic is rendered materialist' (Adorno, 1973a: 192). On the other hand, the last thing which Adorno urges is a liquidation or 'end' of the subject, the effect of which 'would be regression – not just of consciousness, but a regression to real barbarism' (Adorno, 1978: 499). Adorno requires a form of critical analysis which evades the metaphysical endorsement of subjectivism without collapsing into a nihilistic endorsement of social and psychic degeneration.

On the first arm of the dilemma, Hegelian thinking in aesthetics, philosophy and social theory is perhaps the most obvious candidate for Adorno's critical attention. The Hegelian unity of subject and object offers subjectivity as the pattern for a 'universal and total identity' (Adorno, 1973a: 329). But Adorno is insistent that the temptations of subjectivism do not end with Hegelianism. Varieties of phenomenalism or empiricism can appear to assert the priority of the object in their various denials to the subject of any active role in knowledge. But this kind of objectivism is bogus: it fragments the object into elements ('sense data' or 'facts') defined by the capacity of a subject to register them. It rests, for Adorno, on a 'latent and thus much more fatal subjectivism' (Adorno, 1978: 505). This paradox finds its mirror image in the overt subjectivism of phenomenology, which 'does not touch the substance of naive realism; it only needs to state formal criteria for its validity' (ibid.: 503). Adorno draws the lesson that so long as relations between subject and object are thought on the model of constitutive relations between concepts, no coherent assertion of the primacy of the object is possible. One kind of response to this difficulty is to assert the existence of an ur-objectivity 'beyond' the subject–object duality, and Adorno's critique of Heidegger's version of this response will be considered shortly. The response also characterises much postmodernist writing and (as will be argued in chapter five) pitches it into nihilism. Adorno's response is different. The assertion of the primacy of the object which is so critical to the dialectic of non-identity cannot amount to a denial of the role of subjectivity, since 'if the object lacked the moment of subjectivity, its own objectivity would be nonsensical' (Adorno, 1978: 509). But the role of the subject is not to be found in the repetitions and circuits of relations between concepts, which can only produce paradox. It is the 'empirical' and not the 'formal' subject which plays a part in knowledge of the object, so that 'the subject is the object's agent, not its constituent' (ibid.: 506). It is the human individual shaped by processes of social and natural development which is of concern to critical theory.[12]

Identity thinking is not a philosophical error, in the sense of a formulated doctrine which some philosophers promulgate and others oppose. It is a tendency inherent in the self-conception of philosophy as the study of the foundational relations between concepts. To the extent that philosophy thinks that its formulae have exhausted the antinomies of subject–object, thought–reality, universal–particular, and the rest, it resolves into identity thinking. It is around this insight that Adorno's critique of identity articulates itself as an anti-foundationalist 'critical rhetorics'. Dialectic must recognise what philosophy denies, its 'linguistic nature', whose forgetting leads to the hubris of identity thinking (Adorno, 1973a: 55). So, in a formula which converges with Horkheimer's underdeveloped rhetorics, 'dialectics – literally: language as the organon of thought – would mean to attempt a critical rescue of the rhetorical element, a mutual approximation of thing and expression to the point where the difference fades' (ibid.: 56).

Benjamin's antidote to identity is to deal in fragments, to 'seize hold of a memory as it flashes up at a moment of danger' (Benjamin, 1970a: 257). He draws on both Proust and Freud to support the idea of the 'trace' through which 'what has not happened to the subject as an experience can become a component of the *mémoire involuntaire*' (Benjamin, 1970b: 163). Adorno writes of Benjamin that 'the task he bequeathed was ... to bring the intentionless within the realm of concepts: the obligation to think at the same time dialectically and undialectically (Adorno, 1974: 152). But this tribute is at the same time a critique, testifying to Adorno's continual insistence on the necessity to think theore-

92

tically even amid the wreckage of theoretical systems. The discussion of Adorno's Wagner study below will illustrate the wedge which this issue drove between Adorno and Benjamin. Adorno may agree with Benjamin's principle that the particular is not to be absorbed under the universal, but he differs on its methodological implications.

A similar caution is required in the matter of Adorno's Nietzschean pedigree, which was also briefly mentioned above. Many commentators[13] regard Nietzsche as a major influence on Adorno's critique of identity, with some justice. 'The will to a system is a lack of integrity' (Nietzsche, 1968: 25) could be the motto for a dialectic of non-identity. But while Adorno's convergences with Nietzsche are openly acknowledged, they are never uncritical. Nietzsche is a victim of, as well as a resource for, Adorno's critical rhetorics. For example, Adorno credits Nietzsche with the 'strongest argument' against theology and metaphysics: 'That hope is mistaken for truth; that the impossibility of living happily, or even of living at all, does not vouch for the legitimacy of the thought' (Adorno, 1974: 97). But his argument is then turned against the Nietzschean doctrine of *amor fati*, when Adorno asks whether it is 'not the same false inference that leads from the existence of stubborn facts to their erection as the highest value, as he criticises in the leap from hope to truth' (ibid.: 98). Both the syndrome which Nietzsche criticises and his own doctrine are forms of 'ignominious adaption' (ibid.). Against both, Adorno insists that 'hope, wrested from reality by negating it, is the only form in which truth appears' (ibid.).

This example typifies Adorno's insistence on the critique of not only the enemies of a dialectic of non-identity but also of its allies. For dialectic to embrace Nietzsche, or Benjamin, or Adorno himself, as a canonical authority would be to lapse into affirmation and its own denial. Only in a continual critical movement can Adorno's rhetorics disclose the 'will to identify' of discourse. A dialectic of non-identity requires a recognition of identity as a rhetorical effect worked by the discourses of aesthetics, philosophy and social theory. At the same time, it requires dialectic to be constituted as a *critical* rhetorics. Nietzsche was well aware of the danger of an unwitting complicity with the 'grammar' of identity: 'I fear we are not getting rid of God because we still believe in grammar' (Nietzsche, 1968: 38). For Adorno, the danger can be averted only in linguistic devices (rhetorics) which deliver a 'shock' to conventional habits of writing and reading. This is why he is so suspicious of texts which look finished and systematic, and why he leans so heavily on figures such as chiasmus.

If Adorno's critique of identity has made one quite decisive move, it consists in linking an unremitting hostility to metaphysical unities and reconciliations to the recognition that both metaphysics *and* its dialectical critique are effects of the movement of discourse. The conception of critique as artful textuality combines the concerns of dialectic, rhetoric and aesthetics.

> Properly written texts are like spiders' webs: tight, concentric, transparent, well-spun and firm. They draw into themselves all the creatures of the air. Metaphors flitting hastily through them become their nourishing prey. Subject matter comes winging towards them. (Adorno, 1974: 87)

It remains to see how Adorno makes use of this conception of a critical rhetorics and, indeed, how faithful he remains to its spirit.

(b) Ontology

Adorno's critique of Heidegger might appear to be a rather abstruse matter to consider in a book about the prospects for a radical social theory. The rationale lies in the 'end of philosophy' theme. Heidegger's 'deconstruction' of the philosophical tradition is radical in the strict sense that it purports to penetrate 'beneath' the level of philosophical categories and their relations. This project has spawned a variety of 'left Heideggerianisms' in radical social and cultural theory: Marcuse attempted to find a Heideggerian foundation for critical theory at one point; the 'reflexive sociology' of the 1970s deployed Heideggerian themes in exploring the relations between language and Being; and Derrida's project of 'deconstruction' can be understood as a critical appropriation of Heidegger. There are also some convergences between Heidegger and Adorno. As Rose (1978: 70) notes, both insist that the categorical oppositions of philosophy cannot capture the dominance of objectivity. In the post-war period, at least, both relate this problem of objectivity (or 'Being', for Heidegger) to questions about the movement of language. Perhaps it is because Heidegger comes so close to a diagnosis of the problems of philosophy, objectivity and language that Adorno is determined to refute his fatal wrong turning towards an ur-objectivity. The apparently abstruse conflict between Adorno and Heidegger goes to the heart of the question of the type of 'end' which a post-foundational radicalism should make of philosophy. It will have implications for those postmodernist would-be radicalisms which also pursue the mirage of an ur-objectivity.

Adorno offers two kinds of critique of Heidegger's project. In the first, located mainly but not exclusively in *The Jargon of Authenticity*, he offers an account of the broad socio-cultural location and consequences of Heidegger's work. The second, located mainly but not exclusively in *Negative Dialectics*,[14] subjects Heidegger to a rigorous 'immanent critique'. The first, sociological, critique turns on the claim that Heidegger's philosophical terminology is a jargon, a 'rhetoric' in the derogatory sense of the term. The vocabulary of 'authenticity', 'innermost concern', 'commitment', 'Man', 'dialogue', and the rest are treated as an early form of psycho-babble. In an argument which harks back to Horkheimer's concerns in the 1930s, Adorno claims that 'the bourgeois form of rationality has always needed irrational supplements, in order to maintain itself as what it is' (Adorno, 1973b: 47). The jargon provides just such a supplement, it 'fills the breach created by the societally necessary disintegration of language' (ibid.: 48). Lacking any specific content, it adapts easily to social requirements. 'Administration is its essence' Adorno argues, citing a parody of the jargon (ibid.: 89–91).

Adorno's sociological critique echoes standard Marxian concerns, and does not move far from a conventional treatment of the 'ideology' theme.[15] However, *The Jargon of Authenticity* also begins an immanent critique, in which the degeneration of language is analysed in its own terms, and it is here that Adorno's proximity to an anti-foundationalist critical rhetorics becomes clear. The indifference to content of the jargon, noted above, becomes a 'metaphysics of language' (ibid.: 87). It emerges from the collapse of systematic philosophies, so that 'linguistic nonsense is the heir to the disintegrated strictness of the system' (ibid.). Even here, it might be noted, Adorno agrees with Heidegger that thinking, or dialectic, must face up to the end, or the sudden visibility of the *clôture*, of philosophical systems. Adorno's critical rhetorics is alert to Heidegger's recourse to stylistic and rhetorical 'tricks'. In his celebration of the virtues of 'simplicity' and 'genuine rootedness', Heidegger can simulate 'simplicity' in his own writing only by literary artifice. The evocation of the archaic and of the poetic character of thinking resembles 'some trusty folk-art, which after all is not used to speaking well about these things' (ibid.: 53). The prose which intimates Heidegger's own 'rootedness' is a form of Kitsch which 'reminds us of the most washed-out clichés in plough-and-furrow novels' (ibid.: 55).

The main philosophical thrust of Adorno's immanent critique is directed at the 'question of Being', the problems associated with the alleged emergence of particular 'beings' from a primordial, undivided 'Being'. Rose sums up Adorno's case:

> Heidegger's being is antinomical: if it is immediate, primeval and non-conceptual, it is meaningless; if it acquires a meaning it is not immediate, primordial and non-conceptual, but is (equal to) its essence, and is thus a concept of reflection. (Rose, 1978: 72)

This summary also indicates why the critique of Heidegger is such a difficult task for Adorno. Heidegger is accused, as he will be again by Derrida, of recognising but failing to break out of the *clôture* of metaphysics: the attempt to crash through traditional antinomies catches Heidegger in an antinomical paradox. But such a critique inevitably runs the risk of seeming simply to endorse antinomical thinking. Of course, Adorno does not want to do this, and, interestingly, he ascribes to philosophy itself the insight that antinomies are not absolute. Heidegger deserves a limited credit for retaining 'the fundament of the entire philosophical history [he] slanders, notably Kant's and Hegel's: the view that the dualisms of within and without, of subject and object, of essence and appearance, of concept and fact are not absolute' (Adorno, 1973a: 91). Equally, Heidegger is correct to attempt to break out of the phenomenological universalisation of consciousness. The problems begin with the way Heidegger brings together his rejection of antinomical thinking and his suspicion of the immanence of consciousness: 'He pursues dialectics to the point of saying that neither the subject nor the object are immediate and ultimate; but he deserts dialectics in reaching for something immediate and primary beyond subject and object' (ibid.: 106). Such a move can only produce an irrationalist regression, 'a mere parody of the supernatural' (ibid.).

From this point, the form of the critique is familiar: Heidegger's ontology resolves into another case of 'identity thinking'. In appearing to establish an ur-objectivity of 'Being' beyond the subject–object dualism, it actually re-instates subjectivity as its governing principle. Through the concept of *Dasein*,[16] 'Heidegger secretly reinstates the creator quality of the absolute subject' (Adorno, 1973b: 120), so that objectivity becomes a form of 'mine-ness'. This critique does seem to return Adorno, time and again, to antinomical thinking and, particularly, to Kant as a foil for Heidegger. So, he argues that only Heidegger's 'pathos' differentiates his 'Being' from Kant's 'thing in itself'. The 'thinking' of which Heidegger makes so much is 'as un-substantial as the thing to be thought: thinking without a concept is not thinking at all' (Adorno, 1973a: 98). Again, the primacy of the object must be asserted within, rather than beyond, dialectic. In contrast to Heidegger, 'Kant refused to be talked out of the moment of objective preponderance ... he does not sacrifice the idea of otherness' (ibid.: 184). Adorno's general judgement on Heidegger is Kantian, too: 'Heidegger's moment of truth levels into an irrationalist *Weltanschauung*. Today, as in Kant's time, philosophy demands a rational critique of reason, not its banishment or abolition' (ibid.: 85).

Has Adorno simply followed Horkheimer's path of a return to philosophy in the face of the ambiguities of critical theory? The case is not exactly the same. Adorno's conceptions of 'identity thinking' and of a '(negative) dialectic of non-identity' give a much sharper sense of the fundamental tasks of critical theory than anything Horkheimer provides. Those passages in which negative dialectic most nearly approximates to a critical rhetorics represent a high-water mark in the auto-critique of modernist radicalism. What Adorno cannot do, however, is to shake a critical rhetorics free from the tradition of critical philosophy. In effect, he throws the modernist radical 'end of philosophy' into reverse: he is not interested in dialectic as the 'end' of philosophy, but in philosophy as the 'beginning' of dialectic. Adorno's frequent appeals to Kant, or to Hegel, can be misleading, then. He does not wish to restore the plenitude of traditional philosophy; rather, critical philosophy is re-modelled as a site for the assertion of the claims of non-identity. This conception grants Adorno a certain immunity from the temptation to make a radical modernist 'end of philosophy'. The problem is whether it does not also serve as an alibi for Adorno's failure, in the end, to develop the tools of a non-philosophical critical rhetorics.

(c) Aesthetics

Aesthetic debates within Frankfurt critical theory parallel those about philosophy, turning on the extent to which art continues to be a potentially emancipatory tradition. Adorno's position on this issue, as on most others, remained remarkably consistent. As he puts it in *Aesthetic Theory*, 'Pure and immanently elaborated art is a tacit critique of the debasement of man by a condition that is moving towards a total-exchange society where everything is a for-other' (Adorno, 1984: 321). Adorno's development of an 'aesthetic of non-identity' involved him in constant, complex and overlapping debates. During the 1930s, and later, he argued against what he saw as an over-politicised conception of art, exemplified by Brecht. During the same period he began a critique of the regressive products of the 'culture industry', whose most famous (or notorious) expression was his total hostility to all popular music. He defended the classical tradition in music as the bearer of humane values, but argued that any attempt to re-capture the spirit of classical affirmation must be regressive and authoritarian (as in the case of Stravinsky's neo-classicism). Adorno advocated a severe aesthetic modernism, exemplified in literature by Beckett and in music by Schönberg's pre-serialist work.[17]

In Search of Wagner, written in 1937–8, occupies a pivotal position within Adorno's aesthetic project, and is similar in some ways to the critique of Heidegger. Wagner, too, is accused of setting out to overcome the contradictions of modernity and then resolving into a regressive identarian subjectivism. The critique is directed against the theory and practice of the Wagnerian *Gesamtkunstwerk*, the attempt to unify visual art, drama, poetry, and music within a single work. Adorno faces an initial methodological and rhetorical dilemma. He requires a form of writing which will allow him to analyse the effects of Wagner's attempt at artistic synthesis, but which will not recapitulate, and thus legitimate, Wagner's own model. Such would be the effect of structuring the critique around successive discussions of Wagner's visual art, drama, poetry and music, for example.

A similar problem faced Benjamin, who was working on a study of Baudelaire while Adorno was grappling with Wagner.

Benjamin's preferred solution was to construct 'constellations' out of the 'concrete traces' of a culture, ignoring the question of intention. Adorno and Benjamin corresponded about the Baudelaire project, and Adorno came to the view that Benjamin's method threatened to resolve into a refined positivism which, compelled by the logic of identity, must fall under the spell of subjectivism. As Adorno wrote in a much-quoted passage,[18] 'your study is located at the crossroads of magic and positivism. That spot is bewitched. Only theory could break the spell' (Adorno, 1977a: 129). Despite these radical doubts, the method of *In Search of Wagner* does echo Benjamin's, and harks back to the influence of Simmel. Adorno identifies, and structures the text around, a number of Wagnerian 'figures', or forms: Wagner as 'composer', *Leitmotiv*, sonority, the character of Wotan, etc. The analysis of each figure establishes a specific perspective on the Wagnerian totality and on theoretical issues. Adorno intends that this method will preserve the spell-breaking potential of theory without relapsing into either the seductions of identity thinking or the fragmentation of Benjamin's 'traces'.

Wagner presents the *Gesamtkunstwerk* as a protest against the increasing fragmentation of subjective, cultural and social life. The first paradox of the venture, for Adorno, is that it is to be accomplished by a single individual. It is 'founded on the bourgeois "individual" with his soul, whose origins and substance are rooted in the self-same alienation against which the *Gesamtkunstwerk* rebels' (Adorno, 1981: 110). In consequence, any Wagnerian 're-unification' can only be an illusion: 'What the individual conceives as an organic, living unity, stands revealed objectively as a mere agglomerate' (ibid.: 111). This pretended unity rests on two further paradoxes. First, at the level of production, the music-drama depends on a high level of technical rationalisation, upon the strict delineation of formally equivalent, interchangeable, musical and dramatic 'parts' susceptible of easy integration into a 'whole'. Second, it follows that the supposedly progressive unity of music-drama is an effect of objective regression. Wagner's use of *Leitmotiv*[19] exhibits the 'dynamics of permanent regression', each *Motiv* constituting a 'particle of congealed meaning' which can be interchanged with other particles according to the demands of the moment. In effect, Wagner abandons specifically musical form, the 'generally binding musical logic' which Adorno regards as the major achievement of European music. Without such a logic, Wagner's musical time is reduced to mere duration (a point with which all anti-Wagnerians will have an intuitive sympathy), so that 'there is really nothing to analyse in Wagner's music' (ibid.: 41).

Wagnerian drama is as regressive as the music which is, in the end, no more than its accompaniment (Wagner is the direct ancestor of film music, for Adorno). Wagner's characters rarely possess any historical specificity, but function as symbols in a phantasmagoric mythical time and are differentiated merely by gesture. 'The only reason why Wagner's characters can function as universal symbols is that they dissolve into the phantasmagoria like mist' (ibid.: 89). Adorno's use of the term 'phantasmagoria' rather than 'dream' to identify the scene of Wagnerian drama is a further measure of his methodological dispute with Benjamin. The phantasmagoria is an objective, technically produced, piece of stage-craft. To refer to it as a 'dream' or a 'dream-world' is to become complicit in the Wagnerian illusion of interiority and subjectivism. As Adorno wrote to Benjamin, 'The dialectical image should not be transferred into consciousness as a dream, but in its dialectical construction the dream should be externalised and the immanence of consciousness itself be understood as a constellation of reality' (Adorno, 1977a: 112). The weakness of Wagner's characterisation, 'which always subordinates subjective animation to tangible gesture and the outward effect' (Adorno, 1981: 116), conveys a partial recognition of the bankruptcy of the category of the subject. But the fragmentation of both music and drama which are necessary for the phantasmagoric effect signal the failure of the *Gesamtkunstwerk*, which must 'regress to a sort of archaic melange' (ibid.: 104).

If Adorno's discussion of Wagnerian regression places him in a debate with Benjamin, it also emphasises the importance of his connection with Horkheimer and, particularly, the themes of 'Egoism and the Freedom Movement', a connection acknowledged in the preface to *In Search of Wagner*. Wagner's music-dramas stand at the end of the brief reign of bourgeois individualism and at the beginning of its decline into mere conformism. They offer an illusory resolution of two contradictions faced by their audience: that between asceticism and sensuality, and that between rebellion and conformism. Wagner's *Rienzi* takes as its theme the Cola di Rienzo revolt which is the historical starting point for Horkheimer's narrative. Wagner's Rienzo, 'the last

Roman tribune and the first bourgeois terrorist' (Adorno, 1981: 12), directs his attack against the 'decadence' of the Roman ruling class. His radicalism, characterised by a taste for 'self praise and pomp', is a prefiguration of fascism: 'behind Wagner's facade of liberty, death and destruction stand waiting in the wings' (ibid.: 14).

In later works such as *Tristan and Isolde*, Wagner accommodates both asceticism and sensuality by projecting their unity to a moment beyond death and the annihilation of self. For Wagner, 'pleasure assumes the features of death and destruction, in return death is celebrated in the mirror of the work as "soaring joy" and "greatest good"' (ibid.: 146). This 'sinister sentimentality' has a political parallel. After Wagner's desertion of the revolutionary camp in 1848, his attitude to the bourgeoisie is a 'configuration of envy, sentimentality and destructiveness' (ibid.: 17). His 'critique' of the bourgeoisie is carried in anti-semitic caricatures of decadent and degenerate bourgeois types. In contrast, Wagnerian heroes are innocents and natural ascetics, representatives of 'a proletariat modelled on a woodcutter' (ibid.: 131). In between stand the bemused mass of bourgeois, represented in *The Ring* by Wotan, who sets the motion in action but falls silent and becomes a mere spectator. Rebellion, like sensuality, is to be projected beyond death, this time a collective death of the bourgeoisie. 'In Wagner the bourgeoisie dreams of its own destruction, conceiving it as the only road to salvation, even though all it ever sees of the salvation is the destruction' (ibid.: 142).

Adorno's critique of Wagner brings into juxtaposition some of the most important influences on his conception of radical theory. At the level of substantive social theory and ideology critique, Adorno is drawing on Horkheimer's account of the regressive dimension of bourgeois revolutions and also (particularly on the question of anti-semitism) on Nietzsche's critique of Wagner. At the level of method and the critique of form, Adorno is placed in a debate with Benjamin and, by implication, with the ghost of Simmel. The judgement which Adorno reaches about Wagner is parallel to that which he reaches about Heidegger, and has the same air of paradox. The attempt to unify the arts under the aegis of subjectivity is intertwined with a logic of reification and identity: '(The more reification, the more subjectivity: the maxim holds good in orchestration as in epistemology' (Adorno, 1981: 74). The unity which Wagner seeks can only be the fraudulent unity of identity. Just as Adorno's critique of Heidegger comes close to endorsing antinomical philosophy, his critique of Wagner comes close to endorsing the classical tradition.

> The older opera, which Wagner accused of lacking unity because it failed to integrate the different arts, was superior to him in at least one respect: it sought unity not in the assimilation of one art to the other, but in complying with the laws governing each separate realm. Mozartian unity is that of configuration, not identification. (ibid.: 104)[20]

(d) Sociology, philosophy and critique

Adorno's 1931 'Inaugural Lecture' offers an account of the relations between philosophy and sociology. The general thesis of the lecture runs close to a version of the 'end of philosophy'. Adorno urges a model of philosophy as interpretation which 'does not shrink back from that liquidation of philosophy which to me seems signalled by the collapse of the last philosophic claims to totality' (Adorno, 1977b: 129). The connection with Benjamin is clear in Adorno's insistence that (post?) philosophical 'interpretation' is far from hermeneutics. Materialism requires 'interpretation of the unintentional through a juxtaposition of the analytically isolated elements and illumination of the real by the power of such interpretation' in a programme which 'distances itself from every "meaning" of its objects' (ibid.: 127).

This kind of non-totalising interpretation requires a constant communication with new problems, and will 'take its specific scientific material preponderantly from sociology' (ibid.: 130). A little earlier, Adorno provides the formula for the division of labour between philosophy and sociology: 'the idea of science ... is research; that of philosophy is interpretation' (ibid.: 126). The 'end of philosophy' here is close to Wittgenstein's: a purged philosophy lives on after its renunciation of past pretensions. The requirement for a new articulation between philosophy and sociology is closer to Simmel than to the modernist radical image of social science as a successor discipline to philosophy.

Adorno opens a theoretical space in which a materialist hermeneutic articulates with social research. Might this also be the space of a post-foundational radicalism? Certainly, the model of a materialist hermeneutic converges with that of a critical rhetorics which acknowledges the finitude of language. Equally, the recognition that the moment of research, of substantive enquiry, cannot be pre-empted by philosophical reflection is congenial. A residual difficulty concerns the way in which the line between research and interpretation is drawn. It re-capitulates a qualitative distinction between orders of discourse which is a pre-supposition of foundationalist conceptions of enquiry (see chapter 6.5). This problem may reflect a lingering reluctance on Adorno's part finally to abandon philosophy and foundationalism. However, Adorno had no resources to hand with which to model a *research* practice which could meet the requirements of a materialist hermeneutic. In chapter 7.2 the resources of ethnomethodology are mobilised to draw a distinction between 'mundane' and 'orthogonal' enquiry. This distinction retains some of the sense of that between 'research' and 'interpretation' while evading foundational entanglements.

Adorno returned to the question of sociology in the late 1950s and 1960s, in essays which cannot rank as his most impressive work. His three contributions to *The Positivist Dispute in German Sociology* are wordy, repetitive and querulous, representing Adorno's style at its worst. More importantly, they are all too easily read as evidence for the view that Adorno advocates an 'Hegelian' sociology. On his return to Germany, Adorno urged a critical appropriation of the techniques of empirical social research against two kinds of enemy: those who would reject empirical research techniques out of hand, in the name of the 'sciences of culture', and those who would appropriate them entirely *un*critically (see Jay, 1984a: 97). The contributions to the 'Positivist Dispute' volume are all directed overwhelmingly against the second enemy, a broadly drawn 'positivism'[21] allegedly dedicated to the reduction of sociology to social research and to the marginalisation (or worse) of theoretical reflection on society. Unless the reader is already alive to the nuances of Adorno's critique of identity, and to the ambiguities of his relation to the philosophical tradition, it can seem as if he is simply urging Hegel against the 'positivists'.

In these later essays Adorno has become more suspicious of sociology, contrasting it not only with philosophy but with a 'critical theory of society'. The latter is 'orientated towards the idea of society as subject, whilst sociology accepts reification', a characteristic related to 'the sociological claim to domination raised by Comte' (Adorno, 1976a: 34). Positivistic sociology is berated for taking a position on 'totality' that does not seem far from Adorno's in 1931. 'Isolated social research becomes untrue as soon as it wishes to extirpate totality as a mere crypto-metaphysical prejudice, since totality cannot, in principle, be apprehended by its methods' (Adorno, 1976b: 79).[22] Adorno defends the idea of totality as 'not an affirmative but rather a critical category' (Adorno, 1976a: 12), and relates that idea to Durkheim's social realism. 'Formulated provocatively, totality is society as a thing-in-itself, with all the guilt of reification' (ibid.). However, since this thing-in-itself 'is not yet the total societal subject', it retains 'an indissoluble moment of objectivity' (ibid.). Adorno echoes Durkheim's critique of Simmel when he asserts that empirical research 'cannot evade the fact that all the given factors investigated, the subjective no less than the objective relations, are mediated through society (Adorno, 1976b: 84).

It is difficult to avoid a sense that Adorno's later texts on sociology mark a falling away from the clarity of earlier and, indeed, contemporary essays on philosophy and aesthetics. That is why they have not been explored at length here. In them, the waters of the 'end of philosophy' are muddied once more, the critique of totality is compromised, and too many questions are obfuscated in a subject–object dialectic which does, indeed, drift close to Hegelian Marxism and foundationalism. Adorno's judgement on sociology is that its 'abandonment of a critical theory of society is resignatory: one no longer dares to conceive of the whole since one must despair of changing it' (Adorno, 1976c: 121). But this begs a series of questions – about critique, about the antidote to 'resignation' and about practice – which Adorno himself poses elsewhere. It is no less important than paradoxical to insist that Adorno's assessments of sociology have less to offer to a post-foundational and sociological radicalism than do his essays on philosophy and aesthetics.

In these areas, Adorno seems to offer a hard lesson to radical theory: it must never imagine that it is 'adequate' to its object, and it must eschew all 'unities' however progressive they may appear to be. To break these injunctions is to relapse into identity thinking, subjectivism, and the denial of the primacy of the object. The image of a rigorous dialectic of non-identity is Adorno's major legacy to the quest for a post-foundational radicalism, and the contribution which sets him apart from Horkheimer and the other Frankfurt critical theorists. That image is entwined with Adorno's insistence that the movement of dialectic is the movement of language, a 'critical rhetorics'. The 'will to a system' whose lack of integrity Nietzsche and Adorno join in condemning has its matrix in the 'grammar' of identarian theoretical discourse. Dialectic must become a rhetoric both in order to trace the rhetorical movement of identarian discourse and in order artfully to construct itself as critique in its very form, or style. And yet, Adorno will not abandon classical traditions as the 'beginning' of dialectic. He will appeal to the memory of classical antinomies and configurational unities, to a Kant or a Mozart, as the most potent critique of the regressive identarianism of a Heidegger or a Wagner. Adorno's classicism can often seem to serve as an alibi for his failure to develop the critical rhetorics which remains as much a blueprint as a practice.

4

THE SWANSONG OF
MODERNIST RADICALISM?

4.1 PRELIMINARIES

Jürgen Habermas is the only contemporary social theorist who
might be compared without hyperbole to a Marx or a Weber. In
the aftermath of the self-destruction of Althusserianism,
Habermas's project is unchallenged in scope and stature. The
project, which he has seen as moving 'toward a reconstruction of
historical materialism' (see the essay of that title in Habermas,
1979), can be regarded as a 'reconstruction of modernist radicalism'. Habermas takes seriously the critiques of modernist radicalism examined above, but attempts to recapture something of
the optimism of Enlightenment and modernist radical concepts of
modernity.

The 'yet' in Habermas's claim that 'the project of modernity has
not yet been fulfilled' (Habermas, 1981: 12) links him with the
ambitions of a Marx or a Durkheim to bring about the completion
of modernity, and beyond them to the Enlightenment. These
ambitions are contested in ironic conceptions of modernity such
as Simmel's and Weber's. The irony is intensified in the thesis of a
'dialectic of enlightenment' in which the 'normative content of
modernity' (to take a phrase from Habermas) falls victim to
regression. This pessimism connects with Adorno's thesis that the
only possible critical theory is a wholly 'negative' dialectic of non-
identity. If Habermas is to rehabilitate the 'project of modernity'
he must overcome the pessimism of these Weberian and critical–
theoretic themes and work to justify a role for an affirmative, non-
ironic moment in critical theory. This task is as delicate as it
is ambitious. Habermas is acutely aware that he cannot simply
re-capitulate the figures of discredited modernist radicalisms.
Each of the three defining themes (the end of philosophy,
ideology, the unity of theory and practice) requires careful re-
working.

On the face of it, Habermas's successive attempts at reconstruction have taken him a long way from the traditional version of modernist radicalism and its critiques. His intellectual resources have moved further and further away from those of Marxism, or the critical theory of an Adorno. In the late 1960s Habermas's concerns with 'theory and practice' and with 'knowledge constituting interests' still connected with familiar Frankfurt School resources such as Kant, Fichte, Hegel, Marx and Freud. By the early 1980s he is drawing on sociology, developmental psychology, linguistics and the philosophy of language. However, this growing eclecticism should not deflect attention from Habermas's continuing commitment to the project-form of modernist radicalism. Indeed, his more recent work marks a return to an almost orthodox modernist radicalism.

In the late 1960s Habermas was drawn to a model of critical theory as a meta-theory of the sciences, a 'non scientivistic philosophy of science' (Habermas, 1971a: 653), which maintained a privileged link to emancipatory self-reflection. Such an open, second-order theory can operate only at a remove from the ambitions of modernist radicalism. But the new model of the early 1980s turns on a conception of critical theory as a 'reconstructive' science (or synthesis of such sciences). Outhwaite (1987: ch. 5) has remarked on the significance of this shift from epistemology to social science, which involves 'strong realist claims for reconstructive sciences' (ibid.: 84). A first-order critical social science empowered to reconstruct the formative processes of modernity is once again able to mobilise the defining themes of modernist radicalism.

The two sections which follow attempt to fill out this argument-sketch, and to consider its implications. The first reviews Habermas's trajectory from the point of view of his continuing concern with the 'public sphere'. This focus can give a sense of the ways in which Habermas has problematised the 'unity of theory and practice' and connected it to the 'ideology' theme. The second section questions the role of 'reconstructive sciences' such as 'formal pragmatics' in Habermas's more recent model, and relates it to the 'end of philosophy' theme and to Habermas's modernist radicalism.

4.2 A CRITICAL SOCIOLOGY OF THE PUBLIC SPHERE

(a) Theory, practice and the public sphere

The slogan of 'the unity of theory and practice' points to problems which have always been near the centre of Habermas's various interests. A theme which remains constant is that the necessary unity of the two is also always a disunity: theory and practice come in more than one complex, and Habermas's concern has been to trace the lines of continuity and discontinuity between the different complexes. This concern is the thread which links a series of distinctions: between the three 'knowledge constituting interests', between *techne* and praxis, between labour and interaction, between cognitive, interactive and expressive communications, or between strategic and communicative action.[1] The differentiation of complexes of theory and practice can serve to rehabilitate modernity and to give critical theory an affirmative turn. If Habermas can show that the pathologies of modernity result from an imbalance between such complexes, he can argue that the completion of modernity requires a correction of the imbalance. The affirmative role of critical theory is thus to speak for the repressed and marginalised complex; for the 'interest in emancipation', for 'praxis' or for 'communicative action'. This approach also requires a re-orientation of the 'ideology' theme. A hard and fast distinction between *epistēmē* and *doxa* is no longer the centre of attention: ideas or discourses become 'ideological' to the extent that they promote, or become complicit in, an imbalance between complexes of theory and practice. So, technological discourse is not ideological in itself, but it becomes so when it is applied to social relationships which it is not appropriate to bring under technical control.

Habermas's first major book[2] takes up this problem in relation to the origins, structure and degeneration of the 'bourgeois public sphere', where 'public sphere' is taken to specify 'a realm of our social life where something approaching public opinion can be formed (Habermas, 1974b: 49). Habermas offers a substantive model of the development of political 'publics' which is based on the English experience and against which other variants can be matched. The institutions of the eighteenth-century public sphere (coffee houses, political clubs, newspapers) develop as vehicles within which those bourgeois members of 'civil society' who are as yet denied a major role within the absolutist 'state' can articulate a reasoned view of their collective interests. Habermas is under no illusions about the class-specific and self-serving origins of this public sphere, but neither does he wish simply to de-bunk it. As a non-private domain which is not integrated into the state, the public sphere enables the formation of 'opinion' on the basis of rational discourse. It is a crucial site of the self-formative processes of individuals and groups. As Figure 1 shows, Habermas places the public sphere(s) topologically as a 'mediation' between major blocs of institutions.

Private domain			Public power
Civil society		Political public sphere	State
		Literary public sphere	
Restricted family		'Town'	'Court'

Figure 1 Civil society, public sphere and state.

These concerns link Habermas to the young Marx. It will be recalled from chapter one that the key to Marx's critique of Hegel's theory of the state is his assertion of the foundational priority of civil society as the site of a universal rationality. Koselleck's (1988) critique of Enlightenment was mobilised to suggest that Marx becomes entangled in the paradoxes of an apolitical politics. Habermas's concern with the public sphere is similarly entangled. The public sphere, in one sense, is the analogue of the proletariat in Marx's 1843/4 'Introduction'. Both are particulars (a particular social class, a particular social space) placed in some way on the margins of civil society. Both particulars are endowed with a universal significance as the bearers of a rationality immanent-but-obscured within civil society. Habermas re-capitulates the Enlightenment programme, and remains vulnerable to Koselleck's critique, to the extent that he prefigures an apolitical politics in which the state is subordinated to the rational discourses of the public sphere.

Habermas's account of the 'degeneration' of this public sphere is better-known than his account of its origins and structure. The twentieth-century public sphere degenerates into a 'public opinion' manipulated by 'publicity'. This degeneration leads to a new and destructive 'de-differentiation' of the public and the private, precipitating a decline in the critical capacities of individuals and groups. The issue is taken up in a 1968 paper, 'The Scientization of Politics/Public Opinion' (Habermas, 1971a: ch. 5), which examines the role of social science and social technologies in the proliferation of destructive complexes of theory and practice. Social science furnishes 'decisionistic' and 'technocratic' models of political action which serve to legitimate the erosion of a democratic public sphere.[3] Technologies of persuasion, opinion sampling and social control increasingly usurp the place of processes of 'rational will formation' in a public sphere.

The only model of rationalised political action which Habermas regards as retaining a necessary link with democratic processes is that which he labels 'pragmatic' and traces to Dewey. Dewey's model pre-supposes, but does not fully articulate, a model of communication 'based on a historically determined preunderstanding, governed by social norms, of what is practically necessary in a concrete situation' (Habermas, 1971a: 68–9). This 'prescientific' knowledge is the key to a benign complex of theory and practice in a public sphere. Following Gadamer, Habermas urges that an effective public sphere, and therefore a democratic polity, must rest on 'a consciousness that can only be enlightened hermeneutically, through articulation in the discourse of citizens in a community' (ibid.: 69).

Habermas's engagement with hermeneutics in this text, and in others of the late 1960s and early 70s,[4] gives a 'twist' to his theory of the public sphere which is consequential for his subsequent trajectory. The public sphere is no longer to be defined solely in terms of its position in an array of institutions, but with reference to the formal characteristics of patterns of communication. This distinction suggests two alternative strategies through which public sphere issues might be analysed. The first is to consider the public sphere as a social institution, and to locate it in relation to other institutions within a 'topology of social spaces'. The second is to follow the hermeneutic theme and to identify the virtues of the public sphere with the virtues of a particular type of communication, which can be located within a 'typology of discourse'. The 'Scientization' paper sits on the threshold of a shift of emphasis towards the second strategy.

The hermeneutic turn of the 'Scientization' paper sows the seeds of a problem to which Habermas constantly recurs: that of the appropriate balance between distinct 'technical' and 'communicative' processes of rationalisation, or enlightenment. The need for a specifically 'critical' theory arises because of destructive imbalances between the two. In an ideal world, there would be no need for critical theory. The pre-scientific and practical communications of the public sphere would be adequate to processes of self-formation and self-reflection, and the public sphere would communicate unproblematically with the specialised sciences. It is this ideal world which Dewey mistakes for the real one, in Habermas's view. The need for a critical theory arises because no basis currently exists

> for the reliable translation of scientific information into the ordinary language of practice and inversely for a translation from the context of practical questions back into the specialised language of technical and strategic recommendations. (Habermas, 1971a: 70)

As a consequence of this lack, technical development takes place in a direct two-way relation with 'social interests that arise spontaneously from the compulsion to reproduce social life (Habermas, 1971a: 73). It is this direct inter-penetration of technology, including social technology, with social reproduction which leads to the 'degeneration' of the public sphere.

On this diagnosis, the function of critical theory is to enable the kind of 'translation' between science and the 'language of practice' which is a pre-condition for the restoration of a public sphere. The translation problem may provide a clear rationale for critical theory as 'mediator', but it also exposes it to the paradoxes of the 'third thing'. If critical theory is not adequately differentiated from both science and 'the language of practice' it risks collapse into one of the two discourses it is supposed to mediate between. But if it *is* so differentiated, it may itself need 'translation' in both directions, and the regression of 'thirds' is under way. Versions of this difficulty afflict all of Habermas's formulations of the tasks of critical theory.

111

(b) Two typologies of discourse

It is usual to divide Habermas's search for typologies of discourse into two phases, one centred on *Knowledge and Human Interests*, the other developing out of concerns with 'communicative competence.'[5] The first phase offers a typology of three types of science which emerge from three 'media' which are activated by three 'knowledge constituting interests', roughly as shown in Figure 2.[6]

Type of science	Medium	Constitutive interest
empirico-analytic	work	technical (control)
historical—hermeneutic	language	practical (understanding)
critically-oriented	power	emancipatory (reflection)

Figure 2 The three knowledge constituting interests.

This model can be seen as a map of complexes of theory and practice, differentiated at the level of their respective 'rationalities'. It derives logics of discourse from 'interests' which enjoy a 'quasi-transcendental' status: they are epistemological *and* anthropological categories. 'The achievements of the transcendental subject have their basis in the natural history of the human species' (Habermas, 1972: 321). Critics saw these claims as no more than an attempt to revive discredited themes from German critical philosophy.[7] In his 1973 postscript Habermas substantially backed away from the 'interests' model, transforming questions about the 'transcendental' foundations of knowledge into questions about the pre-conditions of communication, laying the basis for a second typology to be considered below (see Habermas, 1973: 165).

If the 'interests' typology is considered as a solution to the translation problem, it can show that critical theory will not collapse into (empirico-analytic) science, since it is based on its own 'interest'. However, it is less clear how critical theory will relate to 'the language of practice', since the 'historical–hermeneutic' sciences have a proprietary claim on the 'practical' interest and its medium of language. One possibility would be to re-formulate critical theory as a 'critical hermeneutics',[8] in which the emancipatory interest is the servant of the practical. But this is not the solution which Habermas adopts. Instead of establishing a privileged relation between the emancipatory and the practical interest, he ties the former to a general 'interest in reason'.

Habermas prevaricates as to whether the emancipatory interest is as anthropologically basic as the other two (see Held, 1980: 319), and there are sound reasons for arguing that he cannot consistently maintain that it is.[9] However, if it is derivative of the other two, if it arises when the technical and practical interests are out of balance, it is difficult to see how an emancipatory interest could enjoy even a 'quasi' transcendental status. In a passage which echoes Horkheimer, Habermas warns against a 'naturalism' which would 'tie the emancipatory interest of knowledge to fortuitous historical constellations and would thus relativistically deprive self-reflection of the possibility of a justificatory basis for its claim to validity' (Habermas, 1974a: 14–15). But it is difficult to see how naturalism could be avoided if the emancipatory interest is contingent upon the balance between the other two. Habermas's solution to the problem of the emancipatory interest emerges in chapter nine of *Knowledge and Human Interests*, where the idea of a general 'interest in Reason' is derived from Kant and Fichte, for whom such an interest is the site of a foundational unity between theory and practice.

> The category of cognitive interest is authenticated only by the interest innate in reason. The technical and practical cognitive interests can be comprehended unambiguously *as* knowledge-constituting interests only in connection with the emancipatory cognitive interest of rational reflection. (Habermas, 1972: 198)

That is, the power of emancipatory self-reflection derives from the 'deep' foundational unity of 'knowledge' and 'interest'. 'In self-reflection knowledge for the sake of knowledge attains congruence with the interest in autonomy and responsibility ... in the power of self reflection, knowledge and interest are one' (ibid.: 314).

This claim was not well-received, even by sympathetic commentators such as McCarthy,[10] and Habermas pulls back from it as part of his general shift away from the 'interests' typology. In an important sense, however, this abandoned claim sets the terms for Habermas's later models of critical theory and, in particular, the problem of theory and practice. Habermas retains an image of an emancipation which rests on the 'realisation' of some universal principle whose immanence in both practical and theoretical discourses is the source of their value and ultimate unity. Critical theory cannot be a critical hermeneutics, a servant of the practical discourses of the public sphere, because its deeper loyalty is to the foundational unity of those discourses with theoretical discourse. To put it another way, Habermas's version of the Enlightenment programme requires that the discourses of the public sphere are animated by a legislative and universal reason. Critical theory can address the problems of the public sphere because both are complexes of theory and practice which rest on the same ultimate foundations.

The outline of an alternative typology, this time of communications, begins to emerge in the 1971 introduction to *Theory and Practice*, which raises questions concerning 'the normative implications that lie in the concept of possible understanding with which every speaker (and hearer) is naïvely familiar' (Habermas, 1974a: 17). Habermas's interest in pragmatics turns on a sense that ordinary processes of (first-order) communication are in some way dependent upon a series of implicit claims, or pre-suppositions, which can be problematised and rendered explicit in (second-order) discourses. 'Systematically distorted communication' results when relations of power obstruct the realisation of such claims/pre-suppositions. This doctrine is systematised in texts such as 'What is Universal Pragmatics?', which yields the typology simplified in Figure 3.[11]

Domains of reality	Modes of communication	Validity claims	Functions of speech
External nature	Cognitive	Truth	Representation of facts
Society	Interactive	Rightness	Establishing inter-personal relations
Internal nature	Expressive	Truthfulness	Disclosure of subjectivity
Language	—	Comprehensibility	—

Figure 3 The types and dimensions of communication.

Despite its complexities, Habermas's 'formal pragmatics' turns on a simple central figure. Communication pre-supposes, and discourse specifically aims at, a 'rational consensus' which would realise the four validity claims. While any given speech-act will be primarily concerned with one specific row of the Figure 3, each involves *some* relation to the external world, to society, to the speaker's subjectivity and to language itself. Circumstances in which the claims *are* realised, in which all speakers speak truly, appropriately, sincerely and comprehensibly, constitute the 'Ideal Speech Situation'.

In the late 1970s Habermas's priority was to link formal pragmatics to a 'rational reconstruction' of species development based on the extrapolation of developmental psychology (Piaget for 'cognitive' and Kohlberg for 'moral' development). It was argued that the species learned to handle 'validity claims' successively (from top to bottom in Figure 3) and that a 'universal ethics of speech' marked the highest possible point of normative development. This account of the cognitive/moral development of the species was then mingled with Marx to reconstruct historical materialism.[12] The idea of 'rational reconstruction' allowed Habermas to model critical theory as a form of social science, rather than meta-science. In formal reconstructive analysis Habermas had discovered a scientific procedure which was distinct from those of the empirico-analytic and hermeneutic sciences.

On the face of it, these concerns took Habermas as far as may be from public sphere issues. The connection lies in the way in which the conception of critical theory as a 'reconstructive' social science enables Habermas to move away from a model of emancipatory complexes of theory and practice as forms of 'self-reflection'. While this movement is only completed in the 1980s, the seeds are sown in the 1971 introduction to *Theory and Practice*. Habermas allows that in the past he may have illicitly run together two senses of an 'interest in enlightenment'. One sense demands the 'relentless discursive validation of claims to validity', while the other aims at a 'practical change of established conditions' (Habermas, 1974a: 15). The alternative to this elision is to draw a distinction between 'two legitimate forms of self knowledge' (ibid.: 23): the discursive reconstruction of 'rule systems' and 'self-reflection'. The model for self-reflection is psychoanalysis conceived as an attempt to repair 'systematically distorted communication' within the subject. In terms of the typology in Figure 3, the claim to 'truthfulness' can be redeemed only in self-reflection.

115

In the early 1970s Habermas toyed with the idea of critical theory as psychoanalytic self-reflection writ large, and applied to 'distortions' in society.[13] Two considerations prevent him from embracing this alternative. First, the critique of social distortions requires theoretical reflection, and must draw on rational reconstructions (Habermas, 1974a: 24). Second, Habermas recognises that problems of concrete social and political organisation in a public sphere cannot be subsumed into general processes of self-reflection (ibid.: 25–40).

The typology of communication removes some of the more obvious embarrassments caused by the transcendentalist vocabulary of the typology of interests. It is also the major exemplar of a shift from a critical theory modelled upon meta-science and 'self-reflection' towards a critical social science of 'rational reconstructions'. In many respects, however, the two typologies are very close. In each case, 'the language of practice' is discovered to be a phenomenon of some innate principle of rationality. In each case, the task of critical theory is to remove obstacles to the realisation of that principle. In each case, there is a difficulty about showing how critical theory has a privileged link to rationality, while at the same time having a more specific relevance than that of enlightenment-in-general. This difficulty is compounded by uncertainties about the respective roles of 'self-reflection' and 'rational reconstruction'. The second typology generates a number of further local difficulties. If, as many critics suspect, Habermas illicitly takes the rationality of academic discourse as a model for all communication,[14] then the linkage between 'everyday' communication and critical discourse comes under question. The apparent resolution of Habermas's 'translation problem' can also be challenged. Discourse may seem to be able to mediate between everyday practice, the sciences and strategic planning by 'virtualising' their validity claims, but only because all action is illicitly assimilated to *communicative* action. This problem is taken up as Habermas returns to a topological model of public-sphere issues.

(c) A new topology

The Theory of Communicative Action marks a return to a topology of institutional spaces as the basis for discussion of public-sphere issues. More precisely, Habermas develops a new topology which articulates with a new typology in which communication finds an important role. The account of communication survives from the 1970s with few changes of detail, but the emphasis has shifted. Communication is now placed in a typology of action, which Habermas extracts from Weber (see Figure 4).[15]

	Oriented to success	Oriented to understanding
Non-social	Instrumental action	—
Social	Strategic action	Communicative action

Figure 4 Types of action.

The crucial distinction is that between the two types of social action, one of which (strategic) is coordinated through 'interests', the other (communicative) through 'normative agreement' (see Habermas, 1984: 285).

There are now, broadly, two types of social space: 'lifeworlds' and 'systems'. Systems line up with strategic action, and turn on the development of generalised 'steering media'. Habermas identifies two such: the economic system, which is steered by money, and the administrative system, which is steered by power. Lifeworlds, on the other hand, line up with communicative action as 'communicatively structured spheres of action, which are not held together by systemic means' (Habermas, 1987b: 319). Lifeworlds come in two sizes, as private and public spheres. Habermas argues that the emergence of steering media with the capacity to transcend social and normative contexts of action is the major impetus behind modernisation. Media emerge in response to lifeworld needs, but as they develop they become progressively 'uncoupled' from lifeworlds. This uncoupling becomes problematic with 'the emergence and growth of sub-systems whose independent imperatives turn back destructively upon the lifeworld itself' (Habermas, 1987b: 186).

Destructive 'colonization of the lifeworld' is the defining problem of a critical social science which reconstructs the uncompleted project of modernity. The problem is specified in a re-working of Weber's rationalisation theme. For Weber, the patho-

117

logies of modernity are a loss of meaning as formal rationalisation erodes substantive rationality, and a developing antagonism between increasingly differentiated 'value spheres'. Habermas is concerned to demonstrate that rationalisation and modernity are not pathological *per se*. There is nothing wrong in principle with a rationalisation of lifeworlds and 'a considerably rationalized lifeworld is one of the initial conditions for modernization processes' (Habermas, 1987b: 384). A rationalised lifeworld which has given tasks of material reproduction over to systems and steering media 'can in turn become more differentiated in its symbolic structures and can set free the inner logic of development of cultural modernity' (Habermas, 1987b: 385). The major *pathology* of modernity and rationalisation is the more specific trend to 'colonization', the increasing 'monetarization and bureaucratization of everyday practices both in the private and public spheres' (Habermas, 1987b: 325). In this process mediatisation oversteps 'normal' bounds, attempting to 'instrumentalize an influx from the lifeworld that possesses its own inner logic' (Habermas, 1987b: 323). Habermas insists that his objection to colonisation is not based on a nostalgia for the pre-modern: colonisation is pathological because, in the end, it cannot work. Steering media 'fail to work in domains of cultural reproduction, social integration and socialization; they cannot replace the action coordinating mechanisms of mutual understanding in these functions' (Habermas, 1987b: 322).[16]

Habermas links critical social science to the need to restore a balance in the processes of modernisation. The colonisation of public and private spheres of the lifeworld by the strategic action-complexes of steering media must be rolled back to allow the suppressed rationality of communicative action-complexes in the lifeworld to unfold. While the specifics of this latest Habermasian scheme are novel, the basic figures on which it turns are, again, familiar. First, from the earliest topology of the public sphere Habermas re-animates his claim that degenerative processes enfeeble the 'space' in which communication and the formation of publics takes place. Second, the translation problem from the 1968 'Scientization' paper re-appears as the problem of how to 'balance' strategic action/systems with communicative action/lifeworlds. Third, ghosts of two of the 'knowledge constituting interests', the technical and the practical, hover around the ideas of strategic and communicative action.[17] Fourth, and linking back to the first point, the 'colonization' thesis can be read as a reinscription within a topological model of the typological concept of 'systematically distorted communication'.

With these continuities in mind, the question arises of whether Habermas has finally resolved the problems which have haunted the various formulations of his project. The overall problem of 'theory and practice' is solved in broadly the way Habermas has always tried to solve it: by finding one or more principles of rationality to be 'immanent' in current institutions and practices, but in a 'distorted' form. The task of a critical theory and radical social practice is to 'realise' the potential of the appropriate principle. Critical theory is able to perform this task because, at some level, it shares in the principles of rationality which animate social practice. The latest version of this doctrine is particularly elegant, combining a 'typological' and 'topological' placing of principles of rationality, but it is no less paradoxical than earlier versions. Critical social science cannot be 'for' communicative rationality and 'against' strategic rationality *per se*, since both are crucial elements of a fully realised modernity. But to suggest that it will speak for each in its appropriate place, or for an appropriate balance between the two, is to utter only an abstract and question-begging formula. It seems as if the new topology simply re-capitulates the paradoxes of the 'interests' typology in a different vocabulary: Habermas must either postulate a specifically 'emancipatory' rationality, or argue that rationality 'as such' is emancipatory.

This interpretation might be thought to underestimate the force of two important shifts, from 'self-reflection' to 'rational reconstruction' and from typology to topology. These twin shifts might render the paradoxes of emancipation and rationality less pressing for two related reasons. First, the return to a topology makes it possible to specify the tasks of emancipation in terms of the structure of social spaces, rather than solely in terms of the relations between rationalities. Second, rational reconstruction can objectively specify the appropriate balance between spaces and rationalities with reference to a developmental logic.

In one important respect Habermas has the honesty to make his own problem worse. If diagnosis of the major pathology of modernity, the colonisation of lifeworlds, resurrects the translation problem, what might be termed the minor pathology, which concerns Habermas's version of the Weberian problem of value spheres, compounds it. Everyday communications in modern societies have become 'culturally impoverished'. Pre-modern cultures are eroded and replaced only with 'an elitist splitting off of expert cultures from contexts of communicative action in everyday life' (Habermas, 1987b: 330). As value spheres become separated from each other, and pursue the working out of their own 'inner logics', they become the preserve of expert aesthetic and scientific *avant gardes* who can less and less communicate their concerns to non-experts. The problem of translation between systems and lifeworlds is compounded by a problem of translation between lifeworld and expert cultures. The pathos of this diagnosis must be that critical social science, too, is the product of an 'elitist splitting off': the problems which critical social science sets itself can only be formulated within an expert culture, but they cannot be solved there.

The Philosophical Discourse of Modernity re-opens the question of the prospects for the public sphere in the light of this diagnosis. Modern technologies of communication 'make possible a highly differentiated network of public spheres – local and transregional, literary, scientific and political, within parties or associations, media dependent or sub-cultural' (Habermas, 1987a: 360). The Enlightenment project turns on a belief that these apparently highly differentiated spheres are 'porous', so that 'all partial public spheres point to a comprehensive public sphere in which society as a whole fashions knowledge of itself' (Habermas, 1987a: 360). In its pure form this belief is a little too simple for Habermas. Not only is it complicit with a discredited model of 'self-reflection', but the idea of social 'self-knowledge' breeds the 'idea that society could exercise an influence over itself by the neutral means of political–administrative power' (Habermas, 1987a: 361), an idea which hastens colonisation and what Habermas terms the 'juridification' of everyday life. Nevertheless, the basic figure of Enlightenment can be preserved: it *is* possible for 'centres of concentrated communication' to arise 'out of the micro domain of everyday practice'. If 'the lifeworld potential for self-organization and for the self-organized use of the means of communication are utilized', then 'autonomous public spheres' which can 'consolidate as self-supporting higher-level intersubjectivites' *will* develop (see Habermas, 1987a: 364).

The question arises here of whether Habermas can evade the conservative critique of Enlightenment. His concerns about colonisation and juridification suggest that he has taken to heart at least part of the critique of apolitical politics. Suspicion that the pursuit of a social 'self-knowledge' leads to an encroachment of administration into the lifeworld echoes the older complaint that Enlightenment rationalism generates only terror and totalitarianism. But in drawing back from the implications of an encounter between power and Enlightenment, Habermas impales himself on the other horn of the dilemma: utopianism. It is clear, first of all, that Habermas remains attached to the idea of a universal and legislative morality. He specifically takes German neo-conservatives to task for their determination to 'de-activate' the force of the 'universalistic principle of morality' which 'even subjects political action to moral scrutiny' (Habermas, 1985b: 90–1). Further, he is not prepared to break finally with the 'utopia of reason, formed in the enlightenment'. 'To be sure', writes Habermas (1987b: 329), utopia can be shown to be 'bourgeois ideology', but it is never a 'mere illusion'. These commitments tend towards a highly formal utopianism of the public sphere which gives a peculiar pathos to Habermas's conception of critical social science. He aligns himself with a rationality which is alleged to be immanent in contexts of ordinary practice, which must be understood as possessed of a dual structure.

> The transcendent moment of *universal* validity bursts every provinciality asunder; the obligatory moment of accepted validty claims renders them carriers of a *context bound* everyday practice ... a moment of *unconditionality* is built in to *factual* processes of mutual understanding. (Habermas, 1987a: 322)

The price of this metaphysical, even theological, discovery of the rational in the structures of the real is a peculiar kind of impotence: Habermas's insight cannot easily be put to work in concrete problems which might be experienced in 'everyday practice'. It is notable that Habermas directly links this difficulty to the abandonment of the 'self-reflection' model.

> Because the successive releasing of the rational potential inherent in communicative action is no longer thought as self-reflection writ large, [the] specification of the normative content of modernity can pre-judge neither the conceptual tools for diagnosing crises nor the way of overcoming them. (Habermas, 1987a: 348)

This passage confirms Jay's claim that an 'inadvertent implication' of Habermas's shift to a critical reconstructive social science is 'a widening of the gap between theory and practice which unintentionally revived the dilemma of classical critical theory in its last years' (Jay, 1984b: 482). In another sense, however, the dilemma is Habermas's own, and almost the reverse of Adorno's problem, which results from his emphasis on pure negation. Habermas's difficulties have always stemmed from the attempt to derive 'critique' from a more general rationality. As Habermas has come to lay more and more stress on the role of 'reconstructions', the problem of 'critique' has receded from view but has not disappeared. The distinction between reconstructions and 'methodically carried out self-critique' (Habermas, 1987a: 300) designates a continuing problem without providing a solution.[18] Even if due weight is given to the dual shift from typology to topology, and reflection to reconstruction, Habermas has not evaded the problems of his earlier formulations of critical theory.

4.3 PROBLEMS OF A 'RECONSTRUCTIVE' FORMAL PRAGMATICS

In 'What is Universal Pragmatics?' Habermas argues that a critical theory of language must make use of formal analyses based on 'the methodological attitude we adopt in rational reconstructions of concepts, criteria, rules and schemata' (Habermas, 1979: 8). Such reconstructions 'are characteristic of sciences that systematically reconstruct the intuitive knowledge of competent subjects' (ibid.: 9). That is, reconstructions specify the 'competences' required to produce behaviours. Universal or formal pragmatics and developmental psychology are examples of reconstructive science. Habermas's theory of social evolution is an extrapolation from this idea of a reconstructive science. In what follows, two aspects of these claims are considered. First, the claim that only a formal, as opposed to an empirical, pragmatics can explain communicative action is contested. Second, problems concerning the 'logic' of reconstructive sciences are considered. These considerations lead to the conclusion that Habermas is advancing a modernist radical 'end of philosophy' argument.

(a) Formal pragmatics

The claim that communicative action can only be correctly understood 'reconstructively' raises the question of whether a 'formal' pragmatics is actually required to explain cases of communicative action, or whether an 'empirical pragmatics' which makes no 'reconstructive' claims might not be quite adequate. In barest outline, Habermas's account of 'communicative action' runs roughly as follows. When communicative action (oriented to reaching understanding) is distinguished from strategic action (oriented to success), the former can be divided into three types: Conversation (constative speech-acts representing states of affairs), Normatively Regulated Action (regulative speech-acts establishing inter-personal relations), and Dramaturgical Action (expressive speech-acts representing self). The three types of action invoke universal validity claims to Truth, Rightness and Truthfulness respectively (the typology is fully set out in Habermas, 1984: 329). The full realisation of these claims without distortion constitutes the 'Ideal Speech Situation'.

When validity claims become problematic in any occasion of action, they give rise to 'argumentation', 'that type of speech in which participants thematise contested validity claims and attempt to vindicate or criticise them through arguments' (Habermas, 1984: 18). 'Discourse' is that form of argumentation in which 'the participants have to start from the (often counterfactual) presupposition that conditions for an ideal speech situation are satisfied to a sufficient degree of approximation' (Habermas, 1984: 42). Where this condition does not obtain, where participants recognise constraints on the speech situation, the form of argumentation Habermas terms 'critique' results. Returning to the typology of communicative action, argumention over the claim to Truth produces theoretical discourse and argumentation over the claim to Rightness produces practical discourse. The claim to Truthfulness can be problematised only in therapeutic critique, rather than a form of discourse. To this list, Habermas adds a further type of critique (aesthetic) and a third type of discourse, 'explicative discourse', which problematises the 'comprehensibility or well-formedness of symbolic constructs' (for the full typology see Habermas, 1984: 23).

A first problem concerns the way in which Habermas uses speech-act theory. The typology of speech-acts which he derives from linguistic philosophy and transposes on to communicative action is an a priori construct. It is most unlikely that any actually occurring strip of linguistic activity will fall naturally and unambiguously into just one type of speech act. The priority to be accorded to the standard form became an issue between Thompson (1982) and Habermas (1982: 270–4). After this exchange Habermas changed his position somewhat, urging that formal pragmatics can approximate to the complexities of naturally occurring communications through a series of 'extensions' of the model to admit non-standard and marginal forms. 'These extensions amount to dropping the methodological provisions we began with in introducing standard form speech acts' (1984: 328). But the standard forms remain central to the logic of formal pragmatics as set out in that text. 'Core cases' of communication are still identified a priori, and empirical data are still to be ordered in relation to them.

An example of the substantive consequences of Habermas's commitment to speech-act theory is provided by his strict separation of 'strategic' and 'communicative' action. This corresponds to a distinction between the 'perlocutionary' and 'illocutionary' force of utterances.[19] On a view of communication which is more 'pragmatic' and less 'formal' than Habermas's, it might be thought that to achieve 'illocutionary success' (to be understood as 'evaluating', or 'agreeing', or 'disputing', etc.) must at the same time be to achieve a species of 'perlocutionary success' (to elicit a response from a hearer, to modify the course of an interaction, to reproduce the context of interaction). Ethnomethodological models of the indexicality and reflexivity of communication, for example, rule out any strict demarcation between 'speech-act' and 'context'. Habermas's formalism is insensitive, at the least, to the mingling of illocutionary and perlocutionary force which, arguably, characterises naturally occurring communications.[20] He insists that:

> strategic *elements* within a use of language oriented to reaching understanding can be distinguished from stategic *actions* through the fact that the entire sequence of a stretch of talk stands – on the part of all participants – under the presuppositions of communicative action. (Habermas, 1984: 331)

Like many of Habermas's arguments in favour of his model, this seems simply to pre-suppose the decisiveness of the distinction which is at issue.

A second and similar problem afflicts the distinction between 'action' and 'argumentation'. Once again, the distinction does not seem well-suited to capturing the dynamics of actual examples of language use. Action is, almost by definition, unproblematic (when it becomes problematic, it turns into argumentation). Or, rather, any routine problems can be dismissed as uninteresting and inessential: only *systematic* distortions to communication are of interest. The concept of argumentation, on the other hand, is definitionally tied to the explicit thematisation of putative 'validity claims' in what becomes, in effect, a formalised meta-communication. The concept of 'action' deflects attention from the susceptibility of language use to various forms of 'muffing' and its ability to repair them. On the other hand, the concept of 'argumentation' treats communicative problems in an overly formal and abstract manner. It may well be that examples of language use *can* be trimmed on the Procrustean bed of this distinction, but at too great a cost. An entire literature of studies in conversation analysis shows that 'communicative action' gives rise to situated and practical difficulties which members resolve without recourse to a systematic, 'argumentative', meta-discourse.[21]

Overall, Habermas's insistence on the necessity of 'a formal–pragmatic grounding for an action theory' (Habermas, 1984: 328) seems to be based on a commitment to a particular conception of rationality, rather than on the requirements of empirical analysis. His arguments for 'formal' pragmatics too often turn on a *petitio principii*, as in his critique of Garfinkel. 'Garfinkel treats as *mere phenomena* the validity claims, on whose intersubjective recognition every communicatively achieved agreement does indeed rest – however occasional, feeble, and fragmentary consensus formation may be' (Habermas, 1984: 128). It is the 'does indeed' which is precisely at issue, of course. The possibility of dropping formal pragmatics in favour of empirical analysis, perhaps on conversation–analytic lines, is dismissed in another *petitio principii*. 'An empirical pragmatics without a formal–pragmatic point of departure would not have the conceptual instruments needed to recognise the rational basis of linguistic communication in the confusing complexity of the everyday scenes observed' (Habermas, 1984: 331).

It is at least arguable that 'the confusing complexity of the everyday scenes' can be clarified by dint of a conceptual apparatus which is considerably 'thinner' than Habermas's formal pragmatics. It may well be that the 'rationality' which members routinely put into play in languaged interaction is not easily assimilated to the 'Rationality' of Habermas's universal validity claims. The problem is that Habermas is not really interested in the explanatory tasks of pragmatics. A formal but not an empirical pragmatics can become the bearer of a series of themes about science, philosophy, rationality and the theory–practice nexus. In short, Habermas's formal pragmatics stands or falls with his re-workings of the defining themes of modernist radicalism. If it falls, the question arises of whether an empirical pragmatics may not become relevant for a radical social theory which has discarded its commitments to foundationalism and modernist radicalism. This question is taken up in chapter seven.

(b) Reconstructions

Habermas's idea of reconstructive science is interesting and problematic for two related reasons. First, reconstructive sciences possessed of their own distinct 'logic' could not be collapsed into 'empirico-analytic' or 'hermeneutic' science. They could, however, establish a relation with everyday action and communication, precisely as 'reconstructions' of the competences these latter require of actors and speakers. That is to say, reconstructive science can meet those criteria for the typological placing of a critical theory which proved to be so troublesome in the 'interests' typology.[22] Second, reconstructive science is situated at the bewitched crossroads between science and philosophy: echoes of Kant and of Hegel ricochet through Habermas's reconstructions. Reconstructive science could be specifically designed to be the bearer of a modernist radical 'end' of philosophy.

Habermas once sought to mark out a space for critical theory 'between philosophy and science' (see the paper of that title in Habermas, 1974a). It is clear enough that his more recent re-formulations try to position 'reconstructions' on a similar terrain. In a passage which links the ambitions of the two typologies of interests and communications, Habermas asserts that he has 'tried to take up the universalistic line of questioning of transcendental philosophy, while at the same time detranscendentalising the mode of procedure and the conception of what is to be shown' (Habermas, 1982: 239). Elsewhere, he links Mead, Weber and Durkheim with Piaget as authors of analyses 'which are simultaneously empirical and reconstructive', a form in which 'the operations of empirical science and philosophical conceptual analysis intermesh' (Habermas, 1987b: 399). The label 'quasi-transcendental' seems as well suited to reconstructive sciences as to knowledge-constituting interests. In order to assess this second type of 'quasi-transcendentalism' it will be useful, first of all, to outline briefly what a 'transcendental argument' is supposed to be.

In Kant, transcendental arguments offer answers to questions of the form: 'given that we have x (where x may be knowledge of the external world, or moral judgement, or aesthetic sensibility, or some such), how is x possible?' Such questions seem odd, first of all, because they pre-suppose that we do, indeed, 'have x'. Some kinds of answer to them may not allay doubts that we do not 'have x'. So, where 'x' is 'knowledge of the external world', the answer that 'we learn about the external world through experience' is unlikely to convert anyone who is inclined to doubt that what we have is 'really' knowledge. In this example, the question is being treated as what Kant terms a 'question of fact'. But transcendental arguments proper understand the question in another register. 'How is x possible?' is not asking how, as a matter of fact, people come by x. It is asking by what *right* we can claim that what we have is x. The oddity of transcendental arguments is that they offer an account of the possibility of some 'x' which at the same time demonstrates that it really is an 'x'. So, Kant's account of the possibility of knowledge of the natural world purports to show that we really do have knowledge of the natural world. As Stroud has pointed out, Kant's transcendental arguments can only be understood as a response to radical scepticism about the possibility of knowledge: they are 'supposed to demonstrate the impossibility or illegitimacy of [the] sceptical challenge by proving that certain concepts are necessary for thought or experience' (Stroud, 1969: 55).

Habermas's conception of a reconstructive science is similar to that of a transcendental argument in philosophy in at least two critical respects. Both begin from the assumption that 'we have x': that 'we have' communicative action, or normative structures, or modernity is not in doubt for Habermas. On this basis, both pose a 'question of right': reconstructive sciences ward off sceptical challenges to rationality and modernity. This convergence creates difficulties for the idea of 'developmental logic' which is used in reconstruction. As Schmid (1982: 174) puts it, reconstructions are '*retrospective interpretations* which treat a factual process of development *as if* it were the optimal fulfilment of a specific criterion'. Two related problems arise here. One concerns the difficulty of placing reconstructions 'between' philosophy and empirical science, and will be taken up shortly. The other concerns the scope of the 'as if' in reconstructive arguments.

The reconstructive 'as if' serves a constitutive function which connects it with the earlier constitutive 'interests' and, beyond Habermas, with Weber's account of the constitutive role of values. All three are concerned with the question of how objects of analysis come to be 'constituted' as such. For Weber, it will be recalled, an 'interest' or 'point of view' (defined by values) constitutes an object, or problem, for analysis. But the task of analysis is then to identify causal chains, which are the sole connection between present and antecedent conditions. Habermas's reconstructions, by contrast, specify another kind of connection, that of 'developmental logic'. The reconstructive 'as if' links an 'intuitive knowledge' to a schematism of developing 'competence' in a rational unity. The most immediate problem which this conception poses is that of the relation between 'causal' and 'developmental–logical' sequences. If the two are aligned too closely, the suspicion arises that developmental logic is an a priori pre-emption of empirical enquiry into causal chains. But if they diverge, it becomes unclear how a given phenomenon can be determined by two different orders.[23]

The problematic relation between 'causality' and 'logic' lies at the heart of the question of the relation between empirico-analytic and reconstructive science. Habermas must allow enough similarity between the two to make reconstructive science plausible as science, but not so much as to cast doubt on the distinction itself. For McCarthy, Habermas fails on the first count. He quotes a passage from the 'Universal Pragmatics' paper to the effect that reconstructions cannot be based on the analyst's reflection on her own intuitions, but require procedures for the formulation and testing of hypotheses which are 'in some ways' like those of nomological science. But as McCarthy (1982: 62) notes, in Habermas's own reconstructions 'the construction of the hypotheses he advances ... does not seem to make essential use of such procedures'. Later (ibid.: 64) he refers to 'Habermas's rather a priori arguments in support of what are intended to be judgements a posteriori' within the programme of formal pragmatics.

Hesse (1982) catches Habermas on the other horn of the dilemma. If the claims to scientificity advanced for reconstruction are accepted, the distinction between reconstructive and other sciences becomes blurred when the latter are understood 'nonpositivistically'. Hesse finds the idea of a science which reconstructs competences to explicate, but not in principle alter, patterns of behaviour to be implausible. '"Reconstruction" may feed back into its data, just as theoretical science may' (Hesse, 1982: 112). Further, the claims made for reconstructions require that a given competence admits of only one possible reconstruction. Habermas writes as if 'there is just one correct explication of linguistic competence, of logic, of human action, and even of theory of science and ethics' (ibid.). This is implausible, since a change in the theoretical framework of a science is always possible, as post-positivist theories of science make clear. Neither orthodox nor reconstructive sciences can evade this possibility.[24]

It is notable that Habermas's otherwise wide-ranging 'A Reply to my Critics' leaves to one side the fundamental objections to the idea of 'reconstruction' raised by Schmid (who advises Habermas to dispense with 'developmental logic'), while acknowledging their importance (Habermas, 1982: 220). The issue goes to the heart of Habermas's commitment to a version of modernist radicalism and is the pivot of his 'end of philosophy' theme. Habermas (1985a: 196) argues for a 'third way' between the pure transcendentalism of foundational philosophy and the pure relativism of its pragmatic and postmodernist critique (the context is a reply to Rorty). On this third way, 'philosophy surrenders its claim to be the sole representative in matters of rationality and enters into a nonexclusive division of labor with the reconstructive sciences' (ibid.). Philosophy is to become more like science, submitting its claims to a 'fallibilistic consciousness', while science becomes more like philosophy as it furnishes an empirical basis for universalistic claims. So, it can formulate the 'moment of *unconditionedness* ... built into the *conditions* of action oriented towards reaching understanding' (ibid.: 195).

Habermas insists that his new conception of philosophy 'marks a break with the aspirations of first philosophy (*Ursprungs-philosophie*) in any form ... but it does not mean that philosophy abandons its role as the guardian of rationality' (ibid.: 196). These considerations point to a second convergence between transcendental and reconstructive arguments. Reconstructive questions about competences are closer to the register of the transcendental 'question of right' than to that of the empirical 'question of fact'. Adapting Stroud's point, reconstructions are directed to warding off sceptical challenges to the rationality of actors' competences and of modernity itself.

(c) The end of philosophy and modernist radicalism

To the extent that Habermas explicitly preserves a role for something called 'philosophy', he does not seem to be offering an 'end of philosophy' argument. In all other respects, however, his is a classic of the genre. Habermas examines traditional philosophy, distinguishes 'what is living and what is dead' within it, dispenses with the latter and places the former in an intimate relation with social science. What is living is, of course, the defence of the 'moment' of universality, unconditionedness and rationality in a world of contingencies. Two items particularly stand out in the catalogue of what is dead: foundationalist first-philosophy and the philosophy of the subject. Strict foundationalisms which attempt to specify a priori the guarantees and conditions of scientific knowledge are no longer plausible. They reached their crisis with Kant: 'Since Kant science has no longer been seriously comprehended by philosophy' (Habermas, 1972: 4). Strict foundationalist claims have been historically and conceptually linked with philosophy's 'subject-centredness'. The search for foundations characteristically takes the form of enquiry into the structures of consciousness, from Descartes through Kant to Husserl. An important element in Habermas's project is the claim that critics of foundationalism have also characteristically been caught in the *aporias* of the philosophy of consciousness.

This case is already made in Habermas's 1969 tribute to Adorno. Adorno's relentless critique of identity produces an exaggerated opposition between an absolute negation and an absolute (and impossible) reconciliation. Against this Habermas poses a more modest sense of 'reconciliation'.

If the idea of reconciliation were to 'evaporate' into the idea of maturity, of a life together in communication free from coercion, and if it could be unfolded in a not-yet-determined logic of ordinary language, then this reconciliation would not be universal. (Habermas, 1983: 107)[25]

More recently, Habermas has argued that postmodernist writing remains trapped in a dead-end as the mere negation of philosophies of the subject. This is why, for example, Foucault's historiography 'sees itself compelled to a relativist self-denial and can give no account of the normative foundation of its own rhetoric' (Habermas, 1987a: 294). In this sense, Habermas's 'third way' offers the model of communicative rationality as an alternative to both the philosophy of the subject and its nihilistic negation. Here, the 'transcendental philosophy of the subject' is replaced by reconstructive sciences in which 'the ontological separation between the transcendental and the empirical is no longer applicable' (ibid.: 298).

The strong links between philosophy's foundationalism and its 'subject-centredness' which Habermas emphasises, and his determined rejection of philosophies of the subject, become the alibi for a continuing attachment to foundational figures. Reconstructive sciences are foundationalist and metaphysical to the extent that they attempt to refute scepticism, relativism and nihilism by posing, and answering, a transcendental 'question of right'. Habermas follows the pattern established in early modernist radicalisms move for move when he argues that questions which were once the province of metaphysics must now be posed in co-operation with social science. For Habermas, as for Marx or Durkheim, this 'end of philosophy' allows rational answers to erstwhile philosophical questions to emerge for the first time.

Habermas's modernist radicalism is perhaps at its most evident in his defence of the 'uncompleted project' of modernity. Radical critiques of modernity and reason, caught in the dead-end of subjectivism, 'are all insensitive to the highly *ambivalent* content of cultural and social modernity' (Habermas, 1987a: 338). Reconstructive sciences of social evolution and communicative competence can re-formulate a concept of the 'rationality' of modernity in procedural terms, so that it will be possible to demonstrate how 'the communicative potential of reason has been simultaneously developed and distorted in the course of capitalist modernization' (ibid.: 315). Reconstructive science provides that understanding of the immanent potential of modernity which will allow that potential to be realised, and modernity completed. Critical theory no longer requires the circumspection which led Horkheimer and Adorno to displace the affirmation of positive values into a 'negation of the negation'. Armed with the weapons of reconstructive science, 'social theory need no longer ascertain the normative contents of bourgeois culture, of an art of philosophical thought, in an indirect way, that is, by way of a critique of ideology' (Habermas, 1987b: 397).

In summary, it has been suggested here that a number of Habermas's claims for reconstructive sciences are re-capitulations of defining figures of the critical philosophy, and that the manner of this re-capitulation almost exactly parallels the 'end of philosophy' arguments of a Marx or a Durkheim. The logic of reconstruction follows that of transcendental argument in posing a 'question of right' to ward off sceptical challenges to rationality and modernity. The idea of reconstruction as a transposition of the philosophical defences of rationality and modernity into a scientific and empirical framework could serve as a definition of modernist radicalism's 'end of philosophy'. Reconstructions follow Marxism and Durkheimian sociology in claiming to articulate the rationality immanent-but-distorted in modernity, and in claiming to point the way to its realisation. Against these suggestions, Habermas can counter that his alleged convergences with critical philosophy and modernist radicalism are unimportant. His own break with philosophies of the subject releases him from foundationalism, transcendentalism and idealism. The terrain mapped out by communicative rationality and its reconstructive sciences is free of the infections which have laid low previous radical philosophies and social theories.

These matters call for a judgement as to whether Habermas has provided a framework within which radical social theory can be developed with some reasonable expectation of a fruitful outcome. The way in which the present chapter has been positioned insinuates a more dramatised implication of the judgement. If Habermas's project is the last modernist radicalism, and if previous versions of modernist radicalism have succumbed to their critics, a judgement for or against Habermas is tantamount to a judgement for or against the tradition of modernist radicalism. The judgement here must be a negative one. Habermas falls behind, rather than advances upon, critiques of modernist radicalism of the types outlined in the two previous chapters. Two considerations moderate this judgement. First, no claim is made to have 'refuted' Habermas. Apart from the hubris such a claim would involve, the model of a judgement determined by the inescapable force of a logical demonstration is simply not appropriate to the case. Second, it is the meta-theoretical elements of Habermas's project which are primarily at issue in this judgement. Substantive sociological themes from Habermas's work might find a place in a post-foundational radicalism. However, a strong claim is being made that radical social theory should look to a future outside the framework laid out by Habermas and, *ipso facto*, outside modernist radicalism.

5

THE POSTMODERNIST 'END' OF MODERNIST RADICALISM

5.1 PRELIMINARIES

It will be plain by now that critiques of modernist radicalism are not new. Alternative conceptions of the nature and tasks of social theory have been available at least since the work of Simmel and Weber. Specifically radical critiques have been available at least since the work of Adorno. And yet modernist radicalism has survived: its defining ambitions and figures seem to have permeated the grammar of radical social theory to the degree that any break with them appears as a betrayal of radicalism itself. Habermas's justification of his own, remarkably orthodox, version of modernist radicalism in terms of its connection with the 'uncompleted project of modernity' is a vivid expression of this spirit. In another sense, however, Habermas's belief that the project of modernity requires a justification betrays a growing sense of unease.

Since, roughly, the mid-1970s the work of a diverse group of French theorists including Baudrillard, Deleuze, Derrida, Foucault, Lyotard and their epigones has attracted increasing attention. These writers would all reject the programmes and figures of modernist radicalism, but would all (more or less) claim credentials as radical theorists. When 'French Theory' first came to the attention of anglophone radical theorists it was, by and large, received as an interesting supplement to a programme defined by Althusserian Marxism (of which more shortly). Only gradually did it become apparent that more far-reaching claims were in play,[1] claims that a wholly new kind of radical theory was now required. Such claims could increasingly draw on a diffused but potent belief that massive historical shifts and dislocations are under way in culture and society. This atmosphere gives rise to Habermas's fear 'that the ideas of anti-modernity, together with an additional touch of pre-modernity, are becoming popular in the circles of alternative culture' (Habermas, 1981: 14). So, critiques of

134

modernist radicalism have emerged which have points in common with their predecessors,[2] but which also draw on a new sense that the exhaustion of modernist radicalism is a symptom of the exhaustion of modernity as such.

An assessment of the postmodernist critique of modernist radicalism is pivotal for the project of this book. If the claims of postmodernism in one of its variants were to be accepted *in toto*, then the book could end here. Alternatively, if modernist radicalism can be successfully defended against its postmodernist critique, then the future for radical social theory may yet be shown to lie with some version of the Habermasian project for a 'completion' of modernity. Neither of these comfortable alternatives will be endorsed. Postmodernist theory succeeds to the extent that it reinforces earlier critiques of modernist radicalism. However, it shares with modernist radicalism an inability to break finally with metaphysics.[3] In addition, postmodernist theory traps itself in a nihilistic incapacity to address questions about social and cultural change which must be central to any radicalism. The struggle between modernism and postmodernism in radical theory has produced only the 'mutual ruin of the contending parties'.

A single chapter cannot attempt an exhaustive review of postmodernism. It attempts, rather, to exemplify the claim that postmodernism is both metaphysical and nihilistic. The two central sections of the chapter perform that task. They are framed by two sections which specifically relate postmodernist themes to modernist radicalism. The opening section argues that Althusserian Marxism played a pivotal role in introducing to radical social theory what came to be seen as 'postmodernist' themes. The brief closing section asks whether modernist radicalism is able to refute or to appropriate the postmodernist critique.

5.2 ALTHUSSER: THE TROJAN HORSE OF POSTMODERNISM?

Who now reads Louis Althusser? For a period in the mid- to late 1970s Althusserian Marxism enjoyed an extraordinary dominance in anglophone radical social theory. It dominated not only as a form of theoretical reflection, but as the framework for research programmes in class analysis, political sociology and cultural studies.[4] At the end of that period, Althusser's star waned with extraordinary speed and thoroughness, displaced largely by the increasingly fashionable concerns of postmodernism. It may be that Althusser will become the subject of a revival, but for the present, the judgement must be that his major significance has been as a transitional figure. Within a project which conforms to the formal pattern of modernist radicalism, Althusser introduced a series of themes which later fed into postmodernism. The notorious ferocity of Althusserian critiques of 'empiricism', 'humanism', 'historicism', 'teleology', '(expressive) totality' and the rest in alternative modernist radicalisms prepared the ground for more far-reaching postmodernist versions of those critiques. This assessment of Althusser is developed in three stages. The first outlines Althusser's 'minimalist' modernist radicalism. The second examines his most important contribution to postmodernism, his monistic theories of practice and knowledge. The final stage considers Althusser's own vulnerability to a postmodern critique.

(a) Althusser's modernist radicalism

Althusser's project is a defence of Marxist orthodoxy by unorthodox means. Althusser relates its inception to two related challenges which the orthodoxy of the French Communist Party (PCF) faced in the early 1960s.[5] The first was the need to come to terms with the aftermath of Khrushchev's 'secret speech' to the twentieth Congress of the Communist Party of the Soviet Union. The second concerned the growth of interest among de-Stalinising intellectuals in non-Marxist philosophies, notably Hegelianism and Sartre's version of existential phenomenology. In the hands of Garaudy and others, Marxism sought common ground with these philosophies, and found it in the 'humanism' of Marx's early writings.

The essay which first brought Althusser to prominence was a 1960 defence of a 'scientific' Marxism based on the work of the mature Marx against the arguments of a collection of essays 'On the Young Marx' (Althusser, 1977b). The defence of orthodoxy requires a balancing act of Althusser: he must disentangle Marxism from 'the Stalinian deviation', but he must shift neither too far to the left (in the direction of Trotskyism and ultra-leftism), nor too far to the right (in the direction of humanism, 'Western Marxism' and social democracy). As Benton (1984: 19) puts it, 'Althusser offers a third way – neither Stalinism nor Marxist humanism and opportunism'. Althusser's defence of orthodoxy is a 'thin' modernist radicalism which pares its defining themes to the bone. Those themes can be related to Althusser's conceptions of politics, science and philosophy.

Althusser has no time for those visions of the 'unity of theory and practice' which draw on pre-Marxist critical philosophy and can only compromise the materialism of Marxist theory. One effect of this prohibition is a reluctance to think of Marxist political practice as a movement towards a long-term goal defined theoretically, as the 'expression' of some inner principle. Althusser's political essays evade the problem of what policy objectives the PCF should pursue. He is more interested in questions of organisation, of the necessary relations between Party, class and masses. Marxist politics is defined by the maintenance of 'correct' relations between the points of this triangle, rather than by its goals. Althusser's criticism of the proposal for a 'Union of the French People' which emerged from the twenty-first Congress of the PCF is typical. He insists that there is a difference between 'a union concluded between organisations and a union forged *among the masses*'. For the union to be more than an organisational veneer, the PCF must become 'a vanguard party which is a mass party', and power must be displaced from full-time cadres to the Party branches which are 'at the heart of the masses' (Althusser, 1976: 209, 214, 215).[6]

Althusser's model of the relation between Marxist theory and political practice underwent something of a change in the course of his prolonged 'self-criticism'.[7] One feature at least remained constant: theory and practice are to enjoy the most intimate articulation, but without recourse to idealist conceptions of 'unity'. In Althusser's earlier 'system' the stark opposition between theory and practice collapses since theory itself is a type of practice. Political practice and theoretical practice are both sub-types of 'practice in general', defined as 'any process of *transformation* of a given raw material into a determinate *product*, a transformation effected by a determinate human labour' (Althusser, 1977a: 116). The consequential feature of this model is that it short-circuits the *dualist* problem of how to 'synthesise', 'unite' or 'mediate between' two heterogeneous orders in a *monism* of 'practice'.

The defence of the 'scientificity' of Marxism is at the centre of Althusser's concerns, and his reflections on the 'great divide' between ideology and science are among the best-known parts of his work. They are also a source of unease. Benton (1984: 21–2), for example, worries that Althusser transforms Marxist philosophy into an epistemology shaped by structuralism and the conventionalist philosophy of science. At first sight, there are two routes through which Althusser reaches an account of the specificity of science in his earlier work. The first is the well-known argument that an 'epistemological break' can be located in Marx's intellectual trajectory, dividing ideology from science. In Althusser's fullest account of the 'break' (1977c) Marx's writings are divided into four periods, with his 'mature' (i.e. fully scientific) work commencing in 1857. Althusser argues that the 'break' 'concerns conjointly two distinct theoretical disciplines. By founding the theory of history (historical materialism), Marx simultaneously broke with his erstwhile ideological philosophy and established a new philosophy (dialectical materialism)' (Althusser, 1977a: 33). The doctrine of the break seems to pre-suppose an account of the distinction between ideology and science, and Althusser's second route to the specificity of science looks as if it should be an account of that distinction as between two types of 'theoretical practice'. But at the point where Althusser might be expected to specify the difference, he asserts that 'the theoretical practice of a science is always completely distinct from the ideological practice of its prehistory', and then simply re-capitulates the doctrine of the 'break' (Althusser, 1977a: 167–8). If the principles of Althusser's ideology–science distinction are unclear, its implications are not: concepts drawn from outside the science of history, even concepts from Marx's own early work, such as 'man' and 'alienation', have no place in Marxist science.

Althusser's attitude to the 'end of philosophy' has varied. In his earliest account of the rupture in Marx's theoretical development, Marx breaks with ideology through a 'retreat from myth to reality' (Althusser, 1977b: 81). Marx's breakthrough into science is a 'return to the pre-Hegelian, to the objects themselves' (ibid.: 77). In Althusser's own later view, this account was complicit with 'that great, subtle temptation, the *end of philosophy*' (Althusser, 1977a: 28). In the better-known model rehearsed above, where the 'retreat' becomes an 'epistemological break', philosophy survives, although in a revolutionised form. However, philosophy is always a subordinate form of theoretical practice for Althusser. In his first system, the task of Marxist philosophy is to articulate the general form of Marx's breakthrough into science, and to defend the idea of Marxist science against attacks from 'ideological philosophies'. This is why, for example, Althusser argues that Marx's scientific texts, such as *Capital*, and not his (or Engels') philosophical polemics, are the key to Marxist philosophy (see Althusser and Balibar, 1970: 30–4). This is a modernist radical 'end of philosophy' in all pertinent respects: science is where the action really happens. Indeed, Althusser flirted with the idea of dropping the term 'philosophy' except as a designation for 'ideological philosophies' and substituting 'Theory' for 'Marxist philosophy' (see the 'terminological note' in Althusser, 1977a: 162).[8]

In the period of Althusser's 'self-criticism' the subordination of philosophy is spelled out even more plainly. In 'Lenin and Philosophy' Althusser (1971a: 32) represents himself as taking up from Lenin the task of articulating a 'non-philosophical theory of "philosophy"'. There are two 'nodal points' in this theory. First, there is a 'privileged link between philosophy and the sciences. This link is represented by the materialist thesis of objectivity' (Althusser, 1971a: 53). The second 'nodal point' reveals the 'secret' of the history of philosophy, which is conceived as an endless struggle between 'idealism' and 'materialism': 'Philosophy *represents* the class-struggle' (ibid.: 64).

Althusser's project is a modernist radicalism, defined in terms of the themes of the unity of theory and practice, ideology, and the end of philosophy. In each case, however, Althusser gives the 'thinnest' possible account. So, the 'unity' of theory and practice is an articulation which eschews any metaphysical figures of mediation or synthesis. While there remains a qualitative distinction between ideology and science, it is rooted in what purports to be a model of the actual 'mechanics' of the production of discourse. Althusser's versions of the end of philosophy similarly shun the traditional figures of immanence, realisation and transcendence, insisting on a more straightforward subordination. Two related problems arise for this 'thin' modernist radicalism. The first is that its innocence of metaphysical entanglements is an illusion: Althusser's is a full-blown metaphysical system. The second problem is that 'thin' as Althusser's formulae may seem to be, they are still too 'thick' to withstand the postmodernist critique.

(b) Metaphysical monism

There are a number of reasons why leftist intellectuals should be tempted to equate 'metaphysics' or 'ideological philosophy' with the idealism and dualism of the German critical tradition. Marx formed his own views in a critique of that tradition, and for orthodox Marxists the history of 'Western Marxism' is the history of attempts to subvert materialism through a regression to Hegelian or Kantian positions. Althusser and the postmodernists share this prejudice, and it has a quite specific effect on their work. In their purge of idealist and dualist traces in social theory they smuggle in a series of themes from metaphysical materialisms and monisms. The principle which divides Althusser from the postmodernists is that while Althusser's system is a massive appropriation of Spinoza's *rationalist* monism, postmodernist theories turn on a range of *irrationalist* monisms.

The peculiarities of Althusser's 'system' lead commentators to seek its origins in various earlier philosophies.[9] Anderson regards Althusser's Spinozist borrowings as 'substantially the most sweeping retroactive assimilation ... of a pre-Marxist philosophy into Marxism' (Anderson, 1976: 64). Althusser himself claimed that Spinoza was responsible for 'probably the greatest philosophical revolution of all times. ... We can regard Spinoza as Marx's only direct ancestor, from the philosophical standpoint' (Althusser and Balibar, 1970: 102). In the course of his 'self-criticism', Althusser denied that his earlier 'theoreticism' had been the product of structuralist influences, rather 'we were guilty of an equally powerful and compromising passion: *we were Spinozists*' (Althusser, 1976: 136).

What, then, does Althusser's 'Spinozism' amount to? It is not simply that Althusser was 'influenced' by Spinoza, or that his 'system' borrows one or two arguments or models from Spinoza: there is no Althusserian 'system'. Althusser's essays from the 1960s offer only a rhetoric which alludes to a system, which is the system of Spinoza's *Ethics*. Even commentators who have noted Althusser's early Spinozism have not taken its measure, and a full demonstration of the identity of the Althusserian and Spinozist systems is beyond the scope of this section.[10] Short of a strict demonstration, an examination of the ambiguities of Althusser's theory of knowledge might at least lend the claim some plausibility.

The account of the 'knowledge effect' from the first part of *Reading Capital* (Althusser and Balibar 1970) is notoriously obscure. Very roughly, 'ideological philosophies' of various kinds pose an ideological problem of knowledge, in which questions are asked about how knowledge 'reflects' or 'reproduces' reality. This ideological problem is bound up with the (equally ideological) quest for foundational guarantees of knowledge, which Marx rejected in the 1857 Introduction to *Grundrisse*. The *non*-ideological problem of knowledge substitutes the analysis of the mechanism of the knowledge effect for the quest for guarantees, asking 'by what mechanism does the process of knowledge, which takes place entirely in thought, produce the cognitive appropriation of its real object, which exists outside thought in the real world' Althusser and Balibar, 1970: 56; emphasis throughout in the original. But having posed this question, Althusser does not seem to answer it. Or rather, once the question of knowledge has been posed in this way it does not permit a simple a priori answer. Althusser insists that the 'object of knowledge' and the 'real object' are quite distinct, that knowledge is the 'effect' of a practice which takes place 'in thought', and that '*theoretical practice* is indeed its own criterion, and con-ains in itself definite protocols to *validate* the quality of its product' (ibid.: 59). In his view, once these points are understood, the mystery of knowledge has been dissipated.

Althusser's critics are far from convinced. Thompson (1978: 195) finds the concluding words on the knowledge effect 'disgraceful': 'We have been led all this way only to be offered a re-statement ... of the original question'. Clarke (1980: 40) thinks that Althusser has re-capitulated the 'classical problem of knowledge', while Benton (1977: 185) argues that he has lapsed into neo-Kantianism. All are puzzled as to how knowledge can be knowledge of the 'real object' when it takes place 'in thought'. Callinicos, who does not otherwise make much of Althusser's Spinozism, grasps the answer. 'Theoretical practice can cognitively appropriate its real object ... because thought and the real are homologous – they possess an identical structure, that of practice' (Callinicos, 1976: 76). But this can only be an answer to the problem in the context of Spinoza's system.

Spinoza insists against all dualisms (such as Descartes's) that there can be only one substance, 'God or Nature' (*Deus sive Natura*). In its active mode this substance is 'God in so far as he is considered a free cause' (*Ethics*: pt. I, prop. xxix n.).[11] Its passive mode is 'all that follows from the necessity of God, or of any of his attributes' (ibid.). Creator and creation are not two different substances, but two modes of the same substance. Spinoza later argues that thought and extension must be attributes of a single substance (ibid.: pt II, props. i and ii), and it is this doctrine from which the Althusserian monism of practice draws its credit.

For Spinoza, knowledge (in its passive mode) consists of 'adequate ideas' whose criteria of adequacy are internal to them. An idea is 'adequate' when it possesses 'all the intrinsic marks of a true idea' (ibid.: pt. II, df. iv). In explaining this definition, Spinoza specifically excludes as a criterion the 'compromise between an idea and its *ideatum* [that of which it is an idea]'. Adequate ideas, like scientific theoretical practice, are constituted entirely 'in thought', and have only internal criteria of validity. In the well-known motto, which Althusser cites (1976: 137), 'truth is the standard of itself and falsity' (*Verum index sui et falsi*) (*Ethics*: pt. II, prop. xliii n.). That knowledge also has an active mode, that it is a 'practice', is equally important to Spinoza. He refers to ideas as 'conceptions' rather than 'perceptions' 'for the name perception seems to point out that the mind is passive to the object, while conception seeks to express an action of the mind' (ibid.: pt. II, df. ii expl.). Even the analogy between theoretical practice and material production which underpins Althusser's 'generalities' model[12] has a warrant in Spinoza's analogy between 'instruments of the understanding' and 'artificial instruments' (Spinoza, 1910: 235–6).

The most overtly Spinozist element in Althusser's acount of the 'knowledge effect' is the distinction between the real object (RO) and the object of knowledge (KO). Althusser's 'dissolution' of the problem of epistemology requires, first, that the KO be distinct from the RO and, second, that the articulation between the two be such as to allow the production of 'knowledge effects'. Two Spinozist doctrines resolve what appears to be a tension between these two requirements. In each, KO can be regarded as equivalent to 'idea' and RO to '*ideatum*'. First, in a well-known formulation:

> A true idea is something different from its *ideatum*. For a
> circle is one thing and the idea of one another: for the idea
> of a circle is not something having a circumference and a
> centre, as is a circle. (Spinoza, 1910: 236)

Second, 'the order and connection of ideas is the same as the
order and connection of things', to which Spinoza adds a note
that 'a mode of extension and the idea of that mode are one and
the same thing, but expressed in two manners' (*Ethics*: pt. II,
prop. vii and n.). At first sight, these two doctrines contradict each
other, one asserting that idea/KO is the same as *ideatum*/RO
while the other asserts that it is not. However, the distinction
which Spinoza/Althusser wants to make between a 'circle' and the
'idea of a circle' is a *logical* one: attributes which can be
predicated of the one cannot be predicated of the other. The
proposition from the *Ethics*, in contrast, asserts an *ontological*
parity between idea/KO and *ideatum*/RO.[13]

The dissolution of the problem of knowledge which Althusser
appropriates from Spinoza runs, roughly, as follows. Ideas and
their objects are clearly different in *some* way. If we deny that the
difference is a logical one, if we imagine that the idea of a circle
has the same properties as a circle, two consequences will follow.
First, we will start to imagine that there is an *ontological* rift
between them, that real circles are circles made of extensional
substance while ideas of circles are circles made of mental
substance. Second, once we think of the difference in this way
we are inexorably driven to a series of 'epistemological' problems
about how one substance can be transformed into the other,
about how mental images can 'represent' extensional entities,
about how the relation of representation can be guaranteed, and
so on. Properly understood, Spinoza/Althusser's two theses on
the logical difference and ontological parity between idea/KO and
ideatum/RO require each other, and both are required for the
dissolution of the 'epistemological' problem of knowledge. On
this view, adequate ideas simply are ideas of their *ideata* – that is
what knowledge means and there is no more that can sensibly be
said. In Althusser's vocabulary, the epistemological problem of
the relations between KO and RO is displaced by a question
about the 'mechanism' of the knowledge effect.

So far, Althusser's Spinozism seems to have met his
requirement for a 'thin', anti-epistemological, even 'materialist',

theory of knowledge. This cannot be the end of the matter, however. The transposition of Spinoza's theory of knowledge also involves the doctrine of the 'kinds of knowledge' (*Ethics*: pt. II, props. xl–xlvi), and it is this doctrine which most clearly reveals the metaphysical character of Althusser's position. The three kinds of knowledge can be defined as follows.

The first kind: (*cognitio primi generis*) is constituted on the basis of perception, or the association of ideas. It is mere 'opinion' or the 'imaginary'.

The second kind: (*cognitio secundo generis*) is composed of knowledge from 'common notions and adequate ideas of the properties of things' (*Ethics*: pt. II, prop. xl, n. ii). It is 'reason' (*ratio*).

The third kind: (*scientia intuitiva*) is that which 'proceeds from an adequate idea of the formal essence of certain attributes of God to the adequate knowledge of the essence of things (ibid.).

Althusser makes a number of allusions to this doctrine, equating pre-Marxist political economy with the first kind (Althusser and Balibar, 1970: 159). Later (Althusser, 1976: 135) he cites Spinoza as the first theorist of ideology: Althusser's well-known account of ideology as an 'imaginary lived relation' and 'double misrecognition' owes as much to Spinoza's first kind of knowledge as to Lacan (see Althusser, 1971b). The emphasis on conceptual relations which permeates Althusser's account of 'theoretical practice', and particularly the 'generalities' model, also derives from Spinoza, who 'was involved in this affair too, because of his "three levels of knowledge" and the central role of the second: scientific abstraction' (Althusser, 1976: 190).

The matter on which Althusser maintains a tactful silence is the critical role of the third kind, *scientia intuitiva*. It is tempting to see the third kind as no more than the sum total of adequate ideas, as the second kind of knowledge systematised.[14] However, Spinoza refers to the third kind of knowledge as 'intuition': it is the spontaneous unity of thought and extension, of knowledge and reality, in the 'mind' of God. No finite, individuated being can attain such knowledge of the whole as *self*-knowledge. For Spinoza, knowledge of the second kind, or reason, is only possible under the aegis of the 'unity' of the third kind. This is why reason comprehends the world 'under a certain species of eternity' (*Ethics*: pt. II, prop. xliv, corol. ii), and why adequate ideas are necessarily true.[15] The procedures for the production of adequate ideas, Althusser's theoretical practice, produce knowledge (of the second kind) by virtue of their generality, that is, by virtue of being 'in God' (see *Ethics*: pt. II, props xxxii–xxxviii).

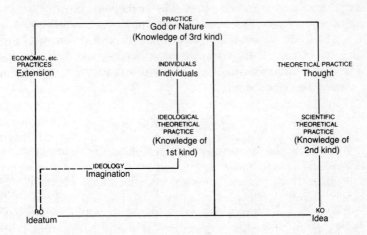

Figure 5 The Spinozist and Althusserian systems of knowledge.

Figure 5 can represent the identity of the Spinozist and Althusserian 'systems'. The most interesting feature, and the most awkward for Althusser, is the line which runs directly from Practice/God or Nature to the relation between RO/*ideatum* and KO/idea. Spinoza/Althusser is concerned to evade the 'epistemological' problem of the relation between the latter two pairs, as already noted. The problem is dissolved in the monism of a general articulation between knowledge/thought and the real/ extension. What makes the monism of Spinoza/Althusser a form of rationalism is that it maintains qualitative distinctions between orders of knowledge: Althusser wants to maintain a distinction between science and ideology which parallels Spinoza's distinction between reason and the imaginary. The directly epistemological problem is displaced, but at the cost of introducing a problem about how the articulation of knowledge/thought and the real/extension can warrant qualitative distinctions. Of course,

Spinoza has a solution to this problem, outlined above: reason is privileged over imagination because the articulation of thought and extension which it requires becomes a rational unity in *scientia intuitiva*. The line which runs directly from top to bottom in the figure above indicates that the unity of *scientia intuitiva* is what ensures that the relation between idea and *ideatum* 'just is' knowledge. Althusser's problem is that if he refuses this solution the distinction between science and ideology looses its qualitative significance, an outcome he could not tolerate. But neither can Althusser embrace this essential element in the Spinozist system. Were he to do so, it would become clear that his polemics against idealist and dualistic conceptions of knowledge turned on a monism which was just as speculative and metaphysical as anything he opposed it to.

(c) Althusser's Achilles' heel

If Althusser's claims are taken at face value, his achievement is considerable. He must be judged to have saved modernist radicalism from the metaphysical entanglements which trap its other variants, while preserving minimal, purified versions of its defining themes. When glossed in this way, Althusser's project seems in tune with the *Zeitgeist* of Paris in the 1960s. He celebrates the end of the metaphysics of 'Man' and the human subject in Marxist theory as does Barthes in literary theory, Foucault in the (anti-) history of ideas and Lacan in psychoanalysis. One problem for such an evaluation has already been addressed: Althusser's modernist radicalism is by no means as 'thin' as it appears to be. But even taken on its own terms, Althusser's minimalist modernist radicalism must remain metaphysical when viewed from the perspective of post-structuralist currents with which it seems to converge.

The metaphor of Althusserian Marxism as the Trojan Horse of postmodernism suggests that Althusser smuggled a series of anti-humanist, anti-idealist, anti-historicist themes into radical social theory, where they were deployed with devastating effectiveness. Althusser's minimalist attachment to modernist radicalism is his Achilles' heel in the sense that it compromises his own immunity to the critiques he uses so effectively. Althusser's own self-criticism marked a partial recognition of this problem, but its most dramatic manifestation was the rapidly accelerating 'auto-critique'

146

of Althusserianism mounted by Hindess, Hirst and their associates during the 1970s. Here, the direction of its own critical method against Althusserianism led rapidly to a retreat from Marxism itself. The 'discourse theory' which this auto-critique led to is considered as a variant of postmodernism in the next section. For now, the vulnerability of Althusser's project can be illustrated by briefly comparing Althusserian and Foucauldian positions on what may appear at first sight to be shared themes.

'Theoretical anti-humanism' can easily appear as the red thread linking Althusser to post-structuralism. For Althusser, the problem of theoretical humanism is linked to the question of the 'break' in Marx. For the young Marx, 'the "Essence of Man" (whether freedom–reason or community) was the basis both for a rigorous theory of history and for a consistent political practice' (Althusser, 1977a: 223). In 1845, however, 'Marx broke radically with every theory that based history and politics on an essence of man' (ibid.: 227). This idea of theoretical humanism has three corollaries. First, humanism is an *error*, closely linked to other errors (empiricism, essentialism, historicism and the rest). Second, Althusser takes it for granted that the intellectual formation 'humanism' was available to be first mobilised and then refuted by Marx. Third, humanism is a *philosophical* error which can be corrected only in the 'discovery' of a science.

Foucault's enquiries into the emergence of the concept of 'Man' contest each of these corollaries. Humanism cannot be understood simply as an error, it did not just happen to be lying around to be picked up by Marx, and it is not primarily a philosophical formation. For Foucault, the 'classical *epistēmē*' did not identify 'a specific domain proper to man' (Foucault, 1970: 309). The modern conception of 'Man' emerges from an inversion of classicism in which an 'analytic of finitude and human existence' opposes a '*metaphysics* of life, labour and language' (ibid.: 317). Man emerges as a split and contradictory being, formed in the 'doubles' of the analytic of finitude (constitutive tensions between transcendental–empirical, *cogito*–unthought and retreat–return of origin). As such, 'Man' is formed not in classical philosophy but in modern human sciences. This theme is repeated in Foucault's later reflections on 'power/knowledge'. 'Knowable man (soul, individuality, consciousness, conduct, whatever it is called) is an effect of the operation of power/knowledge in the human sciences' (Foucault, 1977: 305). Where

147

Althusser sees a unitary and philosophical humanism as an ideological obstacle to science, Foucault traces precisely the contradictory constitution of the 'field' of the human sciences. Althusser's insistence on the primacy of 'structure' over the ideological claims of 'subjectivity' remains subordinated to the 'doubles' of the analytic of finitude: anti-humanism is part of the same formation as humanism.[16]

There is a superficial convergence between Althusser and Foucault in the history of ideas. Althusser insists on the significance of 'breaks' in the development of science, and Foucault, too, rejects the notion of a unitary and continuous history which is an 'indispensable correlative of the founding function of the subject' (Foucault, 1972: 12). His later work evinces a continuing determination 'not to regard the point in time where we are now standing as the outcome of a teleological progression which it would be one's business to reconstruct historically' (Foucault, 1980: 49). But Althusser and Foucault do not stand together for a structuralist approach to history. Foucault's objections to teleological histories do not stop at the idea of continuous progress: his real target is the view that 'mutations' in discourse turn on some innately significant principle. The history of 'ruptures' must be included in this view. Althusser's 'breaks' replace ideological concepts with scientific ones, while Foucault's account of the formation of discourse is to operate 'at a kind of pre-conceptual level ... [determining] ... the field within which concepts can co-exist and the rules to which this field is subject' (Foucault, 1972: 60). From Foucault's point of view, Althusser's attempt to impose a qualitative ideology–science distinction upon the movement of discourse must be rejected. Specifically, Foucault denies that Marx is the site of any fundamental 'break' in the history of thought. 'At the deepest level of Western knowledge, Marxism introduced no real discontinuity; it found its place without difficulty' (Foucault, 1970: 261).

A final example of Althusser's vulnerability to post-structuralist critique can be furnished by the problem of 'reading'. A critical plank of Althusser's platform is his call for 'the dissipation of the religious myth of *reading*' (Althusser and Balibar, 1970: 17). In this myth, texts are transparent windows on to the 'essences' of problems. The correct alternative lies in a 'symptomatic reading' which can obtain access to the 'problematic' which structures both what the text says and does not say. It was through a symptomatic reading that Marx 'managed to read the illegible in Smith' (ibid.: 28), for example. Now, there is clear Foucauldian support for the rejection of the 'myth' of reading. 'Discourse is not the majestically unfolding manifestation of a thinking, knowing, speaking subject' (Foucault, 1972: 55). But Foucault's convergence with Althusser on the rejection of a mythical hermeneutic does not imply agreement on Althussser's alternative 'methodologised' hermeneutic. Foucault rejects not only the interpretation of discourse as the expression of essences and subjectivity, but *any* kind of interpretation. Sheridan (1980: 221) states the matter nicely. 'For the interpreter things are never what they seem. People never say what they mean or mean what they say. ... For Foucault interpretation is reduction, repression, obliteration of fact, discourse and desire.'

Foucault's projected 'archaeology' of discourse rejects the metaphor of 'depth' on which the hermeneutic drive to interpretation turns: it will 'map the flat surfaces' upon which the objects of discourse emerge (Foucault, 1972: 41). Archaeology sets free a 'field' or a 'positivity', it is 'the project of a *pure description of discursive events*' (ibid.: 41). Later in the same text Foucault insists that the analysis of discourse should not dig down to 'a silent content that has remained implicit' or 'a sort of sub-discourse that is more fundamental' (ibid.: 67). These formulae seem tailor-made for ideas of the 'problematic' and the 'symptomatic reading'. To the extent that symptomatic reading attempts to capture the 'unity', however contradictory, of a text or discourse, it remains an interpretive 'combinatory'. Foucault rejects any such unity: 'To define a group of statements in terms of its individuality would be to define the dispersion of these objects' (ibid.: 33).

To sum up, Althusser attempts to hold a line between modernist radicalism and its 'post-structuralist' critique; his is a liminal modernist radicalism. This thin, liminal character explains both the phenomenal success of Althusserianism and its rapid demise. Althusser was successful because he seemed to offer an enormously powerful critical organon which could purge Marxist social theory of discrediting metaphysical associations while retaining a purified form of radical theory. In a rather different sense to Habermas, Althusser might be regarded as the last modernist radical. The demise of Althusserianism owes much to a growing realisation, first, that it was not as thin as it seemed to be and, second, that it was vulnerable to its own critical apparatus. For many leftist intellectuals who embraced Althusserianism, it was the only defensible form of modernist radicalism. When it collapsed, the only alternatives lay outside modernist radicalism in those projects which have come to be labelled 'postmodern'.

5.3 POSTMODERNISM, METAPHYSICS AND NIHILISM

As Kellner has recently noted, 'there is nothing like a unified "postmodern social theory"' (Kellner, 1988: 241). Still less, one might add, is there anything like an agreement on the appropriate use of terms like 'postmodern', 'postmodernity' and other cognates. To follow Featherstone (1988: 197) in regarding postmodernism as constituted both after and against modernism is to survey a very wide terrain indeed. The problem of a definition of postmodernism arises from time to time in what follows, but no attempt is made to map Featherstone's broad terrain. The term is used here to designate a narrower range of developments, continuous with post-structuralism, in what has also been called 'French Theory'. Although writers such as Baudrillard, Deleuze, Foucault and Lyotard form a diverse group, the argument here is that they share a commitment to monism and that as a result their work contrives to be at once metaphysical and nihilistic.[17] The pathologies define the genre, as it were, and warrant an extension of its range across the channel to the 'discourse theory' of Hindess and Hirst. A final disclaimer: the restricted use of the term 'postmodernism' here does not imply that other usages are defective. Should a reader decide that this book is postmodernist because it is both 'after' and 'against' modernist radicalism, so be it. Such a usage would be distressing only if it tied the book to the metaphysical and nihilistic monisms reviewed immediately below.

(a) Metaphysics

A basic critical aim of postmodernism is to show that modernist claims to have moved beyond metaphysics are bogus. Lyotard's influential *The Postmodern Condition* develops a critique which is aimed primarily at Habermas. Lyotard identifies three main lines of continuity which fatally link modernist theory to metaphysics and foundationalism. First, and most generally, modernism 'legitimates itself with reference to a meta-discourse making an explicit appeal to some grand narrative' (Lyotard, 1984a: xxiii). Two such 'grand narratives' are later distinguished according to whether they present 'the hero of the narrative as cogitive or practical, a hero of knowledge or a hero of liberty (ibid.: 31). If the vocabulary is unfamiliar, the basic argument is less so: modernism remains metaphysical because it seeks a foundation in history considered as the working out of a purpose (enlightenment or emancipation). Postmodernism moves beyond foundationalism and teleology, defining itself in terms of 'an incredulity towards meta-narratives' (ibid.: xxiv).

Second, Lyotard repeatedly asserts that modernism is tied to the anachronistic pursuit of a 'unity' in which contradictions will be reconciled. Habermas's consensual theory of language is represented as an impossible attempt to impose unity on the diverse range of language games (ibid.: 14). The 'aesthetic of the beautiful' which Lyotard ascribes to Habermas is said to require that art overcome 'the gap between cognitive, ethical and political discourses, thus opening the way to a unity of experience (Lyotard, 1984b: 72). Finally, modernism remains attached to a metaphysical conception of the human subject which infects its view of the function of knowledge. In the light of 'post-industrial' developments in computerisation and information science 'the old principle that the acquisition of knowledge is indissociable from the training (*Bildung*) of minds, or even of individuals is becoming obsolete' (Lyotard, 1984a: 4). These charges that modernism is founded on teleological meta-narratives, pursues essentialist syntheses, and deploys humanist conceptions of the subject, have close affinities with other strands in French social theory. They are prefigured in Althusser's critiques of ideology, and echoed in Deleuze's pursuit of difference, in Derrida's deconstructions and in Foucault's genealogies.

In each of these respects postmodernist theory recapitulates a critique of modernist radicalism represented earlier in the book by Simmel, Weber and Adorno. So, the 'ironic' conception of history advanced by Simmel and Weber is subversive of 'meta-narratives', Simmel's 'aestheticization' of reality subverts essentialism, and Adorno's dialectic of non-identity subverts the illusions of subjectivity. Continuities of this sort have been noted quite often (see note 2), and they give rise to two related questions. The first is whether postmodernism forges a coherent alternative project from its critique of modernist radicalism, and the second is whether postmodernism evades its own strictures against modernism, thereby 'really' breaking with metaphysics and foundationalism. The argument that it does not do either can begin with an observation made earlier in respect of Althusser. French postmodernisms are chronically one-eyed in equating metaphysics with the German critical tradition. Kantian, Hegelian or phenomenological themes are relentlessly pursued and exposed, while the critique of evolutionism, positivism and physicalism is, to say the least, underdeveloped.

In the absence of a critique of these tendencies, they have become a resource through which postmodernisms articulate their distinctiveness. The pattern is established in some of the earliest attacks on modernist radicalism, so that as Lepenies (1988: 71) notes, Péguy was among those who turned to Bergson as a resource for the critique of sociology. The suggestion below is that postmodernisms fall into either a 'physicalist' or 'formalist' version of metaphysical monism. While the immediate concern is to develop a critique of both versions, the possibility is held out at the end of the chapter of a third and more fruitful possibility. If postmodernist concerns with the movement of discourse can be detached from monism and formalism, they can open the way to a 'phase two' postmodernism which converges with critical rhetorics and post-foundationalism.

Debates about *aesthetic* postmodernity are the home turf of postmodernism, and form a useful starting point for an account of its difficulties. In fact, the label 'postmodernist' has been used for virtually all major developments since the 1940s or 50s which have sought to distance themselves from aesthetic modernism, from Pollock to Warhol, from Stockhausen to Glass. If postmodernisms, in the plural, have in common only that they are constituted in varying degrees after and against the modernist 'school', the concept of a coherent postmodern aesthetic must seem very weak.[18] Attempts by Jameson and Lyotard to save the concept illustrate two strategies which set a pattern for more general claims.

Jameson (1983: 113) regards postmodernism as 'a periodising concept whose function is to correlate the emergence of new formal features in culture with the emergence of a new type of social life and a new economic order'. His difficulty lies in squaring this claim with the evident internal diversity of postmodernism. He identifies four constitutive features of postmodernism: a reaction against high-modernism, the erosion of disciplinary boundaries, a tendency to pastiche, and a 'schizophrenic' isolation of the present and immediate.[19] Jameson allows that these features may also be present in modernist work, and asserts that 'radical breaks between periods' turn on a shift in the arrangement of elements, rather than a transformation of the elements themselves. This nuanced account of the postmodern lacks the clarity and unity which an historical-cum-theoretical concept requires. In the end, Jameson saves the unity of the concept through a reductionist appeal to socio-economic developments. The 'reality' of postmodernism, in a later formulation, is 'a third great expansion of capitalism around the globe' (Jameson, 1984: 88). Its constitutive features are 'closely related to' or 'extraordinarily consonant with' consumerism, advertising, suburbanism and so on (Jameson, 1983: 123–5). Postmodern culture is not so much correlated with a new socio-economic order as defined by it: the cliché of the unity of capitalism is the only principle of unity which Jameson can offer to the postmodern.

Lyotard's account of aesthetic postmodernity begins by drawing on Kant's distinction between 'beauty' and 'sublimity'.

> The beautiful in nature is a question of the form of the object, and this consists in limitation, whereas the sublime is to be found in an object even devoid of form ... [as] ... a representation of limitlessness, yet with a super-added thought of its totality. (Kant, 1952: 90)

An alignment of postmodernism with an aesthetic of sublimity is in tune with the postmodern rejection of the modernist quest for unities. However, modernism cannot directly be aligned with an aesthetic of beauty, since it clearly offers its own critique of traditionally beautiful representations. Rather, modernism approaches the sublime in an attempt 'to represent the fact that the non-representable exists' (Lyotard, 1984b: 78), and thereby becomes 'nostalgic'. Postmodernism breaks with this final illusion, and 'denies itself the solace of good forms' in its intimations of the sublime. Drawing on Kant again, Lyotard formalises the distinction: postmodernism refuses to apply 'determining' judgements which subsume the particular under a 'given' universal or form.[20]

Modernism and postmodernism are both very close and very far apart: 'The nuance which distinguishes these two modes may be infinitesimal; they often coexist in the same piece ... and yet they testify to a difference (*un différend*) on which the fate of thought depends' (Lyotard, 1984b: 80). The paradox here is that Lyotard differentiates an anti-formalist postmodernism from a formalist modernism in a manner which is definitively formalist. The 'unity' of postmodernism is that of a shared formal relation to the sublime. This formalism achieves its clarity by excluding any historical dimension, and reinforces the suspicion that postmodernism can be defined only through the resources of the modernism it claims to supersede. The case could equally be made against other attempts to define postmodernism, such as Lash's (1985) juxtaposition of a postmodernism of 'desire' against formalist modernisms and his later (1988) differentiation, adapted from Lyotard, of a 'discursive' modernism and a 'figurative' postmodernism.

Jameson's 'reductionism' and Lyotard's 'formalism' can stand for the options facing attempts to define a more general theoretical postmodernism. Each strategy constitutes postmodernism as a form of metaphysical monism. One further ingredient in the postmodernist salad needs to be noted here. Postmodernisms gain their particular flavour by linking together questions about theoretical and epochal thresholds. However, it will be clear by now that this linkage also characterises modernist radicalisms. It follows that the self-definition of postmodernism is a delicate matter. Hassan's remarks on the idea of a 'period' in literature state the problem. 'A period is generally not a period at all; it is rather both a diachronic and synchronic construct. Post modernism is no exception; it requires both historical and theoretical definition' (Hassan, 1985: 122). Postmodernisms are required to show that they are both 'historically' and 'theoretically' distinct from modernism in ways which are more than accidentally related. But, of course, they must not simply replicate the historicist formulae of modernist radicalism. The difficulties involved in this task help to explain the paradox that the 'suggestiveness' of the idea of the postmodern has increased as its 'technical and temporal clarity' has decreased (Honneth, 1985: 147).

Many postmodern projects seek the solution in the appropriation of evolutionisms in which the periodising schemes of positivist philosophy constantly re-appear. So, Lyotard's distinction between a modernism which depends on 'meta-narratives' and a postmodernism which manages without them seems close to that between the 'metaphysical' and the 'positive' stages of Comte's triad. Lyotard's entire attack on Habermas's critical concept of modernity draws quite uncritically on the most problematic periodisations of 'post industrialism' and the 'information revolution' in American sociology (Lyotard, 1984a: 3–6). As Kellner (1988: 252) puts it, Lyotard's account of the shift from modernity to postmodernity is 'undertheorised and underdeveloped'. In a powerful assault on this aspect of postmodernist thinking, Rose has noted that Foucault's 'bio-history' also recapitulates the 'law of three stages' while the concept of 'disciplinary power' 'merely adds a third stage to Durkheim's two laws of penal evolution' (Rose, 1984: 169, 176). Monism and evolutionism may convey the impression that postmodernisms can meet Hassan's requirement for a self-definition without relapsing into modernism, but they might equally well be seen as traces of a pre-critical modernism.

The reductionist strain in postmodernism urges a form of materialist social analysis which frequently degenerates into an overt physicalism or vitalism. This is clearly the case for the concept of 'intensity' developed by Deleuze and deployed by Guattari, who asserts that 'with both nature and signs, we are concerned with the same type of machinism and the same semiotic of material intensities' (Guattari, 1984: 120). Baudrillard (1983a and b) represents the most florid case of a postmodernism dominated by physicalism, urging the impossibility of any social theory, be it sociological, Marxist or Foucauldian. The argument is carried entirely by a series of physicalist tropes. Its theme is that 'the mass', the material which composes the putative object 'the social', cannot be the object of a science. The mass is 'an opaque nebula whose growing density absorbs all the surrounding energy and light rays, to collapse finally under its weight. A black hole which engulfs the social' (Baudrillard, 1983b: 4).

Baudrillard's theme of the growing invisibility of the mass, and hence of the social, is linked to a metaphor for change: modern society was once based on a principle of expansion, or explosion, but having reached a certain 'critical mass' it has begun to implode.

> The notion of critical mass usually associated with the process of nuclear explosion, is reapplied here with reference to nuclear *implosion*. What we are witnessing in the domain of the social ... is a kind of inverse explosion through the force of inertia. (Baudrillard, 1983a: 88n.)

Any attempt to save the principle of expansion, even Guattari's model of 'molecular revolution' or Foucault's hope for 'resistance' to power, is now 'archaic, regressive or nostalgic' (ibid.: 60). This position echoes Baudrillard's objection to Foucauldian 'power', that it remains a structural concept. It 'is an irreversible principle of organisation because it fabricates the real ... nowhere does it cancel itself out, become entangled in itself, or mingle with death (Baudrillard, 1980: 100–1). The reality of the social, in an inversion of Durkheim's realism, can only be 'hyper-simulated' in an imaginary 'pataphysics of the social'. Physicalism is the beginning and end of Baudrillard's models of the social and of social change, forming the basis of an explicit rejection of the possibility of any radical social theory. But physicalism traps the argument in a curious loop. If a physicalist model of the social is valid, there is no reason why there cannot be a science of the social. 'Black holes' are objects of scientific enquiry. But if the parallel between nuclear and social processes is not valid, Baudrillard's argument collapses entirely. This oddity adds to a sense that despite Baudrillard's enthusiasm for metaphors drawn from natural science, his project is *meta*physical. The idea of the physical is a formal one, designating some wholly 'other' postmodern 'object = x'.[21]

It is unsurprising, then, that appeals to what Rose has termed a 'transcendent principle of the physical' have an analogue in formalist postmodernisms. For example, Lash draws on Foucauldian themes to identify a 'fold' in language which 'is the space of a non-discursive "literature", where language takes on an opacity, an "ontological weight". It is in this *pli*, this fold, that the postmodern is constituted' (Lash, 1985: 4). In the attempt to mark out this 'space', the only alternative to a critical metaphysics of *constitution* must be a naturalistic metaphysics of *givenness*. Indeed, Lash sees no problem in the claim that postmodernists 'subscribe to a (more or less weak) form of foundationalism' (ibid.: 29) since it enables him to suggest a convergence between Habermas and postmodernism: 'communicative rationality' and the 'problematics of desire' both mark a gratifying break with relativism, for Lash.

Many of the themes of formalist postmodernism were introduced into Anglophone social theory through the form of analysis which Hindess, Hirst and their associates developed in the 1970s. Their critiques of Althusserian rationalism issued in a model of 'discourse' as the medium of theoretical and practical knowledge, where discourse is conceived as a grid of concepts linked by 'logical' relations. In this formalism 'the entities specified in discourse must be referred to solely in and through the forms of discourse, theoretical, political, etc, in which they are constituted' (Hindess and Hirst, 1977: 19). The 'etc' here links 'forms of discourse' with Lash's 'fold' and, beyond that, with the physicalisms of 'intensity' and 'implosion'. For all their emphasis on 'rigour', Hindess and Hirst's analyses rest on a covert and *ad hoc* assumption of the 'givenness' of discourses.

The submerged link between those postmodernist strategies which have been termed 'reductionist' and 'formalist' is a metaphysical monism (whether of 'intensity' or 'discourse') which serves as the foundation for critiques of modernist radicalism. Modernism is always searching for ways to reconcile contradiction: that is why it demands metanarratives, searches for unities and stresses the role of subjectivity. Contradiction is seen to pervade a world constituted in a whole series of dualisms: mind and body, knowledge and reality, potential and actuality, theory and practice. The postmodernist critique undercuts the problem of contradiction by dissolving dualisms in some single world-constituting substance. Now, the discussion of Althusser's appropriation of Spinoza's monism has suggested that monism is far from being an alternative to metaphysics. But Spinoza's *Deus sive natura* is a 'rational' unity, capable of sustaining qualitative distinctions between, for example, reason and imagination (which becomes science and ideology, for Althusser). Postmodernist monisms of intensity or discourse, by contrast, deliberately shun qualitative distinctions of this kind as residually idealistic and dualistic, and this slippage from rationalist to irrationalist monism is intimately connected with the nihilism of postmodernist theory.

(b) Nihilism

Social theory becomes 'radical' in taking up the responsibility of giving reasons why change is required, of making the demand for change accountable in terms of some standards of judgement. Modernist radicalisms are suspect because they claim a foundational 'privilege' for particular versions of accountability and judgement, but at least they grapple with the problem. When radical social theory entirely loses its accountability, when it can no longer give reasons, something has gone very wrong. But this is just what happens to postmodernism, and it is appropriate to use the over-stretched term 'nihilism' as a label for such a degeneration. This nihilism shows itself in two symptoms: an inability to specify possible mechanisms of change, and an inability to state why change is better than no change.

The first symptom afflicts a wide range of projects. Most notoriously, Foucault's model of 'Power/Knowledge' seems able to articulate 'resistance' only as an embodiment of the power which it is supposed to resist. Jameson concludes his account of the new age of postmodernity with the remark that it is an open question whether any sources of opposition to the new age will be found (Jameson, 1983: 125). His later hopes for 'the invention and projection of a global cognitive mapping' (Jameson, 1984: 92) appear weak and unfocused, Kellner's endorsement (1988: 159) notwithstanding. Baudrillard offers a vision of a 'one dimensional' system impenetrable to change, of 'all secrets, spaces and scenes abolished in a single dimension of information' (Baudrillard, 1983b: 131). The only paradoxical hope he offers is of a hopeless 'challenge' which is both 'unremitting and invisible' (Baudrillard, 1980: 107). This difficulty is clearly related to the monism of postmodernism. To divide 'intensity' or 'discourse' into two moments, one of which is the foundation of opposition, or to posit some external foundation, is to reintroduce dualism and with it the modernist problems of contradiction and reconciliation. In resisting this kind of relapse into modernism, postmodernisms exclude that sense of 'tension' which is critical for radical theory. This issue will be taken up again in the final chapter. For now, it will suffice to show that the monistic slackening of the tension of theory induces the second of the two symptoms of nihilism, an inability to justify the demand for change. Examples taken from Guattari, from Hindess and Hirst, and from Lyotard can make the point.

For Guattari, the conditions of postmodernity call for a 'micropolitics' which will set loose 'a whole host of expressions and experimentations – those of children, of schizophrenics, of homosexuals, or prisoners, of misfits of every kind – that all work to penetrate and enter into the semiology of the dominant order' (Guattari, 1984: 184). Opposition is a natural force to be unleashed, a quantitative rather than a qualitative phenomenon. This naturalisation may cure the first symptom of nihilism, specifying the quantity that will produce change, but it induces the second. There can be no *reason* inherent in Guattari's argument why the 'experimentations' of rapists, or child murderers, or racist fanatics should be excluded from the carnival. Any qualitative principle of differentiation, any sense of a tension between 'is' and 'ought', would undermine Guattari's naturalism and pitch him back into some modernist 'grand narrative'. The choice of 'experimentations' is instructive, clearly being shaped by Guattari's view of which 'misfits' will attract the sympathy of his readers. But that choice could be made *accountable* only with reference to a continuous and developing progressive tradition which Guattari's reductionism is quite unable to articulate.

In the formalism of Hindess and Hirst the collapse into nihilism flows from the exclusion of any sense that the significance of discourse results from a production, or movement. 'A rigorous separation should be maintained between problems concerned with the logical properties of the order of concepts of a discourse and those concerned with its process of production' (Hindess, 1977: 190). Significance becomes a function of a single principle of logical order in a strategy which is as nihilistic as Guattari's naturalism. The political implications of this model are presented as a Nietzschean emancipation: the fantasy that Marxism is a science of practice can be dispensed with as socialists face the reality that 'there are no "socialist" issues and areas of struggle *per se* assigned as "socialist" by class-interests and experience' (Cutler *et al.*, 1978: 258). 'Socialism' can no longer 'evade questions about the objectives of its practice and the content of its political programmes' (Hirst, 1979: 6). But the re-thinking of socialism which is put in train issues in an instrumentalisation, rather than a re-valuation, of political values. The constraints of discourse theory tie political theory and practice to a logic of 'calculation'.

While theory can 'begin to investigate the conditions and limits of forms of political calculation [it] can never itself step outside of the conditions of calculation' (ibid.: 11). Forms of discourse, governed by one-dimensional 'logics', are treated as givens which cannot be coherently assessed in other than their own terms. The accountability of theory is transformed into a self-enclosed form of 'calculation', and a formalist monism produces the same incapacity to give reasons as a physicalist monism. No reasons can be adduced for engaging in socialist rather than, say, fascist discourse.[22]

Lyotard draws on concepts of system performance developed by writers such as Luhmann, and also on the Austin/Searle account of linguistic performance, to construct a model of 'performativity' as the dominant, and questionable, value of postmodernity. Opposition to performativity cannot be founded on Habermas's attempt to homogenise language in a consensus. Instead, opposition should celebrate the irreducible diversity of language games, limited only by a rejection of 'terror', defined as 'the efficiency gained by eliminating, or threatening to eliminate, a player from the language game one shares with him' (Lyotard, 1984a: 63). The rejection of terror is suspect on several grounds. First, even if Lyotard's argument is conceded, he has not excluded terror against third parties (barbarians, *Untermenschen*, women) whom the participants in a game deem to be excluded from their *agon*.[23] Only by stretching the concepts of 'game' and 'rules of the game' to an extent that would constitute a new 'grand narrative' (e.g. 'all rational beings are potential members of the game') could Lyotard exclude such terror. Even in relations between mutually acknowledged participants, the exclusion of terror seems arbitrary and external. It is plausible only for a game constituted between two players, so that the elimination of one player destroys rather than wins the game, and is in that sense contradictory. But if games are constituted by institutionally embedded rules which outlive any players, or even by a large number of players, the sense of contradiction dissipates. The 'game' of gladiatorial combat can survive the 'elimination' of any number of players.

Lyotard must exclude terror because it represents a denial of the 'heteromorphy', or diversity, of language. If he does not, a potentially terrorist opposition to performativity cannot be preferred to performativity itself, which also represents a denial of the diversity of language in the name of globalising 'efficiency'. The problem is similar to that facing Foucault's concepts of 'power' and 'resistance'. But in order to make the exclusion, Lyotard must either stretch the 'rules of the game', or restrict the concept of 'game' itself, in a way that transforms them into normative principles of the modernist type. The reflections on 'justice' in the final pages of *The Postmodern Condition* suggest that, in the end, Lyotard prefers an accountable modernism to a nihilistic postmodernism. He seeks to rehabilitate the concept of 'justice' by cutting its ties with 'consensus', so that 'justice as a value is neither outmoded nor suspect' and has a place in 'a politics which would respect both the desire for justice and the desire for the unknown' (Lyotard, 1984a: 66, 67). In contrast, Baudrillard's discussion of terrorism opts for the other arm of the dilemma. Terrorism 'represents' nothing, and between terror and the masses there passes a 'reverse energy ... of absorbtion and annulment of the political' (Baudrillard, 1983a: 56). Terror is naturalised by Baudrillard so that in its 'defiance of sense' terror is 'akin to the natural catastrophe'.

In summary, the postmodernist reliance on either reductionist or formalist monisms generates nihilism in the sense discussed at the beginning of this section. To identify language and social life with a single principle of proliferation is to conjure up the image of a bad totality which must absorb all opposition. Attempts to find a 'natural' ground for opposition are either unable to give any reasons for preferring opposition to compliance (Baudrillard, Guattari, Hindess and Hirst), or are able to do so only in a reversion to modernist regulative principles (Lyotard).

5.4 RESPONDING TO POSTMODERNISM

Contributions to the modernism versus postmodernism debates which have attracted so much recent attention can generally be placed on a continuum. At one end is the argument that postmodernisms are so discredited as to allow the rehabilitation of some version of modernist radicalism, with only minimal adjustment. At the other end is the more or less complete endorsement of some version of postmodernism, while in between come a range of proposed juxtapositions, or syntheses, of elements of each. Some sense of how these alternatives arrange themselves can be gained from brief reviews of the question of Marxism's relation to postmodernism and of Haber-mas's defence of modernity against a conservative post-modernism.

There has been no shortage of defenders of Marxism against post-structuralist or postmodernist critique. For Eagleton, for example, Lyotard offers only 'reactionary celebrations of narrative as an eternal present rather than a revolutionary recollection of the unjustly quelled', while Deleuze and Guattari fall back to the 'banal anarchist rhetoric' of revolution as disorder (Eagleton, 1985: 64, 69). Eagleton does not underestimate the scope of the postmodern challenge: 'What is at stake ... under the guise of a debate about history and modernity, is nothing less than the dialectical relation of theory and practice' (ibid.: 65). Eagleton's 'nothing less than' articulates a belief that once the 'real' issue is revealed, it can only possibly be settled in favour of Marxism. Many Marxists fall back on this sense that once the achievements of Marxism are set alongside the paltry rag-bag of postmodernist fragments, the superiority of the former will be beyond question. Anderson, for example, judges that the (temporary) theoretical defeat of Marxism by structuralisms and post-structuralisms can only be due to extra-theoretical factors. The 'terrain' of the structure/subject relationship which Marxism shares with its competitors is never occupied 'in sufficient depth by structuralism to present any real challenge to a historical materialism confident of itself' (Anderson, 1984: 56). On a more specific issue, Callinicos announces that 'the superiority of Marxism ... over Foucauldian genealogy seems to me evident' (Callinicos, 1982: 162).

Anderson and Callinicos both have interesting critical cases to mount against variants of postmodernism. Anderson characterises 'structuralism and post-structuralism' in terms of four 'operations' within a logical field: the exorbitation of language, the attenuation of truth, the randomisation of history, and the capsizal of structures (Anderson, 1984: 40–51). Callinicos draws on a number of resources from the philosophy of language to argue that a recognition that all access to reality is by way of discourse 'does not lead to scepticism, but merely to fallibilism' (Callinicos, 1982: 178). But the re-endorsement of Marxism is 'underdetermined' by the argument in both Anderson and Callinicos. Anderson's four-point characterisation and critique articulates no more than what 'structuralism and post-structuralism' must look like from the vantage point of historical materialism. Callinicos's defence turns on rather circular claims for two privileged links; one between an adequate theory of language and 'new' realism, the other between 'new' realism and Marxist materialism. From the standpoint of the present argument, Anderson, Callinicos and other strong defenders of Marxism against postmodernism fail, in the end, to confront the increasingly visible metaphysical entanglements of Marxism's version of modernist radicalism. The doubts they raise about postmodernism do not amount to a successful defence of Marxism.

A stronger sense that all is not well with Marxism animates a variety of attempts to combine Marxism and postmodernism. As Smart points out, in support of his own such attempt, 'a history of Marxism reveals the irregular presence of a discriminating openness towards particular non-Marxist forms of analysis and enquiry' (Smart, 1983: 3). Poulantzas's cautious integration, in *State, Power, Socialism* (1978), of elements of a Foucauldian analysis of power/knowledge into the Marxist theory of the state set a precedent for other attempts. Smart argues that deficiencies in Marxist approaches to (particularly) problems of power and rationality might be remedied by taking Foucault seriously. He is clear, however, that this can be no simple 'synthesis': what makes Foucault's analyses of rationality superior to those of the Frankfurt School is, precisely, that they offer 'a critical interrogation, in contrast to a basically internal revision and reformulation, of the political rationality underlying Marxism' (Smart, 1983: 134). A rather similar strategy is evident in Ryan's (1982) 'critical articulation' of Marxism and deconstruction. For Ryan (1982: 61), 'in both Marx and Derrida, the critique of the misconceptions of metaphysics makes necessary the working out of a new practice of differential analysis'. Deconstructive analysis could help Marxism to evade the metaphysical temptations which ensnare, for example, Marcuse and Habermas. A different kind of accommodation is sought by Jameson, whose (1983, 1984) attempts to understand postmodernism as the 'cultural logic' of late capitalism have been considered above. Jameson (1984: 85) hopes this approach will avoid both 'complacent (yet delirious) camp-following celebration' and 'moralizing condemnation' of postmodernism.

There are two major, and related, flaws in responses of these kinds. First, they tend to be relatively uncritical of the postmodern resources they appropriate, and second, they do not take the measure of the incompatibility between Marxism and post-modernism. This second difficulty is nicely caught in the quotation from Ryan above: Marx and Derrida may, indeed, both offer a 'critique' of metaphysics, but the two senses of 'critique' are very different. Marx aims to 'overcome' metaphysics in the manner of a modernist radical end of philosophy: Marxist materialism can make an historical end of metaphysics. For Derrida, metaphysics is a far more subtle and pervasive temptation, capable of surviving any number of alleged 'ends'. To transform Marxism into a deconstructive practice in anything like Derrida's sense would be to destroy it as a project of modernist radicalism. On the question of Foucault, the brief comparison of Althusserian and Foucauldian themes above has suggested a similar incompatibility. In many respects the more orthodox defenders of Marxism such as Anderson and Callinicos have a clearer sense of the threat from postmodernism.

The outline of Habermas's defence of the 'uncompleted project' of modernity against its postmodern critiques will be familiar from the previous chapter.[24] Postmodernist critiques take their cue from Nietzsche's anti-humanism, which is the 'real challenge for the discourse of modernity' (Habermas, 1987a: 74), in launching an assault upon the pretensions of 'subject-centred' reason. In Nietzsche, and Nietzschean postmodernisms, 'subject centred reason is confronted with reason's absolute other' (ibid.: 94). Habermas's riposte (which turns largely on a critique of Foucault) is that both the crisis of subject-centred reason and the inadequacies of its postmodernist critique are symptoms of the 'exhaustion' of the philosophy of consciousness (ibid.: 296). The appropriate way out of this syndrome is not through en-dorsement of the 'absolute other' of reason, but through a shift from subject-centred reason to communicative rationality. In this shift, transcendental philosophies of the subject are displaced by reconstructive sciences which are not subject to the Nietzschean critique. This argument is accompanied by a vigorous polemic against the 'alliance of postmodernists with premodernists' (Habermas, 1981: 14), in which the anti-modernism of 'young conservatives' (i.e. postmodernists) is placed in relation to that of 'old conservatives' and 'neoconservatives' (ibid.: 13).[25]

This response to postmodernism has received a rather mixed press. Kellner, for example, remarks that while an earlier generation of critical theorists responded to new conditions and ideas in a positive way, 'the response of Habermas and his followers to the discourse of postmodernism was defensive and hostile' (Kellner, 1988: 263). But at least one 'follower', Wellmer, has attempted to reconcile Habermas's basic position with a rather more open attitude to postmodernism. Wellmer offers a defence of Habermas's idea of a 'rational consensus' against the 'left-Aristotelian' argument that 'there is no *rational* solution to the problem of an institutionalization of freedom' (Wellmer, 1985a: 59). But this 'defence' entails an implicit shift away from Habermas's overt transcendentalism, as Wellmer argues that

> the utopian perspective inherent in the democratic tradition should not so much be considered in an analogy to geometrical idealizations, which can never be perfectly embodied in the recalcitrant material of physical bodies ... but rather as the center of gravitation of democratic forms of organization. (ibid.: 61)

Elsewhere, Wellmer links this de-transcendentalising turn to an 'ordinary language' variant of Habermas's critique of post-modernism. If we 'give words back their normal use ... it becomes clear that the philosophy of total unmasking still lives from the very rationalistic metaphysics which it set out to destroy' (Wellmer, 1985b: 353). On this basis, some convergence between Habermas and Lyotard is possible. It must be conceded, first, that the 'practical–political' meaning of democratic universalism cannot be reduced to 'a "project" of modernity in the sense of an "identity-logical" reason' (ibid.: 359). But it becomes possible to think of democratic universalism under conditions of post-modernity (as analysed by Lyotard) on the basis of 'a common ground of habits of a second order: habits of rational self-determination, of democratic decision making and of the violence free solution of conflicts' (ibid.).

A broadly similar strategy is endorsed by Dews, who cites Wellmer extensively. The paradigm shift from subjectivity and its critique to intersubjectivity which Habermas sets in train enables a productive re-alignment of a number of post-structuralist/post-modernist themes with those of critical theory. Thus, 'post-structuralist thought is not in any simple sense opposed to critical theory, but rather consists of a mosaic of theories which cover very similar ground' (Dews, 1987: 244). Given the argument of the previous chapter, which rejected Habermas's pretensions to

165

have moved 'beyond' transcendentalism and foundationalism, his overall response to postmodernism cannot be endorsed. As with Anderson and Callinicos, Habermas's valuable critical insights into postmodernism do not warrant acceptance of his own alternative.[26]

It can often seem as if the modernism versus postmodernism debate is trapped in an endless cycle of metaphysics and nihilism. Metaphysical modernisms generate effective critiques of the nihilism of postmodernism, while nihilistic postmodernisms ruthlessly expose the metaphysical dependencies of modernism. Wellmer and Dews explore interesting possibilities for a break out of these cycles into a 'phase two' postmodernism. However, it is incumbent on them to show that they are not parasitic on Habermas's transcendentalism, or glossing transcendentalist formulae in a more sober vocabulary. Placed within the argument of this book, any proposal for accommodation or synthesis between modernism and postmodernism must be premature, at best. Two crucial steps remain to be taken. First, it is necessary to show how both modernist radicalism and postmodernism become caught in the syndrome of 'foundationalism' which is responsible for so many of their infelicities. Second, the question must be posed of how, if at all, a 'post-foundational radicalism' might be set in train in social theory. These tasks are taken up in the two remaining chapters.

6

FOUNDATIONALISM AND RADICALISM

6.1 PRELIMINARIES

The argument of the previous chapter was that 'postmodernist' projects do not point the way to a productive future for radical social theory, offering only regressive amalgams of metaphysics and nihilism. On the face of it, this is an ominous judgement. Earlier chapters have argued that modernist radicalisms are discredited by their continuing and irremediable dependence on the figures of critical philosophy. But postmodernisms set out their stalls as the only viable alternatives to discredited modernisms, so that if they are discredited in turn, it is not clear what is left for radical social theory. One possibility is that there is nothing left. A convincing argument can be mounted that the conjunction 'radical social theory' and each of its component terms are definitionally linked to modernist radicalism. On this view 'radical' gains its meaning from the ideas of enlightenment and an emancipatory unity of theory and practice. 'Social' designates the modernist radical 'discovery' of society as an autonomous reality, the analysis of which can point the way to the completion of modernity. 'Theory' understands itself as the form of post-philosophical reflection adequate to the cognitive tasks of modernity. Once the defining themes of modernist radicalism are dispensed with, 'radical social theory' becomes an empty formula. Postmodernisms of various types can then be understood as symptoms of the collapse of modernist radicalism, as impossible attempts to specify some content for a radical social theory which will not share the fate of modernist radicalism.

This diagnosis is not easily evaded. It may well be that 'radical', 'social' and 'theory' need to be understood in very different senses if the idea of a radical social theory is to be any more than a nostalgic anachronism. In order to be able to specify what those senses might be it is necessary to pay more attention to the 'foundationalism' which is implicated in the pathologies of modernist radicalism and, in a rather different way, postmodernism. The next section introduces the idea of foundationalism as a pervasive syndrome in philosophy and social theory. Later sections consider what are termed the 'instances' and 'modes' of the appeal to foundations in a little more detail. The final section outlines two broad types of strategy which can be pursued in relation to foundational questions. Strategies of 'closure' are characteristic of the foundationalist syndrome proper, while strategies of 'disclosure' have the capacity to point towards a 'post-foundationalism'.

6.2 THE FOUNDATIONALIST SYNDROME

The quest for secure 'foundations of knowledge' derives from a sense that knowledge (in general) is under some kind of threat. Foundationalism emerges in response to sceptical critiques of knowledge: 'Impressed by the possibility of doubt and by the supposal that if doubt be allowed its head this will undermine the foundations of knowledge, philosophers have sought to make those foundations unshakeable' (Hamlyn, 1970: 10).

Descartes becomes the paragon of modern foundationalism in his dramatisation of the confrontation between doubt and certainty. At the end of the 'First Meditation', he conjures the 'demon' of scepticism.

> I shall suppose ... that there is, not a true God, who is the sovereign source of truth, but some evil demon, no less cunning and deceiving than powerful, who has used all his artifice to deceive me. I will suppose that the heavens, the air, the earth, colours, shapes, sounds and all external things that we see, are only deceptions which he uses to take me in. I will consider myself as having no hands, eyes, flesh, blood or senses, but as believing wrongly that I have all these things. (Descartes, 1968: 100)

Of course, Descartes' sceptical nightmare does not last long. Early in the 'Second Meditation' he comes upon the foundational principle which is immune from doubt.

There is ... no doubt that I exist, if [the demon] deceives
me; and let him deceive me as much as he likes, he can
never cause me to be nothing, so long as I think I am
something ... *I am, I exist*, is necessarily true, every time I
express it or conceive of it in my mind. (ibid.: 103)

With this foundation secure, Descartes is able to prove the
existence of God (twice), establish a dualist ontology of mental
and material substance, and discover a criterion of truth ('clear
and distinct ideas').

It is a matter of debate whether the term 'foundationalism'
should be reserved for a restricted range of 'core' philosophies
such as Descartes', or whether it usefully designates a tendency in
a much wider range of epistemological (and ontological)
arguments. Chisholm, for example, would restrict the term to
doctrines which assert that 'those "truths of fact" that are known
but are not directly evident' can be justified 'by certain relations
that they bear to what is *directly* evident' (Chisholm, 1977: 62,
63).[1] However, he acknowledges that in other usages all attempts
to offer any kind of 'justification' of knowledge are regarded as
foundationalist. This problem of how to circumscribe
foundationalism has become particularly contentious in the
ramified and often highly technical debates about language, truth,
ontology and the claims of 'realism' which have issued from the
work of Quine, Davidson and others. Putnam and Margolis, for
example, each attempt to find a space in which more or less
traditional philosophical questions can be pursued in a non-
foundationalist manner. Putnam (1978) urges the claims of an
'internal realism' which evades the foundationalist tropes of
'metaphysical realism', while Margolis (1986) maintains that a
philosophical enquiry into the foundations of knowledge need
not be foundational*ist*. For Rorty (1982), on the other hand, these
would be distinctions without a difference, bound to become
complicit in the counter-productive attempt to maintain the *Fach*
of a 'pure' Philosophy.

These uncertainties help to explain the ambiguity about
whether or not Habermas, for example, is a foundationalist. On a
strict definition (such as Chisholm's), Habermas's Kantianism must
be anti-foundationalist: knowledge and communication are the
products of synthetic activity rather than of some direct and
privileged access to self-evident truth. Habermas clearly has a

strict definition in mind when he rejects the 'foundationalist' tag.[2]
On a broader view, which sees any and all attempts to legitimate
knowledge as objectionable and foundationalist, Habermas's
inability to escape the Kantian 'question of right' commits him to
a foundationalist strategy which displaces, but does not efface, its
commitment to metaphysical guarantees of knowledge. For Rorty,
Kant's attempt simultaneously to differentiate and justify science,
morality and art is a critical episode in the professionalisation and
purification of philosophy. Habermas remains attached to this
differentiating and justifying project, and thinks it requires him to
replace the discredited foundationalism of philosophies of the
subject with a reconstructive theory of 'communication'. But
Habermas is trapped in 'an artificial problem created by taking
Kant too seriously' (Rorty, 1985: 167).

Margolis's 'foundationless pragmatism' looks very Kantian. He
urges that once we grant that there is 'knowledge' 'it is hopeless
to try to deny the admissibility of the Kantian-like questions'
(Margolis, 1986: 165), going on to offer a re-formulation of the
idea of a transcendental enquiry into the foundations of
knowledge (ibid.: 291). Of course, this is just what Habermas
does with the ideas of 'knowledge constituting interests' and
'reconstructive sciences'. But in Margolis's view, Habermas offers
only 'the most attenuated form of foundationalism that can be
found at present' (ibid.: 178). His attempt to balance historical
relativity with universal truth leads him to, but not across, the
brink of facing up to 'the stubborn empirical contingency with
which transcendental reflection ... must be undertaken' (ibid.:
179). Habermas does not take the final step out of foundationalism.

One way to maintain a sensitivity to these ambiguities is to
regard foundationalism as not so much a doctrine, but a
syndrome in which assumptions and questions about knowledge
are linked together in a variety of possible ways. By proceeding
in this way, two useful insights into foundationalism can be
drawn together. The first is that the foundationalist temptation is
strong, plastic and pervasive. Foundationalist assumptions
pervade the figures of speech which articulate what both
common sense and expert cultures mean by 'knowledge': theories
are 'built', conceptual frameworks are 'constructed', arguments are
'supported' and an 'edifice' of knowledge emerges. The
metaphoric character of these figures is rarely noticed, so that the

view of knowledge as a founded construct is peculiarly difficult to break with, and quite capable of subverting well-intentioned attempts to do so. In Margolis's (1986: 166) formula, 'foundationalist views are rather more protean and persistent than the standard examples suggest'. Two particular kind of 'persistence' are important here. Modernist radicalisms have a preference for post-Kantian foundationalisms of 'constitution', in which knowledge (or whatever) is the product of a synthesis of disparate elements. Postmodernist critiques take these foundationalisms to task for their dualism and idealism, but are themselves premissed on alternative and monistic foundationalisms of 'givenness' which identify a world-and-knowledge-making 'substance' (intensity, or discourse). That is, the debate between modernist radicalism and postmodernism is between two different foundationalist strategies, not between foundationalism and antifoundationalism.

It is tempting to take the idea of foundationalism as a syndrome embedded in the grammar of 'knowledge-talk' as a warrant for a 'deconstructionist' critique, drawing credit from Derrida. In one sense, this temptation can be productive: deconstructionist themes can serve as important resources for anti-foundationalism. In another sense, which produces the second promised insight, it is important to resist absorption of the foundationalist syndrome into some more general 'logocentrism' of Western culture. To scramble some philosophical vocabulary, if we have an intuition that foundationalism is inescapable within our form of cognitive life, we have an equal and opposite intuition that foundationalist assumptions and questions are really rather odd. Hamlyn captures this sense of oddity.

> It does not matter that it would scarcely occur to the experts to doubt that knowledge is attainable in their field. ... There is still the suggestion that if certain particular things are not known, nothing else will deserve the title of knowledge. (Hamlyn, 1970: 11)[5]

The oddity, of course, is that the effective production of particular knowledges, in the sciences and in daily life, proceeds in more or less complete indifference to the course of philosophical debates about the foundations of KNOWLEDGE.[4] It is important to note that this indifference extends to both modernist and postmodernist foundationalisms: producers of knowledges are un-

171

likely to react with the wonder of a Monsieur Jourdain to the assertion that they have been producing 'discourse' all along. As is particularly clear in the cases of the specialised sciences, this indifference is not a simple lack of reflexivity: the sciences generate an enormous quantity and variety of knowledge-talk, from formal texts on method to 'hands-on' recipes for effective practice. Our foundationalist intuition about knowledge is opposed by a pragmatist one to the effect that by and large knowledge works. In particular cases where it does not, there will be particular reasons why this should be so. If we follow this intuition, it is difficult to see the quest for The Foundations of KNOWLEDGE as other than pointless. In Rorty's vivid phrase, the foundationalist Philosopher scratches where it does not itch.

How, then, does this syndrome which is at once so general and so singular come to infiltrate both projects of modernist radicalism in social theory and their postmodernist critiques? Modernist radicalism has been identified here with a programme articulated around the three themes of 'ideology', the 'end of philosophy' and the 'unity of theory and practice'. It is difficult to imagine how these themes could be addressed in a non-foundationalist way. The 'ideology' theme requires a universal and qualitative distinction between two orders of knowledge (one upper, one lower case). The modernist radical 'end of philosophy' inaugurates a form of post-philosophical theory which enjoys privileged access to the 'real', as opposed to 'imaginary' foundations of modernity. The 'unity of theory and practice' invokes a double privilege, that of the qualitatively unique THEORY and the qualitatively unique PRACTICE which combine to complete modernity. The accounts of Marx, Durkheim, Habermas and Althusser in earlier chapters lend support to this diagnosis. This section opened by citing Hamlyn's claim that foundationalism in the theory of KNOWLEDGE emerges in response to what it takes to be the threat of scepticism. Modernist radicalisms are prone to versions of Descartes' sceptical nightmare: without the guarantees which they alone can furnish, KNOWLEDGE of modernity will fragment under the pressures of contingency and relativism, and the completion of modernity will be aborted.[5]

Modernist radicalisms resort to foundationalism in order to

privilege qualitative distinctions, as between KNOWLEDGE and knowledge. By contrast, postmodernisms turn to monistic foundationalisms precisely in order to *deny* qualitative distinctions of the modernist sort. Monisms can found claims that there are no qualitative distinctions between knowledge and error, virtue and vice, emancipation and repression, because there is 'nothing but' the will to power, or the pulsation of intensities, or the proliferation of discourse, in the world. One of the oddities of the postmodernisms considered in the previous chapter is the reluctance of, say, Baudrillard or Guattari to embrace fully the consequences of this kind of monism. They, and others, are driven to search for ersatz 'quantitative' versions of the qualitative distinctions they deny: even Baudrillard allows the possibility of 'challenge', however hopeless. The claim that postmodernism leads to nihilism functions as a critique because, in the end, postmodernists do not want to be nihilists.

Lyotard is a particularly interesting figure in this regard. Dews suggests that the debate between Lyotard and Thébaud in *Just Gaming* is pivotal in that Lyotard has to concede that the idea of a 'libidinal politics' which he had previously advanced was based on a monistic 'philosophy of the will'. In the end, searches for quantitative variations of intensity cannot ground a political practice (see Dews, 1987: 220). After this, Lyotard shifts to the better-known positions of *The Postmodern Condition,* with its emphasis on the preservation of diversity and justice, and of *The Differend* with its insistence on incommensurability. For Dews (ibid.) this shift (together with a similar movement on the part of Foucault) represents the eclipse of Nietzschean post-structuralism. It is not so clear that it also signals a retreat from monist foundationalisms in postmodernisms such as Lyotard's. One way to deny qualitative and dualistic distinctions is to assert that 'everything' comes from a single source, but another is to insist on the infinite and untameable diversity of 'everything'. These two strategies of denial appear to be polar opposites, but they have similar consequences. Lyotard's celebration of the diversity of language games has as much difficulty in excluding 'terror' as does Guattari's politics of intensity in excluding the 'experimentations' of rapists. One reason for this convergence may be that the superficial emphasis of 'diversity' in Lyotard and others conceals a latent monism. Postmodernisms of diversity are tempted to specify the privileged single medium in which

173

diversity proliferates. This medium is usually language, or some part of it: 'language games' for Lyotard, 'discourse' for Hindess and Hirst. Formalisms of 'discourse' are as monistic and as foundationalist as physicalisms of 'intensity'.

6.3 FOUNDATIONAL INSTANCES

(a) Origin

For the strictest foundationalisms, such as Descartes', enquiry can only be held to produce KNOWLEDGE if it can be shown to *begin* from a starting-point whose own status as KNOWLEDGE cannot be questioned. The *Cogito* is to serve as the indubitable beginning, and the ultimate support, of an axiomatic science in which the strictest logical derivation allows every part of the whole to share the certainty of its origin. The problem of beginnings is an urgent one for projects of modernist radicalism, although not one which can be solved with quite a Cartesian clarity. So, the beginning of Marx's critical theory of the state lies in a recognition of the priority of civil society 'as it is', which can overturn the Hegelian mis-recognition. For Durkheim, too, a science of the social must begin from an engagement with the reality of the social object 'as it is'. Habermas searches for the jointly socio-historical and cognitive points of origin of differentiated complexes of KNOWLEDGE or action, finding them in 'interests' or 'competences'. These examples serve as a reminder that at least two of the defining themes of modernist radicalism are implicated in the problem of beginnings: the 'ideology' theme insists that KNOWLEDGE requires a beginning which is not that of the defective knowledges of everyday life, while the 'end of philosophy' theme requires that a new, specifically modern KNOWLEDGE make a new beginning.

Althusserians and postmodernists profess contempt for the hopelessly metaphysical 'problematic of origins', but do not quite so easily evade it. Most obviously, the Althusserian doctrine of 'the break' insists that sciences have a specific historical moment of emergence which is also a qualitative rupture. Although Foucault subverts qualitative ruptures of this kind, his 'archaeologies' and 'genealogies' problematise the beginnings of specific 'positivities' or regimes of 'power/knowledge'. Less historically

174

oriented postmodernisms remain committed to the view that the pulsation of intensity or the proliferation of discourse is the only 'real' beginning of knowledges.

But by now, some of the ambiguities of the instance of origin will be apparent: Marx and Durkheim may claim to mark a new beginning for KNOWLEDGE of the social, but they also 'realise' the rational potential of philosophy. Scientific KNOWLEDGE may demand a different beginning to the knowledges of everyday life, but its claims to relevance also require a measure of continuity. Suspicion of the category of origin is nicely caught and generalised in Derrida's doctrine of the 'supplement'. In the course of a discussion of Rousseau's *Essay on the Origin of Languages*, Derrida notes a paradox.

> The desire for the origin becomes an indispensable and indestructible function situated within a syntax without origin. Rousseau would like to separate originarity from supplementarity. All the rights constituted by our logos are on his side: it is unthinkable and intolerable that the name of *origin* should be no more than a point situated within the system of supplementarity. (Derrida, 1976: 243)

Thus, Rousseau seeks a natural origin for language, and finds it in 'passion', but his assertion, or simulation, of the 'presence' of the origin can only turn on an effacing of its (non-)origin in the chain of supplements of his own writing.[6] It is important to realise that Derrida's critique applies with as much, if not more, force to postmodernist as to modernist radical 'beginnings': Rousseau's 'passion' is closer to the monisms of 'intensity' or 'discourse' than to the dualisms of modernist radicalism.

Some of the paradoxes of the 'instance of origin' can be explored with reference to two examples which should be familiar. The Cartesian *Cogito*, the 'I think', has already been considered here as the archetypal strong foundationalism, while Dawe's account of the 'two sociologies' has acquired a classic status as an exploration of sociological origins. At first glance, the 'originarity' of the *Cogito* is clear enough, but in a number of senses it cannot be the beginning of Descartes' enquiries. The *Meditations* take the form of a narrative, which purports to trace the course of Descartes' philosophical reflections over a period of six days. Taking this narrative form at face value, for the moment, the *Cogito* is not the beginning of the story. The textual starting point is a claim about the biographical origins of Descartes' concerns.

> It is some time ago now since I perceived that, from my earliest years, I had accepted many false opinions as being true, and that what I had since based on such insecure principles could only be most doubtful and uncertain; so that I had to undertake seriously once in my life to rid myself of all the opinions I had adopted up to then, and to begin again from the foundations. (Descartes, 1968: 95)

In the biographical sense, at least, the 'origin' of Cartesian science lies outside the text and in the past. This beginning also makes it clear that within his narrative, Descartes' commitment to the necessity of a new foundation pre-dates his 'discovery' of that foundation in the *Cogito*. Further on it emerges that Descartes also has a prior commitment to the criteria which a new foundation must fulfil: 'my reason has already persuaded me to withdraw my assent from whatever is less than indubitable' (ibid.). The 'First Meditation' goes on to adumbrate the very wide range of apparently settled beliefs from which Descartes now feels obliged to withdraw his assent.

The 'Second Meditation' begins, it would seem, with complete scepticism a real possibility for Descartes:

> The meditation of yesterday has filled my mind with so many doubts that it is no longer in my power to forget them. And yet I do not see how I shall be able to resolve them. (Descartes, 1968: 102)

However, Descartes stiffens his resolve, and determines to

> continue always in this path until I have encountered something which is certain, or at least, if I can do nothing else, until I have learned with certainty that there is nothing certain in the world. (ibid.)

As this word-play makes clear, the only sceptical conclusion which Descartes would accept is a rationalist's scepticism in which uncertainty is itself certain. By the time the scene is set for the *Cogtito*, then, its originarity is caught in a series of paradoxes. The *Cogito* is to serve as a new beginning for KNOWLEDGE, but its fitness for that status must itself be demonstrated: this is why it appears some lines into the 'Second Meditation', rather than at the

176

beginning of the first, of course. The orthodox foundationalist position on possible difficulties of this kind is to posit a clear distinction between two orders of enquiry. On one hand is the epistemological or ontological discourse of foundational reflection, and on the other is the substantive discourse of founded scientific enquiry. The end of the former order is to serve as the beginning of the latter: foundational reflection must always be in some sense prior to the substantive enquiry which it founds.

However, one of the obstacles to accepting the *Cogito* as the beginning of enquiry is a suspicion that it is not a genuine 'end' of foundational reflection. The radical doubt of the 'First Meditation' can appear as a simulation, a literary artifice which nearly succeeds in disguising the way in which the formal criteria which define the *Cogito* as an origin for enquiry are pre-supposed from the outset.[7] The passages quoted above would seem to provide some basis for that suspicion. Such a critique could proceed in at least three registers. In the normal register of philosophical debate, questions of logical priority, consistency and inference have been raised against Descartes from the first appearance of the *Meditations* (e.g. see the account in Kenny, 1968: chs 2 and 3). Alternatively, it would be possible to raise the question of priority in a biographical sense: is Descartes narrative account of the sequence of events leading to the 'discovery' of the *Cogito* to be believed? What are the implications for his foundational claims if, for example, his commitment to the *Cogito* preceded the alleged episodes of radical doubt? Finally, the question of origin can be posed in a register of textuality, asking how the selection and sequencing of particular textual figures accomplish the appearance of the *Cogito* as the end of foundational reflection and the origin of founded enquiry. Whether the *Cogito* is considered within each of these registers individually, or in its complex placing in the relations between them, it seems that something like Derrida's argument holds: when a claim to originarity is scrutinised, it dissolves into chains of logical, biographical or textual supplements.

The instance of origin plays a crucial role in the foundational reflection of would-be radical projects, where it is necessary to differentiate between the radical project and its non-radical adversaries. The postulate of different origins can offer a vivid icon of foundational difference. In this spirit, Dawe's 'The Two

Sociologies' takes issue with those accounts of the origins of sociology according to which a 'reaction' to the enlightenment 'created a language which, at once, defined the solution to the problem of order and the sociological perspective' (Dawe, 1971: 542). For Dawe, this account traces only half of the archaeology of sociology. The missing half leads back to the Enlightenment project itself, for which 'the application of reason and the scientific method to social analysis was merely a means to the solution of the problem ... of how human beings could regain *control* over essentially man-made institutions' (ibid.: 547).

Dawe's exploration of the history of sociology stops at the point at which he can locate and differentiate the twin originary instances of the discipline. Henceforth, the discourses of enlightenment and reaction are rendered as mutually exclusive and contradictory, and are referred to by Dawe variously as 'essences', 'views of human nature', 'problems' and 'doctrines'. Once traced to their origins, these pairs of essences, or whatever, become fixed and attain a presence in sociological discourse as foundational principles which govern enquiry by a 'logical progression'. Dawe's 'archaeological' investigations seem to open the possibility that the movement of a discourse is shaped in complex ways by the movement of its history. However, Dawe denegates this possibility in the claim that history is present in the discourses of sociology as an instance of origin for twin 'logics' of discourse. Just as Rousseau's attempt to found language upon its natural origin in passion simply opens a gap between that origin and the supplementarity of discourse, so Dawe's foundational efforts fall into the gap between the movement of history and the logics of discourse.[8]

Descartes and Dawe may be an unlikely pair, but their efforts to specify a foundational originarity for their respective concerns fall prey to the same paradox of the idea of origin. Origins supposedly exert a foundational authority through some direct continuity with that which they found (logical implication, for example). But the attempt to specify an origin finds itself operating in a different discursive 'register': perhaps biography, or history, rather than logic. The foundationalist problem of origin first opens up, and then attempts to bridge, a gap between the register in which the origin is located and described and the register in which it is to function *as* an origin.

(b) Autonomy

The foundationalist syndrome promises to projects of enquiry a unity under the rule of a law (*nomos*) which is the law of their own identity (*autos*), and of that alone. The instance of autonomy encompasses two moments: one of *in*clusion, of establishing the crucial relation between enquiry and its foundation, and one of *ex*clusion, of insulating enquiry from the possibility of contamination by shameful dependencies or associations. When stated in this way, the concerns of the instance of autonomy are clearly co-extensive with many of the central concerns of philosophy in the modern period. The array of metaphors through which the instance of autonomy has been articulated in philosophy forms a crucial part of the inheritance of modernist radicalism.

The Cartesian figures which secure autonomy have already been considered: foundational reflection discovers the starting point of a science which can enjoy the exclusive privileges of an axiomatic system. It may not be too fanciful to see this pattern for the instance of autonomy at work in Durkheim's 'discovery' of the reality of the social, which serves as the starting-point for a methodologically regulated science of sociology. Locke's 'empiricism'[9] appears to be a far more modest alternative to Cartesianism. It offers a self-effacing supplement to the enquiries of 'the great Huygenius and the incomparable Mr Newton' in which it is 'ambition enough to be employed as an under-labourer in clearing the ground a little, and removing some of the rubbish that lies in the way to knowledge' (Locke, 1961: xxxv). However, this modestly belies the foundationalism of Locke's project: when the rubbish of 'vague and insignificant forms of speech' has been cleared away from the sciences, it is possible to demonstrate the possibilities and limits of KNOWLEDGE of the 'inner constitution' of phenomena. The 'under-labourer' conception of foundational reflection has made little impact on modernist radicalism, but has defined the self-understanding of much Anglophone philosophy of science and social science.

Spinoza moves away from Cartesian rationalism in the opposite direction, as it were. For Spinoza, the certainty of the *Cogito* is purchased at the cost of an inconsistent and incoherent dualism of mind and body. The only alternative to this incoherence is a thoroughgoing monism, in which the unitary *Deus sive Natura* admits no distinction of substance between creator and created. The way in which Althusser appropriates this strongest of all foundational defences of the autonomy of KNOWLEDGE has already been considered.

Kant links the instance of autonomy with the idea of the rule of law in his celebrated image of the critique of reason as a 'tribunal'. His demand for a new beginning in philosophy is to be understood as

> a call to reason to undertake anew the most difficult of all its tasks, namely, that of self-knowledge, and to institute a tribunal which will assure to reason its rightful claims, and dismiss all groundless pretensions, not by despotic decrees, but in accordance with its own eternal and unalterable laws. (Kant, 1970: 9)

It is a small step from this metaphor of the foundational tasks of critical philosophy to the programmes of modernist radicalism. Here too, the decisive task is 'self-knowledge', but of 'society' rather than reason; here too the image of a rational tribunal shapes many accounts of the (rational) 'unity of theory and practice'. For the Marxist tradition in particular, Hegel's historicisation of the 'eternal and unalterable laws' of reason provides a resource for an all-embracing materialist science which unites foundational reflection and substantive enquiry, and whose autonomy is secured by its capacity to articulate the historical movement of totality.

Modernist radicalisms, then, draw on a philosophical archive of images of the autonomy of founded enquiry, from the Cartesian to the Hegelian. However, the affinity between foundationalism and modernist radicalism is not quite the end of the story, since elements of the oddity, as well as the inescapability, of foundationalism enter into the instance of autonomy. The worm which eats to the heart of the autonomy of founded enquiry, denegating its exclusionary moment, is the suspicion that the forces which move the discourse of enquiry are located in 'another scene' to that accounted for in the foundation. Marx's project most notoriously exemplifies this paradox of modernist radicalism, which has rendered it chronically susceptible to a debunking critique. On the one hand, Marx mobilises and re-works figures from critical philosophy to articulate the programme of a new kind of autonomous and totalising science. On the other hand, *The German Ideology* and other texts anticipate *The Genealogy of Morals* and *The Interpretation of Dreams* as essays in the 'hermeneutics of suspicion', hunting down the displacements and aporias of apparently autonomous discourses to the 'other scenes' of class interest, the play of power and the unconscious. Here, too, is a trace of the latent foundational complicity between modernist radicalism and postmodernism: the monist foundationalisms of the latter are generalised versions of the displacements which threaten to discredit the former.

Dawe's differentiation of the origins of radical and conservative sociologies illustrates the paradox. Dawe offers two mechanisms which account for the movement of discourse: one, 'history', shapes the doctrines of 'control' and 'order'; the other, through which the doctrines found sociologies, is 'logic'. But the genie of 'history' as a motive force of discourse will not so easily return to the bottle, and the suspicion that it continues to be active in respect of sociological enquiry constantly subverts the pretensions of 'logic'. To sum up, there are grounds for believing that both modernist radicalisms and postmodernisms are inextricably entangled with the foundationalist syndrome, but that this entanglement is aporetic and paradoxical.

6.4 FOUNDATIONAL MODES

Foundationalism can be understood to arise out of questions about how the 'origins' and 'autonomy' of projects of enquiry can be secured and guaranteed. Once asked, there are four main registers, or 'modes', within which such questions can be answered. First, it can be asserted that a uniquely powerful *method* of enquiry will guarantee the production of KNOWLEDGE. Second, the orientation of a project towards some uniquely privileged *goal* (e.g. the building of socialism, or the completion of modernity) can be held to give it a special status. Third, attempts can be made to root a project in some uniquely weighty pre-theoretical *ground* (e.g. Durkheim's 'society', Althusser's 'practice', or Guattari's 'intensity'). Finally, the apparent 'gap' between rational method and pre-rational ground might be bridged in an appeal to the force of *tradition* (e.g. 'enlightenment', or 'the working class movement'). While projects of modernist radicalism will differ in the degree of emphasis they place on each of these modes, they will normally offer some account of each. For example, Habermas's recent work raises foundational claims about 'reconstructive' methods, about the goals of modernity, about communicative and strategic action as the ground of social life, and about the modernist tradition's 'uncompleted project'. For postmodernism, the modes of goal and tradition are particularly suspect. Formalist postmodernisms will tend to emphasise a version of 'method', while physicalist variants turn on a particular conception of 'ground'. The brief accounts of the four modes below aim to give a sense, first, of the foundational force of each mode and, second, of the paradoxes in which each is caught.

(a) Relation to method

The foundational claims of method receive almost universal acknowledgement in the social sciences, although agreement notoriously breaks down on the matter of which method has the strongest claim. The foundational power of method is linked to a crucial limitation of its scope: adherence to method guarantees not the truth, but the validity, of enquiry. The best scientist, using the best method, will produce scientific truth only if a number of other factors are favourable (if the hypotheses to be tested are coherent, if the data to be analysed are reliable, for example). What might be termed the 'formality', or the 'indifference', of method can be articulated in two rather different ways which relate to the senses of 'validity' at work in the discourses of logic and law.

In logic, validity is a function of the form, rather than the substance, of an argument. A false conclusion may be arrived at through a valid derivation from false premises, so that in one sense logic is indifferent to truth. In another sense, this indifference becomes a formalisation: logical calculi operationalise truth as 'truth value (or function)', and the latter becomes a token in the calculation of validity.[10] In the logical sense, then, validity is an abstract and formal relationship, admitting only two valences and calculable with absolute precision. A validity guaranteed by a foundational relation to method offers to enquiry an icon of autonomy and power. The limitation of a methodical pursuit of a validity modelled after logic is the indifference, or 'emptiness' of method: valid procedures guarantee the validity of outcomes only, and are blind to other values which cannot be transformed into functions of validity (truth, utility, beauty, or what you will). The rhetoric of 'rigour' which is so characteristic of the Althusserian and post-Althusserian traditions is implicated with this sense of method. The trajectory through which Hindess and Hirst move from an Althusserian rationalism to a postmodernism of 'discourse' is inscribed by a series of purifications of theory, so that all over-full and rationalistic conceptions are purged. In the end, theoretical discourse is no more than the 'effects' of relations between concepts (e.g. see Hindess and Hirst, 1977: 7). Other postmodernisms of discourse have their analogues to a sense of the productive force of validity. In Lyotard (1984a) the analogue lies in the differentiated 'pragmatics' of language games, in Foucault (1980: 109–133) it lies in the intertwining of power and knowledge in 'discursive régimes'.

If validity is modelled after law, rather than logic, a different sense of a foundational relation to method can emerge. A marriage, for example, is 'valid' if specified initial conditions hold (that the persons to be married are not of the same sex, that neither of them is already married, etc.) and if the proper formalities are duly executed (the celebrant being properly licensed, the appointed form of words being uttered, the participants signing the register correctly, etc.).[11] The formalities which secure the validity of a marriage are 'performatives', as it were. Two interesting implications for the idea of a foundational relation to method flow from this model of validity. First, it emphasises that method is activity and performance, rather than simply abstract protocol. Second, it challenges the idea that method can secure an unconditioned foundational autonomy. One of Durkheim's best known arguments demonstrates that contract can have force only within an ongoing society (see Durkheim, 1964b: ch. 7). To adapt and generalise this Durkheimian point, the performative power of a method patterned on legal validity is radically bound by convention and social context: questions of method begin to implicate a range of other questions about the limits and uses of method in context. A 'foundational' reflection which explored, rather than effaced, these questions would press the limits of the foundational syndrome.

(b) Relation to goal

It would seem that relation to method cannot by itself serve as an adequate foundation for projects of enquiry. On the analogy with logic, a supplement is required which can give substance and direction to the formal calculus. On the analogy with law, the power of method is purchased at the cost of a challenge to the foundational image of the autonomy of enquiry. In the former case, the establishment of a relation to goal promises to provide the required supplement. Goals bring direction and topicality to enquiry, moving it beyond the empty certainties of method and giving it the form of a project. Relation to method and to goal constitute a pair which exhaust the foundational concerns of much of the philosophy of science, setting the limits of a type of knowledge-talk which can specify the 'how' and 'why' of enquiry. Despite this apparently neat fit, the foundational conjunction of method and goal is not without its difficulties.

First of all, as many critical analyses of science have pointed out, the dynamics of scientific enquiry seem to eliminate the possibility of any consequential reflection on goals. In variants of the 'rationalisation' theme, the methods, topics and goals of enquiry come to be integrated in the unfolding of a single self-sufficient 'logic'.[12] It comes to be the mark of a successful science that the goals of projects within it can be specified only in the terms of a specialised organon: a foundational relation to goal is absorbed by the relation to method. A second difficulty compounds the first. The goals of enquiry can be formulated in a number of different registers, and at a number of different levels of generality: 'testing the instrumentalisation thesis through a replication of the "Affluent Worker" studies' and 'advancing the cause of world peace' could both count as goals. The former is technical and specific, the second general and practical. The difficulty is precisely that as 'technical' goals of enquiry undergo the integration noted above, they lose their ties to a reflection on 'practical' goals, a reflection which can only become ever more general, abstract and external to enquiry itself.

This 'splitting' in reflection on the goals of enquiry is a particular threat to projects of modernist radicalism, since the definitive 'unity of theory and practice' theme requires an integration of the technical and the practical. The difficulty of achieving any such integration is an index of the fate of modernist radicalism as a project-form. The kind of integration which, say, Marx and Durkheim hoped for required the development of a new kind of practice to realise the goals of the end of class society, or the perfection of organic solidarity. In response to the failure of the new practice to arrive, modernist radicalisms turn more and more to technical and meta-theoretical reflection on the kinds of knowledge and the kinds of practice which might, one day, really form the basis of a new unity. This inescapable turn accelerates the splitting of reflection on goals as it draws further back from the concerns of both day-to-day practice and empirical enquiry.

(c) Relation to ground

The traditional philosophy of science has often asserted proprietary rights over knowledge-talk about the 'how' and 'why' of enquiry. It has been particularly suspicious of claims that such knowledge-talk should shift into the registers of the history, psychology or sociology of science. In Anglophone circles, the work of Kuhn is usually accorded a pivotal place in the development of a 'new' philosophy of science which gives due weight, if not priority, to these registers.[15] This development turns on a recognition of the foundational significance of the non-rational grounds of enquiry. It raises the possibility that questions about the origin and autonomy of enquiry should be answered with reference to historical, psychic or social 'context'. For social enquiry, the question of relation to ground must raise a demand for reflexivity, for a recognition that the topics of enquiry are also its unavoidable resource. Along with relation to method, relation to ground is the favoured mode of postmodernisms which can use the assertion of a single and non-rational ground for all discourse to deny the importance of qualitative distinctions between discourses. Postmodernist groundings issue in a de-bunking reflexion which asserts that there is 'nothing but' power or intensity or the play of discourse in the world.

In one sense, however, the discovery of 'ground' is also definitive of modernist radicalism: the assertion of the foundational reality of the social domain, and its priority over (mere) 'ideas', is crucial to the claims of Marx, Durkheim and their successors to have 'ended' philosophy. But such foundational claims can only be made good if that non-rational

MODERNIST RADICALISM AND ITS AFTERMATH

(social) ground can be shown to have a privileged connection with rational principles. Habermas's successive difficulties with 'knowledge constituting interests' and 'reconstructive sciences' illustrate the inescapable dilemma. The requirement that knowledge-constituting 'interests' be both rational foundation and non-rational ground of knowledge could be met only in the empty formula of a 'quasi-transcendental' status: as foundation the interests are transcendental categories, as ground they are anthropological. The 'competences' which figure in Habermas's later reconstructions are similarly required to answer both 'questions of fact' and 'questions of right'. In the absence of some plausible 'synthesis' between relation to ground and other foundational modes, the gap which Habermas's formulae attempt to cover yawns at the heart of modernist radicalisms. To give priority to method and 'rational' foundation suggests a retreat to traditional philosophy, but to prioritise ground flirts with irrationalist and postmodernist threats to the autonomy of enquiry.

If modernist radicalism requires that relation to ground be treated as a foundational mode, the difficulties encountered by attempts to meet that requirement suggest that grounding cannot be treated adequately within the limits of the foundationalist syndrome. There, ground must appear either as a substitute principle of rationality, or as the discrediting and irrational 'other' of founded enquiry. Heidegger's questioning of metaphysics has been a point of reference for notable attempts to re-formulate grounding, and thereby the question of autonomy, in a non-foundational manner. The Heideggerian 'question of Being', that of the emergence of beings from Being and of the gap which that emergence opens, can be taken as the general form of the problems of autonomy and grounding. That Derrida's version of the Heideggerian problem is relevant to these questions has already been indicated. So too must be the 'reflexive sociology' of the 1970s, which attempts to formulate sociological discourse as a reflexive recovery of Being through attention to the 'intertwining of language and the social relation' (Phillipson, 1976: 26).[14]

(d) Relation to tradition

If it can sometimes seem as if there is a gap between the rational methods and the non-rational grounds of enquiry, concepts such as authority and tradition may promise to bridge it. Such concepts appear to have a foot on each side, conveying the sense of a pre-rational binding force which has taken articulate form. A relation to the legitimate authority of established tradition might save enquiry from the antinomies of method and ground. This question of the relation which enquiry bears to existing, authoritative and effective tradition is most notably explored in Gadamer's work. The task of enquiry is to integrate the strange with the familiar in 'a new and distinct familiarity which belongs to us and we to it' (Gadamer, 1976: 25).

An insistence on the centrality of tradition might easily be taken as the mark of an inherently conservative project, but tradition is crucial for radical projects, too. The point is nicely taken in Ricoeur's comment on the Gadamer/Habermas debate over the 'conservatism' of hermeneutics.

> Critique is also a tradition ... it plunges into the most impressive tradition, that of liberating acts, of the Exodus and the Resurrection. Perhaps there would be no more interest in emancipation ... if the Exodus and the Resurrection were effaced from the memory of mankind. (Ricoeur, 1981: 99–100)

At a more mundane level, the passion with which the title to Marx's legacy is contested (or was contested until recently) in both academic and sectarian debates is a mark of the legitimating force of authority and tradition in radical social theory. It is a mark of a number of postmodernisms that their 'radical' credentials rest on a tacit appeal to a radical tradition which they are quite unable to articulate. In the last chapter this was seen to be the case for both Guattari's radical 'experimentations' and for the pertinence of 'socialist discourse' in the discourse theory of Hindess and Hirst.

There is one sense in which the suspicion that an appeal to tradition is inherently 'conservative' is warranted, however. The foundationalist syndrome requires that the foundation be accomplished in some sense 'prior' to the enquiry (or the practice) which it founds. To think of enquiry's relation to tradition in a foundational way is to construe tradition as something already fixed and accomplished, rather than as open and corrigible. Such a conception must, indeed, produce conservative thinking (whether with a small 'c' on the left, or with a large 'C' on the right), thinking which presses itself into conformity with the authority of the canon. As with the question of grounding, the potential of relation to tradition to illuminate reflection about enquiry can only be realised if it is taken to press 'beyond' the limits of the foundationalist syndrome.

6.5 FOUNDATIONAL STRATEGIES

It is suggested, then, that relations to method, goal, ground and tradition constitute the modes in which the foundations of enquiry can be asserted to be accomplished. In any particular case, different weights will be given to each relation, so that many empirical research programmes may stress the centrality of method, policy-oriented research may have a particular concern for goals, reflexive enquiries may be dominated by the question of grounding, hermeneutics may prioritise tradition, and so on. However, in each case some account will be offered of each relation: policy research, reflexive enquiry and hermeneutics do not simply ignore method, for example, but produce a variety of accounts of its proper nature and limits, accounts shaped by their own dominant foundational concerns. The exception to this rule may be the negative attitude towards goal and tradition in postmodernist projects, but even here the overt critique can conceal a covert dependency. It has also been suggested that the foundational character of each of these allegedly foundational relations is aporetic and paradoxical to some degree. The relations to ground and tradition, in particular, sit uncomfortably within the foundationalist syndrome.

These observations raise once again a question which was broached in the second section of this chapter: that of whether foundational issues can be approached in a way which is not foundational*ist*. This question requires a careful answer. An unqualified 'no' implies that all knowledge-talk about the origin and autonomy of enquiry and about the relations which enquiry bears to method, goal, ground and tradition must be foundationalist, so that the latter concept becomes severely stretched. On the other hand, too swift and sanguine a 'yes' savours of the complacency which allows foundationalist figures and arguments to proliferate in allegedly non-foundational projects. Modernist radicalisms have been particularly prone to this kind of complacency, so that the 'ends' of philosophy which

Marx, Durkheim and the rest accomplish in their discoveries of the autonomy of the social are very far from being the 'end' of foundationalism.

An answer is required which may appear at first sight to be a mere play on words: foundational issues can, indeed, be approached in a non-foundational way, but only on condition that they are no longer regarded as foundational issues. Some substance can be given to this answer by differentiating between two divergent types of strategy for knowledge-talk about the foundational instances and modes of enquiry: strategies of 'closure' and '*dis*closure'. Strategies of closure might be said to turn on four main assumptions and their corollaries. The first is that foundational reflection is (logically and/or temporally) prior to substantive enquiry, while the second is that, in principle, foundational questions admit definitive answers, so that foundational reflection is terminable. The strategic corollary of these two assumptions is that foundational reflection should aim for completeness (or closure) as a prolegomenon to enquiry.[15] A third assumption is that foundational reflection and substantive enquiry operate with different methods on different material. So, foundational reflection might be conceived as the a priori analysis of concepts, while substantive enquiry is the empirical analysis of facts. The fourth, and related, assumption is that the 'possibility' of substantive enquiry is in some sense dependent upon the outcome of foundational reflection: enquiry poses a 'question of right' which can only be, and must be, answered in foundational reflection. The strategic corollary of the two latter assumptions is that the task of foundational reflection is to secure guarantees for the authority of enquiry.

In fine, the 'strategies of closure' which result from the convergence of the assumptions and corollaries noted above are what make the syndrome of foundationalism foundationalist. The origins, autonomy, relation to method, relation to goal, relation to ground and relation to tradition of enquiry become foundational matters, and reflection upon them foundationalist, within the orbit of strategies of closure. Returning to the question of the possibility of a non-foundational*ist* foundational reflection, the word-play of the answer given above can be re-formulated. Foundational issues can cease to be foundational, and reflection on them cease to be foundationalist, if they can be prized out of their embeddedness in strategies of closure and re-constituted as elements of a strategy of *dis*closure. To raise this possibility is to pose once again the problem of the links between the foundationalist syndrome and modernist radicalisms. If compared to, say, falsificationist or hypothetico-deductive models of enquiry, most modernist radicalisms would not seem to exemplify an extreme commitment to closure. On the first two assumptions and their corollary noted above, modernist radicalisms are often notable precisely for the *in*terminability of their foundational reflection, which can seem to take the place of substantive enquiry rather than 'found' it. However, and as has been suggested before, modernist radicalism's paradoxical and aporetic obsession with foundational questions can be understood as a response to the failure of the world to conform to the requirements of theory. That is, the non-closure of foundational issues in modernist radicalisms might best be understood as the product of a failed strategy of closure, rather than of a successful strategy of disclosure.

The rhetoric of openness and diversity in many postmodernist projects might imply that they break out of the foundational closures of modernist radicalism. Particularly, the rejection of a foundational distinction between knowledge and KNOWLEDGE, a refusal to pose the 'question of right', can appear as an emancipation from epistemology. But postmodernisms never rest content with contingency and diversity: both qualities must be glossed as necessary features of the world, and thus become transformed into something other than contingency and diversity. So, it is never enough simply to leave the knowledge/KNOWLEDGE distinction to one side, it must be shown that the distinction is *necessarily* false. It is not enough not to pose a 'question of right', it must be shown that the question *cannot* coherently be posed. Postmodernisms are driven to strategies of foundational closure which are the negative image, as it were, of the modernist closures they contest.

What, then, might a successful strategy of disclosure look like, if it can not look like modernist radicalism or postmodernism? For now, criteria of disclosure can be specified only in the most general and abstract terms. First of all, disclosure requires the negation of each of the assumptions which underpin closure. That is, foundational reflection is intertwined with substantive enquiry, rather than prior to it; foundational reflection does not generate single definitive answers, it is not terminable; a priori distinctions drawn between the materials and methods of foundational reflection and those of substantive enquiry are of limited utility; foundational reflection is not a privileged tribunal whose task is to answer a 'question of right', thereby underwriting the 'question of fact' of enquiry. Second, a strategy of disclosure will try to explore precisely those gaps and paradoxes in the 'instances' and 'modes' examined above which foundationalist approaches require to efface. The larger question is that of how a strategy of foundational disclosure can contribute to the urgent requirement for a post-foundational radicalism: what resources are available to such a project, and what kinds of problem will it be required to address? These matters can now be addressed in the next, and final, chapter.

7

POST-FOUNDATIONAL
RADICALISM

7.1 PRELIMINARIES

The task of this chapter is to draw together the threads of the
argument and to give some account of the prospects of 'post-
foundational radicalism' in social theory. It is a task which poses
severe difficulties of principle, however. The idea of a post-
foundationalism turns on a suspicion of all projected unities and
all pre-emptions of judgement. To attempt to pre-figure the
substantive concerns or specific procedures of a renewed
radicalism would be to relapse into the legislative mythologies of
a philosophical, scientific or aesthetic politics in which a logic of
'theory' binds the conduct of 'practice'. It follows that it would be
self-defeating to build the chapter around a set of stipulations as
to what should now count as 'radical' issues and how they should
be analysed and acted upon.

The discussion which follows tries to avoid these dangers by
operating at the same meta-analytic level as the rest of the book.
This should not be taken to suggest that the practice of a post-
foundational radicalism is only possible at that level, but to
acknowledge that it is not the task of a meta-analytic text to pre-
empt judgements about enquiry and practice. The chapter falls
into three sections. The first rehearses, and relates to contemporary possibilities, three themes of post-foundationalism identified in chapters two and three: relationalism, irony and rhetoric.
The second section relates the radical requirement for 'accountability' in enquiry to contemporary debates about reflexivity and
value, arguing for the possibility of a non-foundational form of
accountability. The final section considers the appropriate orientation of a post-foundational radicalism to historical thresholds and
the 'fate of the times'.

7.2 RELATIONALISM, IRONY AND RHETORIC

(a) Relationalism

The question of how objects of analysis are either 'given' or 'constituted' is critical to the distinction between foundational and non-foundational conceptions of enquiry. On one side, Durkheim's social realism exemplifies a foundationalism in which the 'givenness' of the social object is warranted by a doctrine of its constitution (through 'collective representations'). Simmel, on the other side, offers an alternative and 'relational' account of constitution. The object of sociology is doubly constituted: social relations are subject to a 'first order' synthesis on the part of social actors and a 'second order' synthesis on the part of analysts. The syntheses which constitute objects of analysis cannot claim universal validity since they are conditioned by the 'interest' of the analyst. This Simmelian view of the constitution of objects of analysis is anti-foundationalist to the degree that it undercuts claims to privilege for a particular given object, or a particular interest.

Simmel's relationalism can be developed in two ways which are less helpful to the anti-foundationalist cause, however. In Weber, it combines with a doctrine of 'values' to produce a model of constitution which tacitly rests on the foundational 'givenness' of values, and thereby pre-figures the nihilistic monisms of postmodernism. Habermas's conceptions of constitution by 'quasi-transcendental' interests and (later) by competences and validity claims which are to be 're-constructed' become important planks in his defence of a rationalist modernist radicalism. Post-foundational radicalism requires a relationalism which can resist Weberian and Habermasian appropriations.

A critical post-foundational move is to shift the 'level' at which the issue of constitution is posed. If the search for a general formula for the constitution of analytic objects can only end in foundationalism, an alternative is to regard the problem of constitution as open, empirical and sociological. For many years sociologists of science have investigated and debated the social processes through which research programmes are organised and knowledge-claims are advanced and assessed.[1] However, for a variety of reasons other social theorists have been reluctant to understand their own projects through the sociology of science.[2]

If such reluctance could be overcome, it would be possible, for example, to formulate a concept of 'interest' which was neither irrationalist nor transcendentalist but sociological, and to enquire into the mutual constitution of interests and programmes of theory and research. The concept of 'interest' and its place in the social study of science was a focus of debate in the early 1980s, and there is a considerable literature to draw on.[5] Many of Simmel's insights are still relevant to the project of turning sociology into its own meta-discourse, and his distinction between actors' and sociologists' syntheses can be given an important twist.

Faced with the first and second order syntheses of social actors, the analyst can make one of two broad choices. The first is to co-inhabit, as it were, the 'reality' of the actors to a recognisable degree. On this basis, the analyst can share the interests of actors, or seek to modify them in some way, and can conduct enquiries designed to further those interests (or perhaps to persuade actors that they cannot be furthered except at great cost). Here, the object of analysis is constituted in a constellation whose principle is a pragmatic convergence of interests between actor and analyst. The alternative is for the analyst to approach the interests of actors orthogonally, as it were, and to focus attention on the 'methods' of reality constitution which are in play (as a sociologist of science might attend to the accomplishment of a research programme in science). The analyst's synthesis is of a different order to that of the actor in this case, and the radicalism of such an enquiry is not easily aligned with the radicalism of socio-political practice.

Both strategies have a place in a post-foundational radicalism. In each case, an acceptance that the constitution of objects of analysis is a contingent matter can be understood as a major step away from a 'strategy of closure' on foundational matters, and towards a post-foundational 'strategy of disclosure'. The relations to method, goal, ground and tradition of programmes of research can be considered as open and corrigible issues. They do not need to be understood as aspects of a transcendental 'question of right' in respect of an object of analysis. If the original warrant for this suggestion comes from a reading of Simmel, it can be sharpened with reference to Pollner's conceptions of 'mundaneity' and 'mundane enquiry'.

The idea of 'mundane enquiry' into 'a world (a domain, a field, a region), which is presumed to be independent of the mode and manner in which it is explicated' (Pollner, 1987: 12) has achieved such authority in modern culture that it appears to be self-evidently *the* form of rational enquiry. Naturally enough, sociology has sought to achieve the status of a successful mundane science, and Pollner re-states the familiar ethnomethodological argument that in doing so sociology replicates and parallels the 'mundane reasoning' of social members.

> In entering mundane space and competing with everyday mundane practitioners, sociology incurs a two-fold loss. It naively accepts and thus is oblivious to the mundaneity of its own inquiry [and it] loses sight as well of the mundaneity of everyday life. (ibid.: 11)

In defining for itself a suitable mundane field, 'inquiry gains a world but loses the work of worlding' (ibid.: 7).

Pollner is aware that the reflexive paradox has been an embarrassment to some earlier formulations of the ethnomethodological project: must not that project, too, make 'mundane' pre-suppositions, thus depriving its critique of all force? Taking his cue from McHoul (1982), Pollner suggests that

> while ethnomethodology is condemned to mundane 'structure' and 'practice' as a condition of its intelligibility, its understanding of the nature of those structures and practices must be informed by rigorous and daring efforts to move the 'limits' of the mundane idiom. (Pollner, 1987: 150)

The second of the two strategies differentiated above aligns with a commitment to the study of 'the work of worlding'. In its ability, first, to display the contingency of mundane practices (to call them to account), and second, to shift the limits of mundaneity, such a strategy becomes 'radical'.

The first strategy offers a 'mundane' radicalism. It may be that sociology's mundane resources have a greater potential than Pollner allows. Some advocates, and many critics, of ethnomethodology converge on a variant of what Smith has termed the 'Egalitarian Fallacy' (see p. 210 below). This version of the fallacy holds that if sociology is not *entirely* distinct from common sense at the pre-suppositional and methodological levels (as 'objective' is from 'subjective', or 'science' from 'ideology'), then it is *no* different and *no* better. But such a case rests on just the foundationalist assumptions which are under question here. When those are abandoned, it becomes clear that judgements about which accounts of the world are more or less illuminating, challenging or elegant are part of the basic repertoire of communication. They can be made, quite coherently, without reference to categorical distinctions and foundational guarantees.

It follows that sociologists who care to do so can challenge members' *versions* of mundaneity, even when not challenging the 'mundane idiom' as such, and can thereby help to formulate new ways of conceiving, and solving, mundane problems. It is one of the most stubborn traces of modernist radicalism that analysts are constantly tempted to construe their challenges to members' versions of (say) class, gender or ethnicity as arising from a division at the deepest possible pre-suppositional level. At this deep level, actors' and experts' versions of phenomena are differentiated and it is shown that the 'real' interests of actors are best articulated by the experts' versions.

Only by resisting this temptation, and recognising its mundaneity, can a sociology of the 'great organs and systems' hope to re-capture its relevance to debates outside the academy. A renewed mundane radicalism could pursue not only the traditional agenda of 'social problems' but, crucially, the emergent agenda of problems which challenge sociology by straddling established boundaries between 'social', 'technical' and 'natural' registers: problems of reproductive technology and 'bioethics', or of environmental damage and climatic change. It is imperative to recognise, however, that the auspices of such a mundane sociology are, indeed, mundane and pragmatic. Mundane sociology can rest on no foundational claim to ontological or epistemological privilege.

(b) Irony and causality

Ironists, as characterised by Rorty (1989: 73–4), are 'never quite able to take themselves seriously because always aware that the terms in which they describe themselves are subject to change, always aware of the contingency and frailty of their final vocabularies, and thus of their selves'. A mundane radicalism in social theory requires to be practised by ironists who can attend to the contingencies of social and political arangements without searching for their foundations. Rorty's 'liberal ironists' separate their 'private irony' from their 'public hope', and turn to literature rather than to social theory. It is possible, however, for social theory to develop the relationalism of Simmel and Weber into a tool of 'public irony'.

The conceptions of modernity advanced by Simmel and Weber offer an alternative to the stalemate between modernist foundationalism and its postmodern inversion. The Weberian 'paradox of consequences' turns on a series of ironies deriving from the juxtaposition of different 'syntheses' of historical processes, related to different constitutive interests. On a sympathetic reading, Weber grants the object-constitutive role of 'interests' while maintaining a series of gaps or tensions between interests, objects and outcomes. The causal chains of Weber's historical sociology serve to bridge the gaps in ways which (always from a particular 'point of view') take on an ironic quality. The pathology of Weberian irony is its proximity to a negative historicism, more evident in the later concept of a 'dialectic of enlightenment'. Part of a solution lies to hand in the relationalism of Simmel, which does not rely on the value-doctrine which lures Weber into world-pessimism. Another part of the solution lies in insisting that causal relations have an independence from object-constituting 'interests', even though they operate within object-domains which interests have constituted. Negative historicisms reduce causality to frustration of purpose, just as positive historicisms reduce it to fulfilment of purpose.[4]

As a gross generalisation, the brief notoriety of the Parisian 'New Philosophers' in the late 1970s, and the rather deeper theoretical penetration of postmodernist themes, might be ascribed to the reluctance of the left to take irony seriously. When Levy was joined by more formidable figures such as Foucault in suggesting that 'the Gulag', or 'the killing fields', had come about because of the programme of Marxism, rather than in spite of it, their case was ironic and Weberian. That they appeared to be doing anything other than stating the obvious was due to the assiduity with which the left had obfuscated awkward paradoxes of consequences in the search for more congenial explanations in terms of errors, deviations or external pressures. One of the most important tasks which a post-foundational radicalism can perform in relation to programmes for social and political change is to maintain an awareness of the possibilities for ironic outcomes. In turn, a critical appropriation of elements of Weberian analysis which the left has regarded with suspicion can make an important contribution to that task. Whatever other difficulties they may present, Foucault's genealogies of power/knowledge are exemplary in their Weberian irony about the consequences of revolutionary or reformist zeal.

(c) Critical rhetorics

The question of language lies at the centre of debate about radical social theory. Three major approaches have been considered here. Habermas exemplifies the most ambitious of attempts to found a modernist radicalism on a model of language. His basic principle is that rationality is 'at home' in language, that 'communicative action' can only be understood through the reconstruction of the validity claims on which it is based. Habermas's affirmative conception of communication finds its critical edge in a capacity to pass judgement on contexts of action in which communication is subject to systematic distortion. As on many other matters, postmodernist conceptions of language often seem to be a simple inversion of modernist radicalism. The monistic proliferation of discourse does not conform to the pattern of any immanent rationality. Indeed, the idea of rationality (or value, or emancipation) is de-bunked as an effect of a movement of discourse which has no inherent meaning.

Habermas's theory of language is a rationalist foundationalism, while varieties of postmodernism offer an irrationalist foundationalism of discourse. The third approach considered here, which points the way to a post-foundationalist engagement with language, is the 'critical rhetorics' which Horkheimer tentatively hints at, and which Adorno refines. Adorno is no monist, and his suspicion of the integrating power of language needs to be differentiated from the Nietzschean strains in postmodernism as well as from Habermas. The 'dialectic of non-identity' is formed in a double engagement with the rhetorical, artful character of language. Affirmations of 'identity' are to be shown to be rhetorical effects, the outcome of literary artifice or of stage-craft, as in the cases of Heidegger and Wagner. But dialectic itself cannot be practised outside language: there is no Archimedean point on which dialectic can found its critique of identarian rhetoric.

The critical studies in philosophy and aesthetics through which Adorno advances the programme of a dialectic of non-identity are difficult to surpass as models for a non-foundationalist critical practice: they are, literally, works of art. It is less clear that they can *exhaust* the programme of a post-foundational radicalism, or even its concern with language, however. Three main limitations should be noted. First, Adorno's sensitivity to language never entirely displaces a concern for familiar philosophical oppositions. He does not evade the problems of 'subject-centred reason', and his critiques of identity can seem to prefer a retreat into classical antinomies to a decisive leap into a post-foundational rhetorics. Second, as Habermas notes, Adorno's relentless 'negativity' is sustained by the extreme utopianism of an absolute reconciliation which may never come about, but which remains the only standard of value. Third, Adorno vacillates about the possibility of a radical social science. His 'Inaugural Lecture' is relatively open to the possibilities of empirical research and of sociology in general. His advocacy of a materialist hermeneutic might seem to open the door to a form of analysis which is critical, empirical and oriented to language. But in the post-war period his opposition to 'positivism' seems to close down these possibilities.

Habermas understands his claims for a 'communicative' conception of rationality and a reconstructive formal pragmatics as a movement beyond Adorno. Certainly, he crashes through the three limits noted above: he decisively rejects subject-centred reason, he offers a non-utopian image of reason and reconciliation, and he re-opens the possibility of an empirical and critical social science sensitive to the importance of language. But Habermas's apparent 'overcoming' of Adorno is no more than a reversion to an orthodox modernist radicalism. As matters stand, none of the approaches to language considered so far can be adopted without modification. The most likely candidate for productive development is Adorno, but the prolonged debate between modernist radicalism and its critics has thrown up no definitive resources to complete the task.

This is not a problem which will be solved in the final chapter of a book of this type. The programme pre-figured in Adorno's demands for a materialist hermeneutics, or dialectic of non-identity, or a critical rhetorics, is not to be completed by a page or so of general formulae. However, there are established traditions of research in sociology which converge with the requirements of a post-foundational radicalism, to state the case no more strongly. A critical approach to language which drew on ethnomethodological and conversation-analytic resources might develop Adorno's insights in the direction of an empirical pragmatics, rather than the formal and reconstructive pragmatics which leads Habermas back to modernist radicalism. It is in this sense that resources which were not available to Adorno render obsolete his early, and suggestive, distinction between 'research' and 'interpretation'. The distinction between mundane and orthogonal enquiry sketched above suggests that (orthogonal) research can advance the work of interpretation while interpretation of interests is a critical moment in (mundane) research.

7.3 ACCOUNTABILITY

It was suggested in chapter six that a mark of radical social theory is its attempt to maintain the accountability of enquiry, loosely identified with a capacity to articulate both the desirability and possibility of change. The idea of a radical accountability is related to the problem of value in enquiry. Accountability seeks to establish the 'relation to value' of enquiry, and thereby the value of enquiry itself. The accountability–value nexus is handled in different, but equally problematic ways, by modernist radicalisms and postmodernisms. Modernist radicalisms understand the demand for accountability as a demand for foundational guarantees, so that the problem of accountability is transformed into that of the definitive themes of modernist radicalism. Accountability is a matter of demonstrating that the discourse of enquiry is the direct expression of some value which is immanent-but-obscured in social relations.

Postmodernisms, by contrast, effectively abandon the problems of accountability and value, and are thereby pitched into varieties of nihilism. The de-bunking critique of value reduces it to an illusory effect of a discourse whose monistic principle of movement can be traced to some discrediting and valueless 'other scene'. The question of accountability cannot arise other than as nostalgia. In relation to accountability and value, then, a post-foundational radicalism faces the familiar challenge of evading the mirror-image pathologies of modernist radicalism and postmodernism. The ways in which that challenge might be met are considered in two sub-sections. The first considers the ways in which enquiry can become reflexive, while the second relates the requirement of accountability to a view of the contingency of value in which the act of judgement is decisive. Accountability is not a matter of producing a special kind of founded knowledge which is guaranteed to be emancipatory. Reflexivity and judgement are a shorthand for a recognition that accountability and radicalism are a matter of the ways in which *any* kind of knowledge is put to use. If reflexivity and judgement in a post-foundational configuration are implicated in the pragmatics of knowledge, it must also be recognised that they are rhetorical accomplishments. As radical demands, reflexivity and judgement convey some sense of the specific tasks of post-foundationalism considered as a critical rhetorics.

(a) Reflexivity

It is a truism that reflexivity is a pre-condition of accountability, in enquiry as elsewhere. An actor who entirely lacked self-awareness could not be held 'accountable' for any of her actions: indeed, she could hardly be accounted an 'actor' at all. Similarly, there can be no wholly 'unreflexive' social theory or enquiry: all researchers have some level of self-awareness, and can give some account of the projects they are engaged on. Claims that a specifically 'reflexive' form of enquiry is required are not so much asserting that 'unreflexive' enquiry is unreflexive *tout court*, but that it accounts for itself in ways that either tell the wrong story, or not the whole story, about itself. So, many versions of empirical enquiry in social science are reflexive only about their 'relation to method'. The accounts which emerge from such enquiries will be unreflexive about their constitutive relations to goal, ground and tradition.

Arguments of this form animated the calls for a 'reflexive sociology' which came to prominence in the early 1970s. Gouldner located two obstacles to an adequate sociological reflexivity. The more important of these is the sociologist's tendency to act 'as if they thought of subjects and objects, sociologists who study and "laymen" who are studied, as two distinct breeds of men' (Gouldner, 1971: 490). The solution to this pathology lies in a 'distinctive conception' of a sociology of sociology (ibid.: 488). The second obstacle is the supposition that such a sociology might be composed of valid bits of information about the 'sociological world' (ibid.: 495). A truly reflexive sociology requires a commitment to 'knowledge as awareness' as well as to 'knowledge as information' (ibid.: 493). A reflexive sociology would be a radical sociology, for Gouldner, because it 'would accept the fact that the roots of sociology pass through the sociologist as a total man, and that the question he must confront, therefore, is not merely how to *work* but how to *live*' (ibid.: 489).

Gouldner's vision of a reflexive radicalism did not find universal favour, even with other advocates of 'reflexivity'. O'Neill objected that Gouldner had produced a naive model of reflexivity, working in ignorance of phenomenology. In trying to think through the problem of reflexivity without the appropriate resources,

> Gouldner comes to the limits of his discipline as a form of theoretical life. Because he has neglected to consider the philosophical foundations of reflexive sociology he is obliged to make his choice of a sociology a political choice.
> (O'Neill, 1972: 219)

For O'Neill, the problem of reflexivity in sociology is, precisely, the problem of the limits of sociology, of 'how it is that we can show the limits of sociology and still be engaged in authentic sociological theorizing' (ibid.: 228). The 'institution' of reflexivity is 'tied to the textual structures of temporality and situation through which subjectivity and objectivity are constituted as the intentional unity and style of the world' (ibid.: 231). O'Neill, too, requires that reflexivity be a feature of radical enquiry. The contribution of phenomenological reflexivity to radical analysis is that 'it grounds critique in membership and tradition' (ibid.: 234).

O'Neill's concerns with the 'auspices' of sociological enquiry were pursued in texts by Blum (1974), McHugh *et al.* (1974) and Sandywell *et al.* (1975), for example. For many, the later work of Heidegger enabled the formulation of reflexivity as reflection on the ways in which the practices of reading and writing sociology are implicated in the dense and constitutive relations between language, social relation and (social) Being. One of the marks of this project was a concern that authorial practice should itself be reflexive, rather than simply 'about' reflexivity.

> A model of reflexive writing must itself become an occasion
> to exemplify the invariant grounds of its production – as an
> occasion to retrieve one's own method, to interrogate the
> wonder of the concept, one's way of transforming text into
> world and vice versa, but without objectifying it in the
> writing. (Sandywell, 1975: 32)

In this project Gouldner's concerns with the transformation of 'the
total man' *(sic)* receive a far from naive re-formulation.

Gouldner himself took a linguistic, or rhetorical, turn in the
mid-1970s. *The Dialectic of Ideology and Technology* (1976)
modelled two different conceptions of the 'rationality' of
discourses. In one, rational discourse is bound by a norm of 'self-
groundedness'. This conception can generate a certain kind of
critical discourse, an enlightenment critique of pre-rational
structures, as it were. But the pursuit of self-groundedness
requires a systematic silence about the 'substantial conditions' of
discourse in language and society (Gouldner, 1976: 49). The
definitive pathology of would-be self-grounded discourse is
'objectivism' 'which conceals the presence of the speaker in the
speech [and] thereby conceals the contingent nature of that
speech and of the world to which it alludes' (ibid.: xv). The
second conception of rationality equates it with reflexivity:
'rationality as reflexivity about our groundings premises an ability
to speak about our speech and the factors which ground it' (ibid.:
49). Reflexivity, or 'self awareness concerning the rules to which
one submits and by which one is bound' (ibid.: 55) is the only
practice which can resist a pathological objectivism in social
theory.[5]

In recent years the demand for reflexivity has been to the fore
within the project of 'social studies of science'. Here, reflexive
questions about sociological practices, particularly writing
practices, are prompted by the attention which researchers pay to
the science-constituting discursive practices of the other researchers whom they study.[6] Experiments with the reflexive
potential of 'new literary forms', exemplified by Mulkay (1985)
and Woolgar (1987), challenge the standard rhetorics of the
academic text. For example, the assumption of a univocal author
developing a single, logically connected argument is challenged
by the device of adopting dialogue form: 'authors' argue with
themselves.

It may be clear enough that a post-foundational radicalism must be reflexive or be nothing, but it is not so clear just how the different versions of reflexivity should be appraised. A first problem concerns the drift towards foundationalism in Gouldner's and O'Neill's early formulations. O'Neill saw phenomenology as an external resource for the 'philosophical foundations' of sociology. Gouldner's earlier version, particularly, seems to argue for the replacement of an inadequate orthodox model of foundations with a reflexive and radical one: the roots of sociology which pass through the 'total man'. His later version is more congenial to post-foundationalism, and its emphasis on the 'contingency' of discourse points to the rhetorical accomplishment of the relations between text and context. While the Heideggerian strain in reflexive theorising is characterised by an analytic sensitivity and complexity which evades crude foundationalisms, Adorno's judgement on the quest for an ur-objectivity may lie in wait for all Heideggerian thinking.

A second problem concerns what might be termed the 'displacement effect' of reflexive theorising, and which underpins much suspicion of calls for reflexivity. To caricature the problem, the naive and pre-reflexive analyst formulates a study of, say, 'class' or 'the practices of natural scientists'. The reflexive analyst then argues that the *real* issues concern the stratifying practices of sociological discourse, or the versions of 'Science' which the sociology of science pre-supposes. To the pre-reflexive analyst it appears as if all her robust questions about 'the social world' are being displaced into an interminable meta-discourse in which sociologists can speak about nothing other than sociology.' This caricature may be unjust, but the distinctiveness, sophistication and complexity of reflexive sociology caught it in a paradox of consequences whereby many sociologists came to see the practice of 'reflexivity' as something outside their interests and competences.

A response can begin by repeating the point that, by definition, no form of enquiry can be entirely 'unreflexive'. But, equally, no form of enquiry could be absolutely reflexive. The idea of an absolute reflexivity seems to imply the simultaneous 'co-presence' of all possible auspices, and can only be a limited concept. All forms of enquiry are ranged between the two limits of no reflexivity on any possible dimension, and complete reflexivity on all possible dimensions. Once this point is taken, the type and degree of reflexivity possessed by a given project of enquiry can be understood as opening a range of analytic possibilities while, by the same token, closing off others. So, the pre-reflexive analyst closes down virtually all possible forms of reflexion (perhaps maintaining an attachment to the idea of method). This sacrifice finds its reward in a capacity to address concrete questions in a social world which overlaps with the social worlds constituted by the 'interests' of social actors. The reflexive analyst, by contrast, opens up wide horizons for reflexion, but pays the price of a disconnection from the pragmatics of sociological and lay social worlds.

The demand for reflexivity can now be refined somewhat. First, if all projects are constituted in a balance of different degrees of reflexivity on different dimensions, a minimal demand might be that any project should be able to *account* for its constitutive balance. This suggests one way of handling the 'displacement' problem. The minimal requirement imposed on the pre-reflexive analyst of class is not a displacement of the topic into a reflexion on the stratifying practices of sociology. It is, rather, a recognition and an account, a justification, of the project's specific balance of reflexivity and un-reflexivity. Second, this formulation of the demand for reflexivity must be understood in a non-foundational way. If foundationalist accounts and justifications of enquiry are accepted, the demand for a minimal reflexivity places no additional burden at all on pre-reflexive analysis: the clichés of 'method' can be mobilised once more.

The apparatus from the previous chapter may be of use here. As a simplifying assumption it might be allowed that the relations of enquiry to method, goal, ground and tradition exhaust the dimensions of reflexivity. Foundationalist versions of enquiry claim that formulae in one or more of these dimensions constitute the privileged 'beginning' of enquiry and guarantee of its autonomy. One or more dimensions will often be excluded as 'external' to serious foundational issues. While foundationalism moves to the 'closure' of foundational matters, the minimal requirement for reflexivity might be equated with the contrasting strategy of 'disclosure', which recognises that enquiry is constituted in contingent and continuing relations to each dimension. Here, 'beginnings' are equally contingent, and autonomy is not de-contextualisation. Understood in this way, the minimal requirement for reflexivity is rather more than a token gesture which leaves everything as it is: projects of enquiry are required to face up to their own contingency, to the rhetorics of their own constitution. The accounts and justifications they are required to give are chronically susceptible to critique and irony.

Similar considerations apply to specifically reflexive projects such as those considered above. Any claims to have discovered in relation to ground or tradition the 'real' and deep foundation which other forms of enquiry fail to recognise must be treated with suspicion. For post-foundationalism the reflexive and rhetorical task is to explore the dimensions of the contingency of enquiry without turning contingency into a metaphysical principle. With that negative point made, a wide variety of reflexive practices have a contribution to make. So, it was suggested above that the 'constitution' of objects of analysis might be studied through the established techniques of recent sociology of science, giving a twist to Gouldner's model of a reflexive 'sociology of sociology'. At a different level, the Heideggerian turn in reflexive sociology offers the most highly developed exploration of the possibilities of reflexivity as a form of intellectual community. The reflexive dimension of textuality itself might be developed in experiments with the textual forms of social theory. The point on which these diverse projects converge is simply the rejection of foundationalist formulae for reflexivity which must appear, from the standpoint of a post-foundationalism, as formulae for its postponement and evasion.

(b) Judgement and value

The sense that all is not well with value discourses finds its classical and problematic sociological expression in the Weberian value doctrine considered in chapter two. Weber posits values as the foundation of world- and science-constituting 'interests', but recognises that they are no longer rationally accountable in a disenchanted modernity. He is concerned to prevent this Nietzschean diagnosis from leading to a nihilistic abandonment of all rational and normative standards. 'Value relevance' and 'value neutrality' work to prevent the inescapable irrationality of foundational values from contaminating the rationality of social science. The doctrine of 'vocation' attempts to make of an individual's consistent articulation of a 'value-orientation', and consistent commitment to a 'value-sphere', a meta-value by reference to which the individual can be held accountable.

Weber's solution is not convincing, and it is far from clear that he evades nihilism. Strauss, for example, is scathing about the Weberian imperative 'thou shalt have ideals'. 'Excellence' and 'baseness' lose their real meanings for Weber: 'excellence now means devotion to a cause, be it good or evil, and baseness means indifference to all causes' (Strauss, 1953: 44–46). From Strauss's standpoint, and not only from there, the line dividing Weber from the franker nihilisms of postmodernism must appear vanishingly thin.

MacIntyre's Aristotelian argument in *After Virtue* converges with Strauss at a number of points, and offers a seductive framework for explaining the crisis of values which Weber confronted, but could not solve. MacIntyre's argument is directed specifically to morality, but with minor modifications it could apply to other realms of value, such as aesthetics.[8] The crisis is implicit in the 'inevitably unsuccessful' Enlightenment project to find a 'rational basis' for morality in human nature (MacIntyre, 1985: 55). This project had to fail because Enlightenment critique had eliminated the Aristotelian 'notion of man-as-he-could-be-if-he-reached-his-telos' (ibid.: 54). Without this notion, the insoluble 'problem' of morality consisted of trying to relate the two remaining elements of the moral complex; a set of injunctions which no longer had a teleological context, and a conception of human nature 'as-it-is' (ibid.).

In the wake of the inevitable failure of the Enlightenment attempt to endow a fragmented and residual moral vocabulary with a rational unity, morality can only become instrumentalised, providing 'a possible mask for almost any face' (ibid.: 110).[9] In MacIntyre's view, it is the 'bad faith' of an instrumentalised moral vocabulary which provokes the Nietzschean critique, which is the only serious competitor to an Aristotelian restoration. MacIntyre spends little time on Weber's value doctrine, but his more general assessment of Weberian thought is that it dominates the 'contemporary vision of the world', while concealing the real nature of the crisis that it cannot resolve (ibid.: 109). Weber is a symptom of nihilism rather than a cure, to revert to a term which MacIntyre rarely uses.

MacIntyre offers an elegant account of why the moral foundationalisms of enlightenment cannot work. He adds a further

dimension to the critique of a moralising and legislative Enlightenment developed by Koselleck and he gives reasons for
suspicion of the Nietzschean anti-Enlightenment. However, the
framework within which the diagnosis is articulated, and the
alternative which MacIntyre presents as the only alternative, are
less attractive. According to MacIntyre, Aristotelianism 'can be
restated in a way that restores intelligibility and rationality to our
moral and social attitudes and commitments' (ibid.: 259). He
proposes a 'new' foundationalism in which moral discourse is
revived by an Aristotelian account of 'the virtues'. As he
summarises the case in his 'Postscript', that account has three
elements: an account of virtues as the qualities which secure
'goods' which are internal to 'practices', an account of virtues as
contributing to 'the good' of a whole life, and an account of the
way in which the first two relate to 'the good for human beings'
(ibid: 272). The question arises here of whether this is, indeed,
the only alternative. It is suggested below that it is not, that there
is a post-foundational alternative which can revive value-
discourses and also preserve what is worthwhile in MacIntyre.

Introducing a collection of 'essays on value and culture', Fekete
(1988: i) claims that 'we may be on the threshold of a new round
of theoretical value discussion in cultural studies'. The new
'postmodern value agenda' is to be distinguished from modernist
and premodernist agenda by its readiness 'to get on without the
Good-God-Gold standards one and all, indeed without any capitalised Standards, while learning to be enriched by the whole
inherited inventory once it is transferred to the lower case' (ibid.:
xi). Fekete speaks for what might be termed 'phase two postmodernism', in relation to which 'phase one' would be the array
of monistic formalisms and physicalisms considered in chapter
five. Phase two shares the enthusiasm of phase one for epochal
horizons, and is equally vigorous in its opposition to Enlightenment rationalisms, but it does not confine itself to a sub-Nietz-
schean de-bunking of value.

Phase two is marked by a convergence on the new 'value
agenda' across a range of traditions. MacIntyre's diagnosis of the
crisis of morality (if not his solution) has been influential, as has
Rorty's critique of professional philosophy. The debate finds some
common ground between erstwhile phase one postmodernists,
such as Lyotard, and modernist radicals such as Wellmer. In a
response to an interview question about 'irrationalism', Lyotard

measures his distance from phase one: 'there is no reason, only reasons' (van Reijen and Veerman, 1988: 278), rather than 'there is no reason, only intensity (or power, or discourse)'. Indeed, Lyotard plays with the archetypally modernist figure of the three spheres of value: 'it is a question of plural rationalities, which are, at the least, respectively theoretical, practical, aesthetic' (ibid.: 279). Elsewhere, Lyotard has extended his anti-monism to the idea of 'language' itself: 'there is no "language" in general, except as the object of an idea' (Lyotard, 1988: xii). This view converges with the conception of contingency developed by Rorty, who urges that 'we treat *everything* – our language, our conscience, our community – as a product of time and chance' (Rorty, 1989: 22).

Wellmer's attempts to reject the 'de-bunking' critique of reason without endorsing transcendentalism were noted in chapter five. A Wittgensteinian account of language allows him to explore the space 'between' Habermas and Lyotard, promising

> a sceptical return so to speak to common sense ... [which] ... destroys the ideals of reason, the foundationalism of ultimate groundings and the utopianism of ultimate solutions, it 'localises' at the same time reason in a web of changing language games without beginning and end and without final certainties. (Wellmer, 1985b: 360)

Between the registers of Goodness, Truth and Beauty there are shifting and porous boundaries, but boundaries nonetheless. If we de-capitalise each register, and do not erect overly formal boundaries between then, we can pose the phase two problem of value.

Suggestive as the convergences of phase two may be, many formulations remain at an abstract and speculative level, establishing a mood or spirit of the times rather than giving clear guidance to programmes of analysis. In this context Smith's 'Value Without Truth Value' is important for its attention to the social contingencies which frame and constitute 'value'. Three elements in her account are particularly relevant to the 'value problem' faced by post-foundational radicalism. First, she rejects any categorical 'fact–value' distinction which, in concert with others such as 'objective–subjective' and 'unconditioned–conditioned', obscures 'the crucially relevant *continuities* between evaluative and other types of discourse and, most significantly, the social dynamics through which *all* utterances, evaluative and otherwise, acquire value' (Smith, 1988: 4).

Second, Smith offers an account of how those 'social dynamics' should be understood. 'Value' is

> the product of the dynamics of some economy or, indeed, of any number of economies (that is, systems of apportionment and circulation of 'goods') in relation to the shifting state of which an object or entity will have a different (shifting) value. (ibid.: 2)

Here, agents act out of self-interest. The 'social economics' of discourse will constrain self-interested speakers to 'serve the interests of their assumed listener(s) in the ways we commonly characterise as "objectivity" and "reliability"' (ibid.: 10). The model generates a critique of Habermas's theory of communication as part of a doomed but recurrent 'impulse to dream an escape from economy, to imagine some special type, realm or mode of value that is beyond economic accounting' (ibid.: 17).

The third element of Smith's analysis is her rejection of the 'Egalitarian Fallacy'. The fallacy asserts that if the idea of an objective, disinterested, impersonal, etc. value is rejected, then all judgements are 'equal', 'equally good' or 'equally valid'. Modernist radicalisms deplore this outcome, while phase one postmodernisms celebrate it. But for Smith, the fallacy turns on precisely the 'vacuous' conception of validity which is under challenge. 'What feeds the fallacy is the objectivists' unshakeable conviction that 'validity' in *his* objectivist, essentialist sense is the only *possible* measure of the value of utterances' (ibid.: 8). 'Foundationalist' can be substituted for 'objectivist' here. The alternative is to reject the idea that 'interests' and 'economies' distort the production and circulation of 'value'. Instead,

> we may better be able to see them as the conditions under which all verbal transactions take place and which *give* them – or are, precisely, the *conditions of possibility* for – whatever value they do have for those actually involved in them. (ibid.: 9)

Smith's analysis is important for its attempt to pin down the new value debate to an account of the specifics of social dynamics. Even more significantly, it lays the basis for a reversal of the Weberian doctrine of values. 'Value' is no longer the pre-rational given which is the constitutive pre-supposition of discourse, but rather the *outcome* of discursive practices. Analytic attention is shifted to the practices of 'judgement' or 'evaluation' which produce and sustain value. That is, the problem of value is linked directly to the rhetorical movement of discourse. In this, the weak link is the model of a 'social economy'. The objection is not that 'economy' subverts 'value', but that the linked concepts of economy and market tend towards an overly formal and abstract conception of discursive and social practices. The image of self-interested actors and speakers constrained into order by market forces performs a closure on enquiry into discursive and social practices which is as marked, in its way, as that which defines action and discourse as regulated by an immanent rationality.

Smith's insights are better served by open and empirical enquiries into the social and discursive production of value than by the a priori imposition of an 'economic' model. It is notable that she supports the extension of her analysis to the 'cognitive' values of science by citing sociologists such as Barnes, Bloor and Collins (Smith, 1988: 11, 19n.). But, of course, they precisely *do not* impose the model of a 'social economy' on practices. Once again, the distinction between 'mundane' and 'orthogonal' enquiries can be useful.

In the latter case, enquiries conceived largely after the pattern of conversation analysis would attend to the ways in which speakers formulate judgements or evaluations which are heard by listeners to be competent exemplars, 'adequate for all practical purposes'. Fine-grained studies of the ways in which judgements are agreed with, disagreed with, insisted upon, modified or abandoned in various modes of languaged interaction are the route to an understanding of the social production, circulation and maintenance of 'values'.[10] Here, the model of a 'social economy' is too gross to be illuminating, and its conception of 'interest' deflects attention from 'methods' of judgement to 'motives'.[11] The radical accountability of such studies lies in a commitment to a reflexive understanding of what Pollner terms 'the work of worlding' as the rhetorical accomplishment of a valued world. Such an understanding pre-figures forms of intellectual, moral and political life over the horizon of foundationalism.

In mundane enquiry, radical accountability is secured in a traceable relation to the values of social actors. That is not to say that radical enquiry becomes nothing but the articulation and service of those values. It may be that one of the more important services which radical enquiry can perform is to foster an ironic perspective on values and their 'fate' among the mundane 'organs and systems' of society. An obvious and instructive objection arises here: this formulation seems to have a weak discriminatory power, and is unable to differentiate between a relation to 'progressive' and to 'reactionary' values. Surely, this failing traps the present argument in just that nihilism of which Guattari and others were accused in chapter five.

But what makes Guattari a nihilist is precisely the pre-emption of any judgement of value in his postulate of a quantitative opposition to established order. A pre-emption of judgement is also typical of those modernist radicalisms which guarantee qualitative distinctions at the foundational level, so that progressive values are immanent-but-obscured in present realities. The weak discriminatory power which may be found questionable in the present model of accountability is no more than a recognition that the need for a judgement is not to be evaded. To accept that 'progressive' and 'reactionary' values cannot be differentiated with logical precision at a foundational level is to face up to the contingency of value. To require a litmus test for the radicalism of values is to remain locked in an impossible foundationalism.

Belief in the need for such a test is linked to the foundationalist 'question of right'. As a 'question of fact', it takes no very great sociological acuity to identify the kinds of issues and values which will engage radical intellectuals in advanced societies. They include (to use crude flags) economic re-distribution, anti-racism, gender politics, welfare rights, democratic politics and (increasingly prominent) green issues. Foundationalism insists on asking by what 'right' these issues form a package, thereby displacing value problems into a meta-analysis of value. By contrast, a post-foundationalist rhetorics denies the utility of a *general* meta-analytic distinction between radical and reactionary values.

Of much greater interest are the very many *particular* value problems which arise within the broad radical tradition. Some of these reflect conflicts of priority between values. The practice of so-called 'female circumcision' may seem objectionable on a number of progressive grounds, but the objection itself may smack of cultural imperialism and even racism. Other problems concern the familiar tensions between ends and means, as in questions about political violence. Still other problems concern values, or programmes, or organisations whose radical status is ambiguous. Can religious values be progressive? Are Solidarity, or Sinn Fein, progressive organisations? It is implausible, to put it no more strongly, that any foundational formula for differentiating the 'radical' from the 'reactionary' could resolve these value problems, while the procedural foundationalism of a Habermas merely displaces the implausibility.

The contribution of mundane radicalism lies elsewhere than in a fruitless search for foundational formulae and rules. The need for a judgement, on the part of both actors and analysts, is not to be evaded, and mundane enquiry can inform judgement by exploring the social contexts and consequences of value debates. Enquiry can challenge and provoke, as well as support, the social actors whose values it relates to. In doing so, it can help to stave off the most potent practical threat to the exercise of judgement in relation to values. This comes not from academic foundationalisms, but from the sclerosis of a 'routinisation' which transforms radical tradition from a vital and corrigible resource into a dead hand of habit.

In short, post-foundational radicalism must insist, with Smith and others, on the contingency of value. This sets it against both the attempt to find foundational guarantees for value and the attempt (in the palpable absence of such guarantees) to deny the possibility of value. A corollary of this recognition of contingency must be a shift away from second-order value problems, from 'enquiry into the *value of value*' (in Fekete's (1988: vi) formulation).[12] That shift affects both orthogonal and mundane enquiry. In the former, the abstract and foundational problem of 'the value of value' is replaced by a series of empirical questions about the rhetorical accomplishment of value by social actors. A mundane enquiry disburdened of the requirement to address second-order foundational issues can engage directly and pragmatically with the first-order value problems faced by social actors and communities.[13]

This dual 'relation' to value can help to reinterpret MacIntyre's solution to the crisis of value. It is a major theme of *After Virtue* that no system of morality is independent of the community in which it is current. This theme is taken up (and extended to

213

include 'rationality' in its scope) in *Whose Justice? Which Rationality?*, where MacIntyre argues the need for a battle on two fronts: against the view that 'contexts' are a mere background to ideas, and the view that ideas are merely 'masks' for self-interest (MacIntyre, 1988: 390). Standards of morality, or of rationality, have a history and belong to a tradition, but to recognise this is not to de-bunk morality and rationality. This argument tends towards the conception of 'contingency' advanced by Smith and taken up here. Many of the differences can be related to Mac-Intyre's preference for the broad historical overview: the relativities he concerns himself with are those between epochs and cultures, rather than within them.

When followed through, MacIntyre's sociology of knowledge and belief converges with a 'phase two' account of the contingency of value. His Aristotelianism then appears in a different light. First, it is clear that the plea for a 'new' moral vocabulary is a plea for a new moral *community*. Second, it follows that his case is better understood as a claim about the way to resolve first-order value problems than as a contribtion to a second-order debate about 'the value of value'. Within a view of the contingency of value, MacIntyre can be read as advancing a series of substantive claims which are subject to empirical scrutiny and value judgement.

7.4 HISTORICAL THRESHOLDS AND THE 'FATE OF THE TIMES'

Modernist radicalism offers social theory a powerful and seductive image of itself as a privileged KNOWLEDGE of reality, qualitatively distinct from the contaminated knowledges of common sense and competitor disciplines. The power of this KNOWLEDGE lies in its capacity to synthesise with social practices, transforming them into a privileged and world-transforming PRACTICE. Through these twin revolutions in KNOWLEDGE and PRACTICE, social theory can accomplish the understanding and the completion of modernity. Social theory can thus fulfil the unrealised emancipatory potential of the philosophical tradition: in social theory, philosophy finds its 'end' as both *finis* and *telos*. This book has attempted to convey some sense of the way in which these three defining themes of modernist radicalism have shaped both classical and contemporary versions of the nature and tasks of radical social theory.

Modernist radicalism has not gone unchallenged: a series of critiques of its pretensions and practices have borne at least partial witness to the possibility of another kind of radicalism. This book has aligned itself with this developing critique of modernist radicalism, sharing the view that modernist radicalism locks social theory into an anachronistic and speculative metaphysics. Two obstacles have seemed to stand in the way of this project for another kind of radical social theory. The first is the tenacity of modernist radicalism itself, while the second has been the rise of far-reaching postmodernist critiques which offer only the nihilistic mirror-image of modernist radicalism. Modernist radicalism and its postmodern critique are both animated by foundationalist conceptions of enquiry. In closing, a final problem posed by the convergence of modernism and postmodernism needs to be addressed: how should post-foundational enquiry orient itself to historical and theoretical 'thresholds'?

Modernist radicalism and postmodernism both place themselves in relation to a threshold which is conceived as at once historical and theoretical. For modernist radicalism, the historical rupture which constitutes modernity as a qualitatively distinct social order can be appropriated only by a form of theory which is itself constituted by a rupture which separates it from previous forms. The convergence of these two ruptures is a pre-supposition of the three defining themes of modernism: a new and powerful form of theory can comprehend and complete the emergence of a new and powerful social order, thereby ending outdated forms of reflection. In this, as in much else, postmodernism mirrors the modernist radicalism it refutes: once again, only the new theory is adequate to the new order. Another kind of difficulty attaches to Bauman's attempt to straddle the divide in his proposal for a sociology animated by 'the intention to preserve the hopes and ambitions of modernity in the age of postmodernity' (Bauman, 1988: 231). This rather begs the question of whether those 'hopes and ambitions' are not definitionally and historically tied to modernity itself.

Some purchase on the ways in which these formulae generate misconceptions of the tasks of social theory can be gained from Blumenberg's (1983) refutation of an anti-modernism which claims that modernity is 'illegitimate' because its principal themes are 'secularisations' of the themes of a pre-modern theology. So, for example, Marxism can be de-bunked as 'just' a secularisation of Christian eschatology. The logic of this critique is very close to many postmodernist arguments. Now, Blumenberg's overall project may appeal to modernist radicals such as Habermas,[14] but two elements of his response to anti-modernism might feed into a post-foundational orientation to 'thresholds'. First, he argues that a real, and problematic, continuity lies in an inability to break with the definitive questions of pre-modern theory. Many modern philosophers and social theorists are drawn towards a 're-occupa-tion of answer-positions that had become vacant and whose corresponding questions could not be eliminated' (Blumenberg, 1983: 65). So, 'What is the meaning of history?' has a clear mean-ing and a clear answer in theology. If we get rid of the theo-logical answer, but not the equally theological question, we are in trouble.

> We are going to have to free ourselves from the idea that there is a firm canon of the 'great questions' that throughout history and with an unchanging urgency have occupied human curiosity and motivated the pretension to world and self interpretation. (ibid.)

The 'end of philosophy' theme which is so central to modernist radicalisms cannot but produce theoretical moves which look like 're-occupations'. Marxism may not be 'just' Christian eschatology, but it does present itself as the 'materialisation' of the idealist demand for 'reason'. In turn, this re-occupation facilitates the alignment of theoretical and historical thresholds in a 'great divide': a transformation of society enables the old questions to be answered in new ways. Postmodernisms become complicit in these moves in two ways. First, as on the question of 'thresholds' itself, they update and repeat modernist figures. On other matters, they simply negate the radical modernist 're-occupation', so that there is no meaning in history, the idea of reason is an illusion, and so on. In each case, postmodernism remains parasitic upon the modernism it contests.

Blumenberg's second thesis insists that the most important transitions in the history of cultures are those in which new questions arise. His defence of modernity turns on the identification of a 'legitimate' conception of 'progress' which does not derive from a re-occupation (progress as the meaning of history), but from the emergence in the late medieval period of the programme of human 'self-assertion'. Here, 'man' *(sic)* 'indicates to himself how he is going to deal with the reality surrounding him, and how he will make use of the possibilities that are open to him' (ibid.: 138). Self-assertion requires the abandonment of all attempts to guarantee the desired outcomes of projects: Nietzsches's insight that there is no necessary connection between truth and human purposes is decisive and irreversible.

It is an implication of these arguments that modernist radicalism and postmodernism both misunderstand the challenges posed by social and intellectual change. Their shared obsession with the foundations of enquiry binds them into regressive 're-occupations' and a continual scratching at old questions. Neither is capable of responding to the challenge of contingency: modernist radicals search for necessity beneath surface contingencies, while postmodernists elevate contingency itself to the status of foundational necessity. A latent failure to break with old questions is obfuscated in an overt insistence on an absolutely new beginning. Like MacIntyre, Blumenberg regards the de-bunking critique of reason and value as the consequence of impossible foundational projects.

Blumenberg singles out Descartes' version, which was considered in chapter six. In Descartes

> the exigency of self-assertion became the sovereignty of self foundation which exposes itself to the risk of being unmasked by the discoveries of historicism, in which beginnings were to be reduced to dependencies. (ibid.: 184)

It might be added that this fate repeats itself in all the bright new beginnings of modernism and postmodernism: historicisms are debunked as dependent on foundational philosophies by postmodernisms which can themselves be de-bunked as parasitic upon historicisms.

In the light of these arguments, post-foundational radicalism cannot announce itself as yet another entirely new beginning. Anti-foundationalist themes have a long history as the 'other' of foundationalism, and radical enquiry must understand itself as a continuation of that history. The capacity to pose new questions does not derive from some single originary rupture with a theoretical past, but from a hard-won and far from guaranteed

217

openness to the contingencies of objects of analysis. If social theory is to retain a capacity to identify and respond to culturally salient shifts, ruptures and thresholds, it must end its romance with 'ends' and 'beginnings'. The co-ordinates between enquiry, the contexts from which it emerges, and its objects of analysis must be understood to be contingent and pragmatic.

There is a notable tendency among writers who have explored anti-foundational themes in social theory to relapse into the kind of global pessimism noted earlier in the chapter. Weber, Horkheimer and Adorno are the most obvious examples. MacIntyre falls into an instructive variant of this syndrome when he reflects on the demands which 'the fate of the times' impose upon the intellectual.

> What matters at this stage is the construction of local forms
> of community within which civility and the intellectual and
> moral life can be sustained through the new dark ages
> which are already upon us. (MacIntyre, 1985: 263)

This formula is both too pessimistic, and not pessimistic enough. It is not pessimistic enough because the figure of a 'new dark ages' is, in the end, a consoling one. 'Dark ages' appear as such in retrospect, from a posterity which considers itself to be illuminated. MacIntyre projects a posterity whose very existence would vindicate the strategy he favours. It is no longer entirely eccentric to imagine a future which admits of no recognisable 'posterity'. The possibly drastic consequences of nuclear conflagration, pollution or climatic change threaten an extinction which is no longer easily dismissed as the hysterical 're-occupation' of answer-positions left vacant by the Book of Revelation.[15] If the possibility of such a future is entertained, MacIntyre's response to the times appears as quite inadequate. But MacIntyre is also too pessimistic in suggesting that only a retreat into enclaves for the preservation of 'civility' is possible for intellectuals. A post-foundational social theory which retains an openness to contingency has the capacity to help cultures to evade worst case outcomes.

MacIntyre's quietist strategy shares two characteristics with foundationalist social theory. First, it shares an over-estimation of the significance of its own concerns in the general scheme of things. For MacIntyre, *the* problem is a moral problem, so *the* solution must be a moral solution. For modernist radicalisms in social theory, the defining pathologies of modernity and the cures for those pathologies are 'social'. This over-estimation, in turn, derives from foundationalist conceptions of the autonomy of social theory as dependent on the autonomy of a social reality. Second, like modernist radicals, MacIntyre smuggles in a guarantee of the effectivity of the solution he proposes (in the implied posterity of the 'dark ages'). However, these claims are increasingly implausible: it is not easy to assimilate what appear to be the major problems facing human individuals and cultures to the classical idea of a 'social problem'.

It is not the least of the advantages of the kind of post-foundational radicalism advocated here that it is not committed to that increasingly problematic view of the autonomy of the social. Its 'orthogonal' enquiries can examine processes of constitution and evaluation taking place across what classical theory would see as the boundaries of social, technical and natural systems.[16] Its 'mundane' enquiries can pragmatically align themselves with lay concerns across those same boundaries. This is very far from saying that a post-foundational radicalism is *the* solution to *the* challenge posed by the fate of the times: such a claim would simply echo the foundationalism it sets out to contest.

Post-foundational radicalism has the capacity to be a part of possible solutions, however. If major problems are not 'purely' social, neither are they 'purely' technical or natural. A social theory which gave up its claims to privilege could trace the movement of social relations in the constitution of natural and technical problems (which is a different matter from asserting that these are 'really' or 'only' social). On this terrain it could re-locate classical social problems of alienation, inequality, violence, and the rest on the boundaries between registers. Most importantly, an outward-looking social theory which is engaged with the critical issues of its day has the capacity to exemplify and, perhaps, to extend the radical demand for the accountability of enquiry, for the maintenance of a reflexive relation to problems of value. To ask social theory to do more than this, or to insist that it provides foundational guarantees of its final success, is to tempt it into a fatal over-extension. Post-foundational radicalism may appear to be thin and timid when compared to the utopianism of modernist radicalism, or the 'dark brilliance' of postmodernism. But it may also be the only form in which the salience of radical social theory can be defended.

NOTES

INTRODUCTION

1 A brief digression on terms may be in order here. 'Social theory' has a broader scope than 'sociology', but it will not be helpful to attempt an over-precise differentiation of the two. Roughly, 'sociology' has a narrow and a broad reference. The narrow reference is to the projected 'sciences' of society pursued by Comte, Durkheim, Simmel and others who applied the term 'sociology' to their work. The broader reference is to what is taught in departments of sociology and published in sociological journals. Many sociologists would find this 'definition' disreputably nominalist, of course, and would prefer rationalised accounts of the legitimate concerns of sociology and its place in the academic division of labour.

'Social theory' can be taken to designate any attempt at systematic reflection on social processes and structures. It comprises work in social and political philosophy, economics, social geography, cultural studies and so forth as well as disciplinary sociology. 'Sociology (narrow)' is a sub-set of 'sociology (broad)', which is a sub-set of 'social theory'. The concerns of this book are probably best understood as falling within 'sociology (broad)'. However, the term 'social theory' is used in the title and throughout in acknowledgement, first, of the past influence of Marxism and, second, of the contemporary influence of 'French theory'. Neither of these falls under 'sociology (narrow)', and although versions of the former are now accommodated in 'sociology (broad)' the position of the latter is ambiguous enough to make the term 'social theory' preferable.

2 The terms 'metaphysics' and 'metaphysical' are used throughout to imply an adverse judgement about a wide range of projects. In the most general sense, to label a project as metaphysical is to suggest that in some important respect it turns on speculative, a priori and

220

tòtalising formulations of its topic. Further, to suggest that Habermas, or Althusser, or the postmodernists, are metaphysicians is also to imply that they work in a discrediting continuity with an historically superseded conception of the tasks of enquiry, that they are anachronistic.

This general and tendentious usage blurs a number of important distinctions, however. While these distinctions are addressed as they arise in the book, a summary version here may be of some use to the reader. The rationalisms of Descartes and Spinoza might be taken to epitomise the modern form of metaphysics. In each case, a priori reflection following rational principles furnishes a systematic knowledge of totality. The critical doctrinal difference is between Descartes's dualism and Spinoza's monism. Of the social theorists considered here, only Althusser's appropriation of Spinoza establishes a direct link with 'metaphysics' in this sense. Two kinds of indirect connection are particularly important, however.

First, the critical metaphysics of Kant is a reference point for both Marxism and sociology. Kant displaces the certainties of dogmatic rationalism in a series of enquiries into the possibility of different spheres of experience and knowledge. Kant 'ends' metaphysics in the way modernist radicalisms 'end' philosophy: what is rational in metaphysics is preserved even as its shell is destroyed. Kantian critique founds metaphysics on 'the possibility of synthetic knowledge a priori' (Kant, 1953: 134).

Habermas's relation to radical social theory closely parallels Kant's relation to metaphysics. He turns from a dogmatic to a procedural radicalism in which the foundations of radical values are entwined with the grounds of the possibility of communication. The metaphysical trace in Habermas is his directly Kantian commitment to a transcendental 'question of right': communication is possible because it activates a 'universal' validity and rationality.

Modernist radicalisms from Marx on are caught in a series of debates with the post-Kantian critical tradition. Their claims to 'end' philosophy often turn on assertions that the antinomies of the critical tradition, such as freedom–necessity or subject–object, have their *real* foundation and resolution on the terrain of 'society', or the 'mode of production'. If the first connection between a dogmatic metaphysics and social theory is one mediated by critical metaphysics, the second connection emerges in critiques of the first. Postmodernist critiques of modernist radicalism can discredit 'end of philosophy' arguments by uncovering a latent antinomical rationalism within them. Althusser is half way to postmodernism, mobilising Spinoza's rationalist monism to contest critical metaphysics. Postmodernisms take the further step into irrationalist monism via nineteenth-century evolutionism and vitalism. The metaphysical trace which they inherit is the speculative assertion that 'everything' is the result of the proliferation of a single principle, perhaps power, or intensity, or discourse. The world becomes a purely quantitative phenomenon, in which the qualitative distinctions of the critical tradition have no place.

To sum up, the term 'metaphysics' is used with reference to dogmatic rationalisms, to critical rationalisms and to irrationalist monisms in philosophy. Its use is extended to their avatars in social theory. While there are important boundaries to be drawn on the very broad terrain of metaphysics thus defined, there are important continuities and traces which cross boundaries and warrant a broad usage.

1 THE IDEA OF MODERNIST RADICALISM

1 'Project' is used here in preference to alternatives such as 'theory' or 'perspective' or 'paradigm'. Its use emphasises that two aspects of the fields which the term designates are particularly important for the argument. These aspects might usefully be contrasted with models in which 'theories', or what you will, are understood as static arrays of concepts, or propositions, linked by logical relations and subsisting in an insulated and rarefied 'logical space'. First, projects are interventions in the world, strategic processes which aim to 'make a difference', they are dynamic rather than static. Second, projects range between different theoretical and practical 'registers' or 'realities'.

2 Sherover-Marcuse (1986: ch. 1) offers a view of Marx's debt to Jacobin themes in his very early work. The classic account of *Capital* as an Hegelian re-working of political economy is provided by Rosdolsky (1977).

3 Useful discussions of Durkheim's entrepreneurial activities within the *république des professeurs* can be found in Besnard (1982), Clarke (1972) and Richter (1960). Lukes provides pithy accounts of Durkheim's relation to Comte (1973: ch. 3) and to Renouvier (ibid.: 2). Lepenies (1988: ch. 2) discusses the controversies surrounding the Durkheimian influence in the 'new Sorbonne'.

4 The 'melting vision' portrays the 'vital powers' of the modern world as 'dazzling, overwhelming', but also as 'swinging wildly out of control, menacing and destroying blindly' (Berman, 1982: 101). This contrasts with a 'stable vision' of the 'sober scenes' of bourgeois society. The links which Berman makes between Marx and aesthetic modernism are enormously suggestive, but it is not this vision or those connections which constitute Marx's project as a modernist radicalism.

5 Foundationalism is discussed in chapter six. Margolis's definition (1986: 38) of foundationalism as 'the belief that we possess a privileged basis for cognitive certainty' outlines the problem area.

6 There is some dispute about where the term originated. Knox, Hegel's translator, cites a claim that Ferguson's *An Essay on the History of Civil Society* influenced Hegel's usage, but points out that the term was commonplace in England from the seventeenth century (Hegel, 1952: x).

7 This is the title which the piece traditionally goes under, and it is retained here although in the edition of the text cited it is referred to as *Critique of Hegel's Doctrine of the State*.

8 The typology of institutions takes up the third part of *The Philosophy of Right*, which makes it clear that they are to be considered as forms

of the 'Ethical Life'. Earlier parts have discussed 'Abstract Right' and 'Morality'. It is important to emphasise that the three terms designate quite complex arrays of institutions in Hegel's argument – they are not just simple tokens for a principle. The section on civil society covers the division of labour, class division, law and justice, and those institutions which Hegel refers to as 'police' and 'corporation'.

9 The heart of the critique, which is drawn on here, lies in Marx's discussion of Hegel's concept of 'mediation' (Marx, 1975b: 150–5). There are marked continuities between this early critique of Hegel's method and later passages from *Grundrisse* (Marx, 1973: 100–8) where the critique of Hegel is linked to that of political economy.

10 Calvert (1982: 45) provides a basic picture of the medieval 'estates'.

> The legally established divisions between the nobles, the clergy and the rest of the citizens were formalized into categories known as 'estates'. Each was regarded as a necessary part of the social whole [and] ... each estate, accordingly, had a proportionate role in the legal business of government.

The category 'the rest of the citizens' does not comprise the entire population, of course.

11 So, Marx makes fun of the obscurities of Hegel's doctrine by contrasting it with the good sense of the 'common man' (Marx, 1975b: 82).

12 This is not to claim that the version of the project considered here is 'the same' as that of Marx's later work. A case can be made for reading Marx's early texts 'in their own right', without the benefit of hindsight. One of the strengths of Sherover-Marcuse (1986) is that she attempts such a reading, whereas many accounts are locked into the game of 'hunt the real Marx' (notoriously, Althusser, 1977a, but also Colletti's 'Introduction' in Marx, 1975a).

13 Coser (1960) and Nisbet (1967) made the 'conservatism' argument into something of an orthodoxy, although Nisbet's view is quite nuanced, allowing Durkheim a 'political' liberalism (Nisbet, 1967: 13). It found a ready echo among left-wing critics of Durkheim such as Zeitlin (1968) and Bauman (1976). Zeitlin's account is particularly forceful: 'Taken as a whole, Durkheim's system bears an overwhelmingly conservative bias' (Zeitlin, 1968: 235).

Richter (1960) is a strong advocate of the 'liberalism' argument, which is taken up by Lukes (1969) and Prager (1981). Giddens, too, is a supporter: 'Durkheim's sociology was rooted in an attempt to reinterpret the claims of political liberalism in the face of a twin challenge: from an anti-rationalist conservatism on the one hand, and from socialism on the other' (Giddens, 1977: 271). Fenton (1984, ch. 1) offers a recent strong statement of the view that Durkheim's substantive social and political views are 'radical'.

14 For Lukes (1973: 227) 'it was precisely in its treatment of the nature of social phenomena that The Rules was least probing and decisive', while for Giddens the idea of 'externality' is ambiguous, or even nonsensical (Giddens, 1977: 249). If the twin criteria of externality

NOTES

and constraint are considered from the standpoint of Durkheim's theory of ideology they appear less odd.

15 On this view, it is a mistake of some consequence to attribute to Durkheim 'a crude empiricist stance ... according to which the natural and social worlds can be described in a theory-free observation language as immediately available to the senses' (Giddens, 1977: 292). Similar difficulties confront Hirst's important attempt to read *The Rules* as an exercise in 'sensationalist' epistemology (see Hirst, 1975: 104).

The argument also casts some doubt on a popular view espoused by Larrain, according to which in *The Rules* 'the social origin of ideology itself is disregarded', so that it is 'an obstacle to science but not an object to science' (Larrain, 1979: 92 and 96). Hirst is also complicit in this view: 'Ideology is unreal. It is suspended unreality which is never anchored in the real itself' (Hirst, 1975: 89).

16 Durkheim explicitly links his discussion of this issue to the Baconian doctrine of *praenotiones*, the pre-scientific ideas from which science emerges (Durkheim, 1964a: 17). The connection is discussed by Bauman (1976: 2), Benton (1977: 95) and Larrain (1979: 92).

17 Spencer falls victim to the illusion that social development represents 'an "innate tendency towards progress" – a metaphysical entity of the very existence of which there is no demonstration' (Durkheim, 1964a: 109). The critique of Spencer illustrates the close connection Durkheim draws between methodological individualism, teleology and ideology.

18 Kant understands empirical knowledge as a work of 'synthesis' in which concepts are applied to intuitions under the principle of the unity of consciousness. A particularly important species of concept are the 'pure concepts of the understanding', or 'categories'. These concepts serve to define a priori the basic characteristics of an object of knowledge. The categories correspond to basic forms of judgement, and both the forms of judgement and the categories fall under four heads (quantity, quality, relation, modality) with three variants under each. It becomes a moot point in the neo-Kantian tradition whether the table of categories can be established a priori for all knowledge. Durkheim argues that the categories must be seen as having a social origin. La Capra (1972) is as clear as may be on Durkheim's neo-Kantian theory of knowledge.

19 Strawbridge (1982: 127) argues that the equation is abandoned, so that in Durkheim's late work 'there is a relatively autonomous level of collective representational life which, while in part manifest in images and concepts, is not reducible to consciousness'. Larrain is a little closer to the mark, arguing that ideology becomes 'a natural bent in the mind of society' (Larrain, 1979: 97).

20 Egoism is a deficiency of social integration, while anomie is a deficiency of regulation. Johnson (1965) argues that the two pathologies are effectively identical in *Suicide*, while Meštrović (1987: 570) makes an interesting case that lack of regulation (*dérèglement*) should be read as a species of 'derangement'.

224

21 Lepenies (1988: 70) argues that critics of Durkheim, sociology and the new Sorbonne', such as Péguy, saw their disputations as a new form of the *Querelle des Anciens et des Modernes*.

22 The centrality of the theme of morality in Durkheim is widely acknowledged: 'from beginning to end, morality constituted the center of Durkheim's thought' (La Capra, 1972: 288). For Lepenies (1988: 62), 'Durkheim's sociology counted not least as a moral science'. This centrality must be maintained against arguments, such as that advanced by Stedman-Jones (1980), that Durkheim takes up only the Kantian concern with science, and not that with morality.

23 See e.g. Durkheim (1974: 93), (1976: 16 and 466), (1960: 337).

24 This view has a natural affinity with those accounts of Durkheim which stress his increasing emphasis on the 'internalisation' of norms and values. Parsons (1968, ch. X) correctly maintains that obligation and respect continue to temper the voluntary character of moral conduct, but perhaps he sails a little too close to the idea that they can be wholly internalised. His (1960) and Coser (1960) also come close to this view.

25 In the formula of Elementary Forms:

> Man is double. There are two beings in him: an individual being which has its foundations in the organism ... and a social being which represents the highest reality in the intellectual and moral order that we can know by observation. (Durkheim, 1976: 16)

This doctrine does not in itself explain why the 'highest reality' must be social, however.

26 Durkheim's best-known defence of 'individualism' makes it clear that his concern is with 'the individualism of Kant and Rousseau, that of the *spiritualistes*' and that these authorities 'are no less sensitive to the rights of the collectivity than they are to those of the individual' (Durkheim, 1969: 20 and 22). Far from being evidence of conservatism, this emphasis on the collectivity is the direct descendant of Enlightenment conceptions of a morality which binds even sovereignty.

27 At least four versions can be differentiated. First, sociology must free itself of philosophy (see Durkheim, 1964a: 141). Second, sociology must provide materials for philosophical reflection (ibid.: 142). Third, sociology can re-formulate, and answer, philosophical problems (see Durkheim 1976: 13 and 1982a: 237). Finally, sociology can synthesise philosophical doctrines (see Durkheim, 1976: 15).

28 Durkheim's objections to socialism draw on the ideology/science division. There can be no 'scientific socialism' since socialism is oriented to the future (Durkheim, 1958: 6). Socialism is a social fact, and therefore an object of science (ibid.: 8). Science can only move 'slowly and laboriously' towards goals which 'emotional and zealous beings' attempt to reach instantly (ibid.: 239).

NOTES

2 THE SOCIOLOGICAL CRITIQUE OF MODERNIST RADICALISM

1 The 'generational' argument is mobilised in *The Structure of Social Action*. The 'Preface' to the paperback edition identifies the work of the generation of Durkheim and Weber as 'a major *movement* in the structure of theoretical thinking' (Parsons, 1968: viii).

2 Frisby (1981: 62) takes this nuance as decisive evidence that Simmel is not the author of a 'neo-Kantian formalism'. However, Simmel continues to take his bearings from contemporary neo-Kantian debates. He offers a version of the distinction between the historical and natural sciences, which are 'two different categories for the analysis of the homogeneous manifold of reality' (Simmel, 1977: 171). This is both more 'formal' and more 'Kantian' than its neo-Kantian alternatives.

3 Simmel considers the possibility that 'an enquiry into the conditions of the process of sociation' would be 'the epistemology of society' (Simmel, 1959b: 341, 342).

4 Simmel outlines a general 'philosophy' of form in 'The Nature of Philosophy' (Simmel 1959c). Weingartner (1959, 1960) offers a systematic account. The key distinction is between 'world forms' (such as art, or religion) which can transform a 'manifold' of contents into an entire world, and more limited forms. Simmel also distinguishes between the 'ideal' of form and its 'partial' historical realisations. Frisby (1981: 63) may be correct to insist that Simmel did not aim for an 'abstract classification' of social forms, but he did have a relatively systematic view of the relations between 'levels' of form.

5 Durkheim (1982b) quotes from essays which appeared in the Durkheimian *Année sociologique* and the neo-Kantian *Revue de métaphysique et de morale*.

6 Rose (1978: ch. 3) offers a useful summary of the 'reification' theme and of Simmel's relation to it.

7 The section of *The Philosophy of Money* which looks as if it will come closest to materialism is that on 'The division of labour as the cause of the divergence of objective and subjective culture' (Simmel, 1978: 453). Even here, however, Simmel turns out to be concerned with issues such as the 'spiritual determinacy' of labour.

8 Ollman (1976: part 2) extracts a systematic theory of 'human nature' from Marx's alienation theme. On the issues of the 'unity of theory and practice' and 'the end of philosophy', the theoretical identification of human 'essence' can inform a practice which will realise the potential of that essence, and thereby redeem the promise which philosophy can only make in the abstract.

9 The text is not without its difficulties. As Oakes (1977) points out, it is not always clear precisely which philosophical doctrine Simmel is arguing against. Again, Simmel often appears to understand 'historical materialism' in an oddly psychologistic way as a theory of motivation (see Simmel, 1977:185–6).

10 On this point, at least, there is a marked convergence between

Simmel and Althusser's gnomic reflections on knowledge (Althusser and Balibar, 1970: 35–68).

11 So, Frisby's reading of 'the total meaning of the world as a whole', quoted above is contentious. Frisby himself (1985: 57) quotes it in context. When aesthetic pre-occupations are pursued to their limit, a world-view of 'aesthetic pantheism' emerges. *Within* this view, 'Every point conceals the possibility of being released into absolute aesthetic significance. To the adequately trained eye, the *total* beauty, the *total* meaning of the world as a whole radiates from every single point'. Simmel is not discussing his own method here.

12 Again, Weingartner (1959, 1960) is a useful guide through the complexities.

13 Weber uses the expression 'the peculiar modern western form of capitalism' in the introduction to *The Protestant Ethic* (1976: 24), and the simpler 'western capitalism' throughout the text.

14 An obvious case in point would be Cutler *et al.* (1977), with its re-discovery of the concept of 'conditions of existence'.

15 The text is interpreted in this way by Collins (1986: ch. 2), for example.

16 This is quite a complex matter, related to the doctrine of 'value relevance'. See, particularly, the discussion of the place of cultural significance and causal efficacy on pages 72-3.

17 Roughly lined up with 'Weber the ethically neutral' and/or 'Weber the liberal' are Parsons (1971), Bendix (1960), Beetham (1974) and Roth and Schluchter (1979), among others. The opposition includes Aron (1971), Habermas (1971b), Giddens (1972) and Turner and Factor (1984), in addition to Mommsen.

18 It may be that the ideal-type of the 'ethic of ultimate ends' has some empirical exemplars which it can illuminate. As a tool for the analysis of modern political ideology and practice it seems quite inappropriate, however. 'Revolutionary syndicalists' may take the view that the (very) long-term consequences of action are more important than immediate consequences, but it is unhelpful to gloss this as an utter indifference to all consequences.

19 Rose places both Weber and Durkheim in relation to this tradition: Durkheim gives priority to validity over values, while Weber gives priority to values over validity. In paradoxical consequence, Durkheim generates an empirical sociology of values, while Weber generates an empirical sociology of validities ('legitimacy') (Rose, 1981: 21).

20 See Brubaker (1984: 62–82) for a discussion of 'orientations' and 'spheres'.

21 For Rickert, value relevance is the key to the distinction between the sciences of nature and of culture. 'The presence or absence of *relevance to values* can ... serve as a reliable criterion for distinguishing between two kinds of scientific *objects*' (Rickert, 1962: 19).

22 Habermas claims that Weber mobilises the doctrine of value-freedom 'to restrict the social sciences to a cognitive interest, valid for the production of knowledge which can be utilized technically' (Habermas,

1971b: 63). For Habermas, communicative and emancipatory 'interests' must also be admitted.

23 Of course, Weber has no resources with which to construe the distinction as problematic. One such resource might be Austin's concept of the 'illocutionary force' of utterances. Searle (1967) argues that the logic of 'performatives' challenges an absolute fact–value distinction.

24 Gouldner's 'Anti-Minatour: the Myth of a Value-Free Sociology' (Gouldner, 1973) reviews and re-works this critique.

25 Dawe (1971), Farganis (1975) and Bauman (1976) offer other examples of the genre. Corrigan (1975) and Benton (1978) offer stern denunciations of such 'dualisms'.

26 Habermas (1971a: ch. 5 and 1971b) offers a critique of Weber's 'decisionism' which Schluchter's 'Value Neutrality and the Ethic of Responsibility' (in Roth and Schluchter, 1979) attempts to refute. Turner and Factor (1984: 47–50) review the argument.

3 THE AUTO-CRITIQUE OF MODERNIST RADICALISM

1 The term designates the group of philosophers, aestheticians and social scientists associated with the Institute for Social Research, officially opened at the University of Frankfurt in 1923 under the directorship of Karl Grünberg. The version of 'critical theory' which is identified with the Institute developed in the period after Max Horkheimer became director in 1931. The Institute was closed down by the Nazis in 1933, and its members and associates went into exile, many to the United States. The Institute's journal, the *Zeitschrift für Sozialforshung* (later *Studies in Philosophy and Social Sciences*), continued publication until 1944. The Institute re-opened in Frankfurt in 1951, and shaped the concerns of a later generation of radicals, most notably Jürgen Habermas. The members of the Institute most closely concerned with the development of the idea of a critical theory which was neither traditional philosophy nor straightforward social science were Theodore Adorno, Max Horkheimer and Herbert Marcuse. An authoritative intellectual history of the Institute up until its return to Germany is provided by Jay (1973).

2 Accordingly, Marcuse (1969) first saw Heidegger's ontology as a 'foundation' for a critical theory, then turned to the Hegelian foundations of Marxism (1977), went through a prolonged phase of 'Freudo-Marxism' (1966), and finally turned to an aesthetics which owed a lot to his very early encounters with Schelling (1979). See Katz (1982) for a serviceable biography.

3 Views on the precise nature of Horkheimer's political trajectory vary. Kellner (1975: 133), for example, maintains that Horkheimer was advancing a Marxist programme throughout the 1930s. Howard (1977: 91) sees the 1942 'Authoritarian State' essay as the 'dizzying zenith of Horkheimer's revolutionary zeal'. On the other side of the fence, Connerton (1980: 36–41) is among those who doubt whether Horkheimer could ever have been considered a Marxist. Part of the

difficulty is Horkheimer's tendency to refer to Marxism, and to specific Marxist theories, in an eliptical and indirect way ('the new constellation of the problem', 'the theory which we regard as correct', and so forth). In any case, by the late 1960s he had reached the view that the distinction between left and right in politics was 'an already outdated bourgeois antithesis', not corresponding to the crucial division between 'respect for and contempt for life' (Horkheimer, 1978a: 230).

4 The choice of these 'aspects' is not random. They correspond to what will be referred to in chapter six as the four 'modes' in which the putative 'foundations' of theoretical projects can be claimed to operate.

5 Wittgenstein's *Tractatus Logico-Philosophicus* had appeared in 1921, and Carnap's *Logical Structure of the World* in 1928. Adorno's 'Inaugural Lecture' (1977b) indicates a rather less dismissive assessment.

6 Thus, in formal logic, the form of the general proposition '$[(x) \phi x]$' is rendered in the hypothetical form '*given any* x in the universe, ϕx'. Only singular propositions make existential claims, '$[(\exists x) \phi x]$' translanting as 'there is at least one x in the universe such that it is ϕx (see Copi, 1967: ch. 4).

7 Van den Berg, writing of critical theory in general, notes an ambivalence between an insistence that a 'higher truth' is available, and a reluctance to reveal what it is. He claims that 'Critical Theory would be doomed by this ambivalence' (van den Berg, 1981: 452). Horkheimer's version of the ambivalence fell increasingly under theological influences (see Jay, 1973: 56 and Held, 1980: 198).

8 The paper was published in 1936, two years before Marcuse's 'On Hedonism' (translated in Marcuse 1968). Marcuse has no patent on hedonistic themes within critical theory.

9 Many commentators see this reluctance to 'ground' critical theory as a major flaw. For orthodox Marxist critics, such as Slater (1976: 63) and Therborn (1977: 73), a return to the grounding of 'class struggle' is required. More interestingly, phenomenologically inclined critics have urged an anchoring of critical theory in the *Lebenswelt* (see Piccone, 1977: 138, Reid, 1977: 113 or Rovatti, 1973: 37). For the purposes of the present argument, any such move would be a retreat into a frank foundationalism.

10 The figure of the 'negation of the negative' is not as minimalist as it may appear. Its force depends on the suspect concept of 'immanence': the negative must be the repression of an immanent value which the 'negation of the negative' can indirectly assert.

11 Jay (1984a: 15–23) identifies five 'primary points of light and energy' in Adorno's 'constellation': Marxism, aesthetic modernism, cultural conservatism, a 'Jewish impulse' and 'deconstructionism'. It is at least arguable that classical and contemporary philosophy, Freudian psychology and varieties of 'bourgeois' social science should be included in lists of this kind.

12 Dews (1987: 39) puts it nicely: 'For Adorno the subject is always a

NOTES

"piece of the world", it is something, despite its transcendent moment, whereas the object is not by the same token a subject'.

13 See, for example, Friedman (1981: 62), Jay (1984a: 22), Held (1980: 208). Rose (1978: 16–26) provides an excellent survey of the relationship.

14 Adorno writes that he had 'conceived the *Jargon of Authenticity* as part of the *Negative Dialectic*', but excluded it because of size and differences of style (Adorno, 1973b: xix).

15 As Piccone (1978: xix), for example, has suggested, Adorno's meta-analytic sophistication is not always incompatible with orthodoxy: 'large chunks of traditional Marxist doctrine resurface wholly un-affected by the *aqua regia* of critical theory'.

16 As lucid and brief account as may be of the doctrine of the 'thrown-ness' of human 'Being-there' in the world is provided by Steiner (1978: 80–9).

17 Within the Frankfurt tradition, Marcuse's position on art was the furthest from Adorno's. During his 'left-Freudian' period, notably in *Eros and Civilization*, Marcuse held an 'end of art' position, according to which the need for art would disappear with the abolition of social and psychic repression. Towards the end of his life he moderated this view, but took a far more 'affirmative' view of art than did Adorno. The final paragraph of Marcuse's *The Aesthetic Dimension* gives a twist to a motto from Adorno and Horkheimer (1979): '"All reification is a forgetting". Art fights reification by making the petrified world speak, sing, perhaps dance' (Marcuse, 1979: 73). Adorno was not a dancer.

18 Buck-Morss (1977: 157) and Rose (1978: 41) both cite the passage, but do not relate it to the problems of the Wagner project. The danger of 'positivism' comes from the empiricism of the 'trace', that of 'magic' from Benjamin's near-theological conception of naming, and also from his use of the concepts of 'dream' and 'dream-world'.

19 The *Leitmotiv* is a brief musical figure which identifies a character (or other element) in a music-drama. Much of the music in *The Ring* con-sists of sequences, combinations and variations of such figures.

20 Adorno is prepared to recognise certain 'progressive' tendencies in Wagnerian technique. Given Adorno's estimation of Schönberg, it is unsurprising that his interest focuses on those passages in *Parsifal* and *Tristan and Isolde* where otherwise 'regressive' tendencies lead Wagner to the brink of atonality.

21 As Popper complained, with some justice, no 'positivists' (in the strict sense) were involved in the dispute (Popper, 1976: 288–91). He ascribes what he sees as a frank error to a mistaken view of his own relations with the Vienna circle. This is rather implausible. There is no reason to assume that Adorno was ignorant of the nuances of Popper's position. His argument is that Popper's critique of positivism converges with positivism in crucial respects (see the reflections on 'refutation' and 'criticism' in, e.g., Adorno, 1976c: 112–13).

22 The 'Inaugural Lecture' (1977b) is less hostile to logical empiricism, and cites earlier empiricists, notably Bacon, with approval.

4 THE SWANSONG OF MODERNIST RADICALISM?

1 On the 'interests' see the appendix to Habermas 1972; on *techne* and praxis see Habermas, 1971a: ch. 4 and Habermas, 1974a: introduction, ch. 1 and ch. 7; on labour and interaction see Habermas, 1974a: ch. 4; on the types of communication see Habermas, 1979: ch. 1; and on strategic and communicative action see Habermas, 1984: ch. III.

2 The new English translation of *Strukturwandel der Öffentlichkeit* (Habermas, 1989) appeared too late to be used here. Habermas 1974b summarises the argument. Figure 1 is taken from the French translation (Habermas, 1978: 41).

3 So, the 'decisionistic' model eleborated by Weber and Schumpeter 'reduces the process of democratic decision-making to a regulated acclamation procedure for elites' (Habermas, 1971a: 68). The widely-drawn 'technocratic' model offers a vision of a 'scientized politics' in which 'the reduction of political power to rational administration can be conceived ... only at the expense of democracy itself' (ibid.).

4 In connection with the critique of positivistic theories of science, see Habermas's contributions to Adorno *et al.* 1976. For an early statement of the theory of 'communicative competence' see Habermas 1970.

5 The assumption that the typology of interests is prior to the typology of communication is adopted here as an heuristic device, but it is misleading as a claim about Habermas's trajectory. For much of the 1960s and early 1970s Habermas was working on the two schemes in tandem.

6 This scheme can be extracted from the appendix to Habermas 1972, which dates from 1965.

7 See, for example, Dallmayr 1972, Lenhardt 1972 and Lobkowicz 1972. Useful and sympathetic critiques which enjoy the benefit of some hindsight include Held, 1980: ch. 11 and McCarthy, 1978: ch. 2.5.

8 The idea of such a re-formulation has exerted a strong appeal to Bleicher 1982, Ricoeur 1981 and Thompson 1982, for example. Outhwaite 1987 is also drawn to a version of this view.

9 Notably because he claims (in Habermas, 1974a: ch. 4 and elsewhere) that 'work' and 'interaction' are the two (and only two) fundamental principles of social development.

10 McCarthy (1978: 94–5) insists on the distinction between 'self-reflection' as the critique of knowledge and as the critique of ideology. Bernstein (1976: 198) captures Habermas's dilemma nicely, suggesting that the emancipatory interest must be 'at once derivative and the most basic constituting interest'.

11 Habermas, 1979: 68. The 'modes of communication' also align with different standard-form speech-acts: cognitive with constatives, interactive with regulatives and expressive with avowals (Habermas, 1979: 58).

12 See Habermas 1979 on moral development (ch. 2), on the evolution of normative structures (ch. 3) and on relations with historical materialism (ch. 4).

13 Habermas's account of Freud is controversial in its own right. See Keat's (1981: ch. 4) 'realist' critique, for example. The difficulties of transferring the psychoanalytic model to problems of social emancipation are discussed in Dallmayr 1972 and McCarthy, 1978: ch. 3.4.

14 Bubner 1982 offers a strong version of this critique, accusing Habermas of sophistry. See also McCarthy 1982 and Posner 1976. Lyotard's rather generalised 1984a critique of Habermas turns on a similar point about the 'homogenisation' of language. Jay shows how this line of criticism can subvert Habermas's rationalism, asking rhetorically 'what if language is not seen as the antidote to nature and man's embeddedness in it, but rather at least in part as an expression of man's irrational "naturalness" itself' (Jay, 1984b: 508).

15 Slightly simplified from Habermas, 1984: 285.

16 Habermas's 'system versus lifeworld' and 'system versus social integration' arguments receive an earlier formulation in his 1976: ch. 1.

17 Habermas remains ambiguous about the 'interests' model. Habermas, 1987b: 326 still refers to the 'inner logics of cognitive–instrumental, moral–practical and aesthetic–expressive complexes of knowledge'. Only the dignity accorded to aesthetics is new. Habermas (1982: 233) argues that the attempt to ground social theory in a theory of knowledge 'did not lead astray' although it was a 'roundabout way'.

18 The same might be said of the attempt to differentiate 'discourse' and 'critique' as forms of argumentation on the basis of participants' 'presuppositions' about whether the Ideal Speech Situation is or is not approximated (see Habermas, 1984: 42).

19 Passmore offers a concise summary of Austin's distinctions. Austin 'distinguishes between three sorts of sentence-using act; the "locutionary" act of using a sentence to express a meaning, as when somebody *tells us* that George is coming, the "illocutionary" act of using an utterance with a certain "force", as when someone *warns* us that George is coming, and the "perlocutionary" act of producing a certain effect by the use of the sentence, as when someone, without actually telling us that George is coming, *succeeds in warning us* that he is on his way' (Passmore, 1966: 456).

20 Habermas seems to regard the issue as unimportant, remarking that 'speech acts … can produce side effects that the actor did not forsee; these are perlocutionary effects in a trivial sense, which I shall not consider any further' (Habermas, 1984: 289). He goes on to relate interesting and serious perlocutions to the strategic 'orientation' of an actor.

21 Such studies can be related back to Garfinkel's well-known accounts of 'psychological autopsies', jurors' decisions, clinical record-keeping and the like (see Garfinkel, 1967: chs 1, 4, 6). More recent (and more specialised) studies include Pomerantz's analysis of 'agreeing and disagreeing with assessments' and other papers collected in Atkinson and Heritage 1984. Pollner (1987) offers a challenging restatement of the ethnomethodological orientation to 'practical reasoning'.

22 Putting to one side the question of whether there is still a place for a 'critique' which is formally differentiated from reconstruction.

23 Habermas does, indeed, want to insist that the two are distinct: reconstructions are not to be re-capitulations of the philosophy of history. See, e.g., Habermas, 1987a: 300 and 1987b: 383.

24 Outhwaite (1987: 86–7) makes a similar case, drawing on Quine's critique of Chomsky. According to Quine, Chomsky's 'reconstructive' depth grammar must pre-suppose that two 'extensionally equivalent' systems of grammatical rules cannot both be correct: one must be 'unconsciously preferred' by speakers.

25 Specifically, Habermas wants to avoid what he sees as the mystical quest for a 'resurrection of fallen nature' and a form of reconciliation with nature which requires an entirely different scientific method. See Habermas, 1971a: 85–6.

5 THE POSTMODERNIST 'END' OF MODERNIST RADICALISM

1 The episode of the Parisian 'New Philosophers' in 1977–8 played a role here. The brief notoriety which surrounded re-born rightists such as André Glucksmann and Bernard-Henri Lévy helped to focus the attention of leftist intellectuals on the political ambivalence of 'French Theory'. See Dews (1980) for a useful review and exemplary reaction.

2 Adorno's persistent opposition to subjectivism and his suspicion of the integrating power of language can be read retrospectively as 'prefiguring' many postmodernist themes, for example. Again, Weber's 'ironisation' of history has more in common with Foucault's project than the latter generally acknowledged. In many respects Nietzsche is the subterranean connection between historically and politically diverse critiques of modernist radicalism. Among recent commentaries, Dews (1987) offers the best discussion of these continuities and discontinuities. For useful collections of essays which attempt to assess postmodern theory, see Boyne and Rattansi (1990) and the two special issues of *Theory, Culture and Society*: 2.3 (1985) and 5.2/3 (1988).

3 Of course, two rather different senses of 'metaphysics' are at issue here. Many modernist radicalisms turn on a post-Kantian 'critical metaphysics' of the 'constitution' of objects of analysis and experience which has already displaced dogmatic rationalism. The antinomies, or dualisms, of critical philosophy are then transformed into the defining problems of social theory (agency and structure, etc.). Postmodernisms are on a different route away from dogmatic rationalism, a route which first offers a monistic critique of dualism and then shifts from rationalist to irrationalist monism. On this basis, assertions of the 'givenness' of matter, or intensity, or discourse can be mobilised in a monistic critique against modernist radical doctrines of 'constitution'.

4 On the questions of class and politics, Therborn (1978) and Poulantzas (1978) represent both the high-points and turning points

of Althusserian influence. Hall and Jefferson (1976) and Hall *et al.* (1980) testify to the centrality of Althusserian themes to the concerns of British cultural studies.

5 Althusser frequently alludes to this context. See, e.g., his (1977a: 10, 1971: 15 and 1976: 167–8).

6 Standing to the left of the PCF, Rancière is deeply suspicious of Althusser's position on these matters, complaining that he 'annexes to communist orthodoxy theses which are the inheritance of *gauchisme*' (Rancière, 1974: 182).

7 Kelly (1982: 184) places the beginning of the 'self-criticism' in a series of 1967 lectures to science students. The preface to the Italian edition of *Reading Capital* also begins a critique of 'theoreticism'. 'Philosophy as a Revolutionary Weapon' and 'Lenin and Philosophy' (in Althusser, 1971a), both dating from early in 1968, set out the elements of the new position on politics, science and philosophy.

8 Althusser (1977a: 168) proposed to differentiate between theory ('any theoretical practice of a scientific character'), 'theory' ('the determinate theoretical system of a real science') and Theory ('the Theory of practice in general'). Perhaps it is no wonder that he changed his mind.

9 Althusser has been variously categorised as a Platonist, a Spinozist, a Kantian, a positivist and a structuralist.

10 Patton (1978) comes closest to identifying the extent of Althusser's Spinozism, but slips up in regarding the Althusserian notion of knowledge as a 'production' as non-Spinozist. The author's D.Phil thesis (Crook, 1984: pt 3) offers an extended version of the argument here.

11 The majority of references to the *Ethics* cite Spinoza's own detailed architechtonic of parts, propositions, corollaries, and so on.

12 This model, from 'On the Materialist Dialectic' (in Althusser, 1977a), might be said to be 'overdetermined' by the 'kinds of knowledge' and Marx's model of the labour process.

13 Kolakowski (1971: 128) argues that the KO/RO distinction in Althusser contradicts Spinoza's monism. Kolakowski seems to be confusing logical and ontological difference.

14 This position is taken by Patton (1978: 12).

15 This point helps to explain the oddity of Althusser's apparently complete identification of 'science' with 'truth'. There is no space in Althusser's system for the idea that scientific theories may be disproved.

16 As Brown and Cousins (1980: 269) put it, Foucault 'can dispense with both humanist and anti-humanist conceptions of the subject because he is not concerned to support either a general concept of the human or the social'.

17 Lyotard's position in this company requires some explanation. His work during the 1970s could be easily assimilated to a monism of 'intensity' in the manner of Deleuze. The later text which is the focus of attention here is rather different, marking a shift away from physi-

calism. A recent interview (van Reijen and Veerman, 1988) expands on the implications of that shift. The argument here will be that Lyotard's position in *The Postmodern Condition* does not evade all the problems of monism, and that Lyotard's attempts to do so require a retreat to modernism.

18 A number of attempts to 'save' the concept split it in two. Butler (1980: ix) distinguishes between a 'rule-dominated' and an 'irrationalist, indeterminate or aleatory' postmodernism, while Foster (1983: xii) separates a 'postmodernism of resistance' and a 'postmodernism of reaction'. Huyssen (1984) places a similar 'radical/reactionary' split in the context of a useful chronology of postmodernism in the USA.

19 In the more widely cited Jameson (1984), which articulates the idea of postmodernism as a 'cultural dominant', the four constitutive features are given rather differently as a new depthlessness, a weakening of historicity, a return to theories of the sublime, and a relation between cultural, technical and social change at the global level. The differences between the two versions highlight the difficulty of Jameson's task.

20 As opposed to a 'merely reflective' judgement in which only the particular is 'given' (Kant, 1952: 18). Lyotard's distinction between modern and postmodern approaches to sublimity is close to that which Kant (ibid.: 94) makes between the 'mathematically' and 'dynamically' sublime. The former exercises the faculty of cognition, the latter that of desire. Lyotard makes no reference to the distinction, however.

21 The term 'object = x' is used by Kant to refer to the noumenal 'thing in itself' which is a condition of phenomenal knowledge, but which cannot be known 'in itself'. For a more sympathetic account of Baudrillard's 'anti-theory' which reads it as 'a tracing out of the Nietzschean regression in Marx' see Kroker (1985: 69).

22 In this, the position of discourse theory comes very close to the 'decisionistic' elements of the Weberian doctrine of value relevance.

23 Lyotard's equation of 'game' with *agon*, or contest, itself pre-empts the specificity of other types of 'game' (games as play, games of chance, games as ritual, etc.). It certainly sits uneasily with his Wittgensteinian references to 'language games'.

24 The main texts are Habermas 1981, 1985b and 1987a.

25 Habermas (1985b) is rather more nuanced, suggesting that the 'neoconservative' conjunction of a rejection of cultural modernism and an endorsement of capitalist modernisation (as in Bell, 1976) encourages the 'return to Nietzsche' among the young conservatives.

26 Such insights would include the comparison between Nietzsche and Adorno and Horkheimer (Habermas, 1987a: ch.5), the reflections on Derrida's treatment of philosophy and literature (ibid.: 209) and the reading of Foucault as combining transcendentalism and empiricism (ibid.: 274).

6 FOUNDATIONALISM AND RADICALISM

1 The two other, non-foundationalist, justifications for 'indirectly evident' propositions identified by Chisholm are 'by certain relations that they bear to *each other*' and 'by their own nature, so to speak' (Chisholm, 1977: 63).

2 See the discussion of the idea of 'reconstruction' in chapter 4.3(b) and of Habermas's version of the 'end of philosophy' in 4.3(c).

3 The gap in the quotation excises one parenthetical exception to this rule: 'it must be admitted that *some* mathematicians, for example, have been led to wonder whether anything within their discipline could rightly be called knowledge' (Hamlyn, 1970: 11).

4 Rorty generally capitalises 'Philosophy' to indicate the pretentions of its practitioners, and Woolgar (1988: 107) capitalises 'SCIENCE' to denote the 'mythic, idealist' connotations of some usages. In what follows 'KNOWLEDGE' is capitalised where allegedly 'founded', and therefore privileged knowledges are at issue.

5 Advocates of so-called 'new' realism are particularly prone to sceptical nightmares, witness the hysterical title of Trigg's (1980) *Reality at Risk*. A sustained refutation of this metaphysical regression is long overdue, but cannot be provided here. From the point of view of the present argument, 'new' realism is just another series of a priori attempts to privilege particular knowledges (often Marxist-ish knowledges) as KNOWLEDGE.

6 Derrida sees 'supplementarity' as ineradicable in writing. Writing-as-supplement presents itself as both 'in addition to' and 'in place of' its topic. For a useful account of Derrida on writing, which places him in relation to Nietzsche, Heidegger and Freud, see Spivak's 'Preface' to Derrida 1976.

7 The same suspicion surrounds Durkheim's *Rules*, where the opening pages seem to pre-suppose criteria of social facticity which have yet to be established. Althusser's doctrine of 'the break' in Marx is equally caught in 'an inescapable circle in which the application of Marxist theory to Marx himself appears to be the absolute precondition even of the constitution and development of Marxist philosophy' (Althusser, 1977a: 38).

8 This paradox is not only Dawe's, of course: it pervades the views he sets out to contest. So, Nisbet's 'unit ideas' are formed in and by history, but are then transubstantiated. An 'idea' becomes 'a *perspective*, a framework, a category (in the Kantian sense)' (Nisbet, 1967: 5).

9 It is rather misleading to portray Locke as an 'empiricist'. Woolhouse advances a strong argument that Locke takes a rationalist view of science which turns on a conception of 'natural necessity'. See Woolhouse, 1971: 28–9.

10 So, in the propositional calculus the validity of arguments is tested by attempting to assign truth values T(rue) or F(alse) to their component propositions such that values of T can be obtained for the premises and F for the conclusion. If this can be done, the argument is invalid (see Copi, 1967: ch. 3.7).

11 A recent story in the Australian press illustrated the importance, and the oddity, of formality in these contexts. It suggested that all Australian marriages performed by clergy since the early 1970s might be 'invalid' because the act under which clergy had been licensed to perform marriages may have been in breach of a provision of the Federal Constitution which prohibits the establishment of a state religion.

12 Most obviously, this argument is developed in the Frankfurt School critique of science. *Dialectic of Enlightenment* sums up one phase of this critique, while the papers collected in Adorno *et al.* 1976 give a sense of the post-war debate. The problem continues to animate Habermas's developing project, of course. Husserl's *The Crisis of the European Sciences* parallels many pre-war Frankfurt School concerns.

13 See Sandywell *et al.*, 1975: 12–14 for a sense of the limits to Kuhn's 'reflexivity' on these matters. Important and controversial work towards non-foundational accounts of scientific knowledge has been produced in the recent development of 'social studies of science'. See Woolgar 1988 for a summary of the issues.

14 Key texts in 1970s 'reflexive sociology' include O'Neill 1972, Blum 1974, McHugh *et al.* 1974 and Sandywell *et al.* 1975.

15 It is one of the defining paradoxes of the foundationalist syndrome that foundational reflection is almost never temporally 'prior' to enquiry. Either the enquiry never materialises, or foundational reflection shares the pathos of Locke's under-labourer who attempts to clear the ground after 'the great Huygenius and the incomparable Mr Newton' have already built on it.

7 POST-FOUNDATIONAL RADICALISM

1 For a statement of the controversial 'strong programme' see Bloor (1976). The papers collected in Barnes and Edge (1982) give a good sense of the concerns of the sociology of science during the 1970s, when the issue of scientific knowledge itself came to the forefront of attention.

2 Perhaps because many social theorists remain attached to the fancy that they are engaged in the production of KNOWLEDGE, or even SCIENCE. It would seem to them a pyrrhic victory if the great achievement of their disciplines was to subvert the ideas of KNOWLEDGE and SCIENCE. For a sample of views about the dangers of 'relativism' in the sociology of science see Brown (1984).

3 Explanations based on 'interests' become problematic when they treat interests as given. For a critique of this tendency, and a useful review of the literature, see Woolgar (1981) and the replies it attracted. It is more useful to regard interests as being constituted at the same time as they are mobilised, as it were. Callon and Law (1982) develop an original argument along these lines. The 'interests' of actors are alluded to in a loose way in what follows. These allusions should not be taken to imply that interests are in any way given, fixed or independent of context.

4 Weber himself would find nothing to object to in principle here, but

he does not always stick to the principle. An emphasis on 'causality' in mundane enquiry does not entail a commitment to the realist meta-physics of 'causal powers' or to any kind of 'natural science' model. Causality is an instrument of irony, and as such cannot escape the condition of a rhetorical device. On these conditions, a 'pessimism' which is not subject to foundational guarantees is quite possible.

5 For some critics Gouldner's earlier version remained superior. Lemert and Piccone (1982) regard Gouldner's linguistic turn as a relapse into objectivism and classicism.

6 A cartoon reproduced as the frontispiece to Knorr-Cetina (1981) shows a scientist at work who is observed by another scientist armed with a clipboard who is observed by yet another scientist ....

7 This objection turns, in important part, on a failure to appreciate the mixture of playfulness and respectfulness which characterised reflexive sociology. Reflexive analysis is not an objectivist critique, whose aim is to blow rival projects out of the water. Its aim is not to prohibit enquiry, but, precisely, to encourage reflexivity about it.

8 MacIntyre hints that a similar disaster may have befallen the dis-courses of 'truth'. See his (1985: ch. 7) treatment of the fetish of 'facts'.

9 MacIntyre relates this to a rather one-dimensional reading of Goffman's sociology (MacIntyre, 1985: 115).

10 Pomerantz (1984) offers an example of the contribution which the techniques of conversation analysis might make to such a pro-gramme. The discussion of audience activity in Crook (1989) ap-proaches the problem in a rather more eclectic manner.

11 The problem here is that addressed in note 3 above. Mills (1963) offers a powerful argument that 'motives' can no more be taken as given than can 'interests'.

12 To quote Fekete in full, the question of the 'validity of values' leads to 'a second order enquiry into the *value of value*. Implicit in this move is the strategy of establishing at the second level of value that objectivity (or that universality) which always remained elusive at the first level' (Fekete, 1988: vi).

13 A danger here is that pragmatism itself might mutate into an ersatz foundationalism. As Smith (1988: 13) warns, pragmatist conceptions of validity become as 'impotent' as any others if they try to close the 'multiple and inevitably diverse appropriations of any verbal/con-ceptual construct'. Lyotard is also alert to the sense in which 'to accord oneself the privilege of the pragmatic ... is finally to get the essential on the cheap' (van Reijen and Veerman, 1988: 306).

14 See the reference in Habermas (1987a: 8). Habermas likes the idea of a 'self-grounded' modernity.

15 In something like this dismissive spirit, Enzensberger (1976) explained ecological concerns in terms of the inability of the bourgeoisie to con-ceive an 'end of capitalism' that was not also an 'end of the world'.

16 The dismantling of such boundaries is an important methodological device in the work of Latour, Callon and Law. See, for example, Law's (1986) study of Portuguese sea power and Callon's (1986) account of the fate of the scallops of St Brieuc Bay.

BIBLIOGRAPHY

Abrams, P. (1982) *Historical Sociology*, Shepton Mallet: Open Books.

Adorno, T. W. (1973a) *Negative Dialectics*, London: Routledge & Kegan Paul.

——(1973b) *The Jargon of Authenticity*, London: Routledge & Kegan Paul.

——(1974) *Minima Moralia*, London: Verso.

——(1976a) 'Introduction', in T. W. Adorno, H. Albert, R. Dahrendorf, J. Habermas, H. Pilot and K. Popper *The Positivist Dispute in German Sociology*, London: Heinemann.

——(1976b) 'Sociology and Empirical Research', in T. W. Adorno, H. Albert, R. Dahrendorf, J. Habermas, H. Pilot and K. Popper *The Positivist Dispute in German Sociology*, London: Heinemann.

——(1976c) 'On the Logic of the Social Sciences', in T. W. Adorno, H. Albert, R. Dahrendorf, J. Habermas, H. Pilot and K. Popper *The Positivist Dispute in German Sociology*, London: Heinemann.

——(1977a) 'Letters to Walter Benjamin', in E. Bloch, G. Lúkacs, B. Brecht, W. Benjamin, T. Adorno *Aesthetics and Politics*, London: New Left Books.

——(1977b) 'The Actuality of Philosophy', *Telos* 31: 120–133.

——(1978) 'Subject and Object', in A. Arato and E. Gebhardt (eds) *The Essential Frankfurt School Reader*, Oxford: Blackwell.

——(1981) *In Search of Wagner*, London: New Left Books.

——(1984) *Aesthetic Theory*, London: Routledge & Kegan Paul.

Adorno, T. W. and Horkheimer, M. (1979) *The Dialect of Enlightenment*, London: Verso.

Agger, B. (1977) 'On Happiness and the Damaged Life', in J. O'Neill (ed) *On Critical Theory*, London: Heinemann.

Albrow, M. (1974) 'Dialectical and Categorical Paradigms in Sociology', *Sociological Review* 22: 183–201.

Althusser, L. (1971a) *Lenin and Philosophy and Other Essays*, London: New Left Books.

——(1971b) 'Ideology and the Ideological State Apparatuses', in L. Althusser *Lenin and Philosophy and Other Essays*, London: New Left Books.

——(1976) *Essays in Self Criticism*, London: New Left Books.

——(1977a) *For Marx*, London: New Left Books.

——(1977b) 'On the Young Marx', in L. Althusser *For Marx*, London: New Left Books.

——(1977c) 'Today', in L. Althusser *For Marx*, London: New Left Books.

Althusser, L. and Balibar, E. (1970) *Reading 'Capital'*, London: New Left Books.

Anderson, P. (1976) *Considerations on Western Marxism*, London: New Left Books.

——(1984) *In the Tracks of Historical Materialism*, Chicago: University of Chicago Press.

Aron, R. (1971) 'Max Weber and Power Politics', in O. Stammer (ed) *Max Weber and Sociology Today*, Oxford: Blackwell.

Atkinson, J. M. and Heritage, J. (eds) (1984) *Structures of Social Action*, Cambridge: Cambridge University Press.

Barnes, B. and Edge, D. (eds) (1982) *Science in Context: Readings in the Sociology of Science*, Milton Keynes: Open University Press.

Baudrillard, J. (1980) 'Forgetting Foucault', *Humanities in Society* 3: 87–111.

——(1983a) *In the Shadow of the Silent Majorities*, New York: Semiotext(e).

——(1983b) 'The Ecstasy of Communication', in H. Foster (ed) *The Anti-Aesthetic*, Port Townsend: Bay Press.

Bauman, Z. (1976) *Towards a Critical Sociology*, London: Routledge & Kegan Paul.

——(1978) *Hermeneutics and Social Science: Approaches to Understanding*, London: Hutchinson.

——(1987) *Legislators and Interpreters*, Cambridge: Polity Press.

——(1988) 'Is There a Postmodern Sociology?', *Theory, Culture and Society* 5: 217–37.

Beetham, D. (1974) *Max Weber and the Theory of Modern Politics*, London: Allen and Unwin.

Bell, D. (1973) *The Coming of Post-Industrial Society: a Venture in Social Forecasting*, New York: Basic Books.

——(1976) *The Cultural Contradictions of Capitalism*, New York: Basic Books.

Bendix, R. (1960) *Max Weber, an Intellectual Portrait*, London: Methuen.

Benjamin, W. (1970a) 'Theses on the Philosophy of History', in W. Benjamin *Illuminations*, London: Fontana.

——(1970b) 'On Some Motifs in Baudelaire', in W. Benjamin *Illuminations*, London: Fontana.

Benton, T. (1977) *Philosophical Foundations of the Three Sociologies*, London: Routledge & Kegan Paul.

——(1978) 'How Many Sociologies'? *Sociological Review* 26: 217–236.

——(1984) *The Rise and Fall of Structural Marxism: Althusser and his Influence*, New York: St Martin's Press.

Berman, M. (1982) *All That is Solid Melts into Air: the Experience of Modernity*, New York: Simon and Schuster.

Bernstein, R. (1976) *The Restructuring of Social and Political Theory*, Oxford: Blackwell.

Besnard, P. (1982) *The Sociological Domain: The Durkheimians and the Founding of French Sociology*, Cambridge: Cambridge University Press.

Bleicher, J. (1982) *The Hermeneutic Imagination*, London: Routledge & Kegan Paul.

Bloor, D. (1976) *Knowledge and Social Imagery*, London: Routledge & Kegan Paul.

Blum, A. (1974) *Theorizing*, London: Heinemann.

Blumenberg, H. (1983) *The Legitimacy of the Modern Age*, Cambridge, Mass.: MIT Press.

Boyne, R. and Rattansi, A. (eds) (1990) *Postmodernism and Society*, London: Macmillan.

Brown, B. and Cousins, M. (1980) 'The Linguistic Fault: the Case of Foucault's Archaeology', *Economy and Society* 9: 251–78.

Brown, J. (ed) (1984) *Scientific Rationality: the Sociological Turn*, Dordrecht: Reidel.

Brubaker, R. (1984) *The Limits of Rationality: an Essay on the Social and Moral Thought of Max Weber*, London: Allen and Unwin.

Bubner, R. (1982) 'Habermas's Concept of Critical Theory', in J. Thompson and D. Held (eds) *Habermas: Critical Debates*, London: Macmillan.

Buck-Morss, S. (1972) 'The Dialectic of T W Adorno', *Telos* 14: 137–44.

——(1977) *The Origin of Negative Dialectics*, Brighton: Harvester.

Bürger, P. (1984) *Theory of the Avant Garde*, Minneapolis: University of Minnesota Press.

Butler, C. (1980) *After the Wake: an Essay on the Contemporary Avant Garde*, Oxford: Oxford University Press.

Callinicos, A. (1976) *Althusser's Marxism*, London: Pluto Press.

——(1982) *Is There a Future for Marxism?*, London: Macmillan.

Callon, M. (1986) 'Some Elements of a Sociology of Translation: Domestication of the Scallops and Fishermen of St Brieuc Bay', in J. Law (ed) *Power, Action and Belief: a New Sociology of Knowledge?*, Sociological Review Monograph 32, London: Routledge & Kegan Paul.

Callon, M. and Law, J. (1982) 'On Interests and their Transformation', *Social Studies of Science* 12: 615–25.

Calvert, P. (1982) *The Concept of Class: an Historical Introduction*, London: Hutchinson.

Chisholm, R. (1977) *Theory of Knowledge*, Englewood Cliffs, NJ: Prentice-Hall.

Clarke, S. (1980) 'Althusserian Marxism', in S. Clarke, T. Lovell, K. McDonnell, K. Robins and V. Seidler (eds) *One Dimensional Marxism*, London: Allison and Busby.

241

Clarke, T. (1972) 'Emile Durkheim and the French University', in A. Oberschall (ed) *The Establishment of Empirical Sociology*, New York: Harper-Row.

Collins, R. (1986) *Weberian Sociological Theory*, Cambridge: Cambridge University Press.

Connerton, P. (1980) *The Tragedy of Enlightenment*, Cambridge: Cambridge University Press.

Copi, I. (1967) *Symbolic Logic* (3rd edn), New York: Macmillan.

Corrigan, P. (1975) 'Dichotomy is Contradiction: on "Society" as Constraint and Construction. Remarks on the Doctrine of the "Two Sociologies"', *Sociological Review* 23: 211–243.

Coser, L. (1960) 'Durkheim's Conservatism and its Implications for Sociological Theory', in K. Wolff (ed) *Emile Durkheim 1858–1917*, Columbus: Ohio University Press.

Crook, S. (1984) 'Beyond Foundationalism: a Critical Analysis of Three Foundational Projects in Radical Social Theory', unpublished D.Phil. thesis, University of York.

——(1989) 'Television and Audience Activity: the Problem of the Television/Viewer Nexus in Audience Research', *Australian and New Zealand Journal of Sociology* 25: 356–80.

Cutler, A. Hindess, B., Hirst, P. and Hussain, A. (1977) *Marx's 'Capital' and Capitalism Today* 1, London: Routledge & Kegan Paul.

Cutler, A. (1978) *Marx's 'Capital' and Capitalism Today* 2, London: Routledge & Kegan Paul.

Dallmayr, F. (1972) 'Critical Theory Criticised: Habermas's *Knowledge and Human Interests* and its Aftermath', *Philosophy of the Social Sciences* 2: 211–29.

Dawe, A. (1971) 'The Two Sociologies', in K. Thompson and J. Tunstall (eds) *Sociological Perspectives*, Harmondsworth: Penguin.

Derrida, J. (1976) *Of Grammatology*, Baltimore: Johns Hopkins University Press.

Descartes, R. (1968) *Discourse on Method and Other Writings*, Harmondsworth: Penguin.

Dews, P. (1980) 'The "New Philosophers" and the End of Leftism', *Radical Philosophy* 24: 2–11.

——(1987) *Logics of Disintegration*, London: Verso.

Durkheim, E. (1958) *Socialism and St Simon*, Yellow Springs, Ohio: Antioch Press.

——(1960) 'The Dualism of Human Nature and its Social Conditions', in K. Wolff (ed) *Emile Durkheim 1858–1917*, Columbus: Ohio University Press.

——(1961) *Moral Education*, New York: Free Press.

——(1964a) *The Rules of Sociological Method* (ed. G. Catlin), New York: Free Press.

——(1964b) *The Division of Labor in Society*, New York: Free Press.

——(1969) 'Individualism and the Intellectuals', *Political Studies* 17: 19–30.

——(1974) *Sociology and Philosophy*, New York: Free Press.

——(1976) *The Elementary Forms of the Religious Life*, London: Allen and Unwin.

——(1982a) *The Rules of Sociological Method and Related Texts on Sociology and its Method* (ed. S. Lukes), London: Macmillan.

——(1982b) 'Sociology and the Social Sciences' (with P. Fauconnet), in E. Durkheim *The Rules of Sociological Method and Related Texts on Sociology and its Method* (ed. S. Lukes), London: Macmillan.

——(1983) *Pragmatism and Sociology*, Cambridge: Cambridge University Press.

Eagleton, T. (1985) 'Capitalism, Modernism and Postmodernism', *New Left Review* 152: 60–73.

Enzensberger, H.M. (1976) 'A Critique of Political Ecology', in H.M. Enzensberger *Raids and Reconstructions: Essays on Politics, Crime and Culture*, London: Pluto Press.

Farganis, J. (1975) 'A Preface to Critical Theory', *Theory and Society* 2: 483–508.

Featherstone, M. (1988) 'In Pursuit of the Postmodern', *Theory, Culture and Society* 5: 195–215.

Fekete, J. (1988) 'Introductory Notes for a Postmodern Value Agenda', in J. Fekete (ed.) *Life After Postmodernism: Essays on Value and Culture*, London: Macmillan.

Fenton, S. (1984) *Durkheim and Modern Sociology*, Cambridge: Cambridge University Press.

Foster, H. (1983) 'Post Modernism: a Preface', in H. Foster (ed.) *The Anti-Aesthetic*, Port Townsend: Bay Press.

Foucault, M. (1970) *The Order of Things*, London: Tavistock.

——(1972) *The Archaeology of Knowledge*, London: Tavistock.

——(1977) *Discipline and Punish*, Harmondsworth: Penguin.

——(1980) *Power/Knowledge*, Brighton: Harvester.

——(1981) *The History of Sexuality Volume One: an Introduction*, Harmondsworth: Penguin.

Friedman, G. (1981) *The Political Philosophy of the Frankfurt School*, Ithica: Cornell University Press.

Frisby, D. (1981) *Sociological Impressionism: a Reassessment of Georg Simmel's Social Theory*, London: Heinemann.

——(1984) *Georg Simmel*, Chichester: Ellis-Horwood.

——(1985) *Fragments of Modernity: Theories of Modernity in the Work of Simmel, Kracauer and Benjamin*, Cambridge: Polity Press.

Gadamer, H. G. (1976) *Philosophical Hermeneutics*, Berkeley: University of California Press.

Garfinkel, H. (1967) *Studies in Ethnomethodology*, Englewood Cliffs, N.J.: Prentice Hall.

Giddens, A. (1971) *Capitalism and Modern Social Theory*, Cambridge: Cambridge University Press.

——(1972) *Politics and Sociology in the Work of Max Weber*, London: Macmillan.

——(1977) *Studies in Social and Political Theory*, London: Hutchinson.

——(1982) *Profiles and Critiques in Social Theory*, London: Macmillan.

Gouldner, A. (1971) *The Coming Crisis of Western Sociology*, London: Heinemann.

——(1973) *For Sociology*, Harmondsworth: Penguin.

——(1976) *The Dialectic of Ideology and Technology*, London: Macmillan.

Guattari, F. (1984) *Molecular Revolution*, Harmondsworth: Penguin.

Habermas, J. (1970.) 'Toward a Theory of Communicative Competence', in H. Dreitzel (ed.) *Recent Sociology Number 2*, New York: Macmillan.

——(1971a) *Toward a Rational Society*, London: Heinemann.

——(1971b) 'Discussion on Value Freedom and Objectivity', in O. Stammer (ed.) *Max Weber and Sociology Today*, Oxford: Blackwell.

——(1972) *Knowledge and Human Interests*, London: Heinemann.

——(1973) 'A Postscript to "Knowledge and Human Interests"', *Philosophy of the Social Sciences*, 3: 157–89.

——(1974a) *Theory and Practice*, London: Heinemann.

——(1974b) 'The Public Sphere: an Encyclopaedia Article', *New German Critique* 3: 49–55.

——(1976) *Legitimation Crisis*, London: Heinemann.

——(1978) *L'Espace public*, Paris: Payot.

——(1979) *Communication and the Evolution of Society*, London: Heinemann

——(1981) 'Modernity versus Postmodernity, *New German Critique* 2: 3–14.

——(1982) 'A Reply to my Critics', in J. Thompson and D. Held (eds) *Habermas: Critical Debates*, London: Heinemann.

——(1983) *Philosophical-Political Profiles*, Cambridge: Polity Press.

——(1984) *The Theory of Communicative Action Volume One: Reason and the Rationalization of Society*, London: Heinemann.

——(1985a) 'Questions and Counterquestions', in R. Bernstein (ed.) *Habermas and Modernity*, Cambridge: Polity Press.

——(1985b) 'Neo-Conservative Cultural Criticism in the United States and Germany: an Intellectual Movement in Two Political Cultures', in R. Bernstein (ed.) *Habermas and Modernity*, Cambridge: Polity Press.

——(1987a) *The Philosophical Discourse of Modernity*, Cambridge: Polity Press.

——(1987b) *The Theory of Communicative Action Volume Two: Lifeworld and System*, Cambridge: Polity Press.

——(1989) *The Structural Transformation of the Public Sphere* (trans. T. Burger), Cambridge: Polity Press.

Hall, S., Hobson, D., Lowe, A. and Willis, P. (1980) *Culture, Media, Language*, London: Hutchinson.

Hall, S. and Jefferson, T. (eds) (1976) *Resistance Through Rituals: Youth Subcultures in Post War Britain*, London: Hutchinson.

Hamlyn, D. (1970) *The Theory of Knowledge*, London: Macmillan

Harvey, D. (1989) *The Condition of Postmodernity: an Enquiry into the Origins of Cultural Change*, Oxford: Blackwell.

Hassan, I. (1985) 'The Culture of Postmodernism', *Theory, Culture and Society* 2: 119–31.

Hegel, G. W. F. (1949) *The Phenomenology of Mind*, London: Allen and Unwin.

——(1952) *Hegel's Philosophy of Right*, Oxford: Oxford University Press.

Held, D. (1980) *Introduction to Critical Theory: Horkheimer to Habermas*, London: Hutchinson.

Hesse, M. (1982) ' Science and Objectivity' in J. Thompson and D. Held (eds) *Habermas: Critical Debates*, London: Macmillan.

Hindess, B. (1977) *Philosophy and Methodology in the Social Sciences*, Brighton: Harvester Press.

Hindess, B. and Hirst, P. (1977) *Mode of Production and Social Formation*, London: Routledge & Kegan Paul.

Hirst, P. (1975) *Durkheim, Bernard and Epistemology*, London: Routledge.

Hirst, P. (1979) *On Law and Ideology*, London: Macmillan.

Honneth, A. (1985) An Aversion Against The Universal: a Commentary on Lyotard's *Postmodern Condition*, Theory, Culture and Society, 2: 147–56.

Horkheimer, M. (1972a) 'Traditional and Critical Theory', in M. Horkheimer *Critical Theory*, New York: Seabury.

——(1972b) 'The Social Function of Philosophy', in M. Horkheimer *Critical Theory*, New York: Seabury.

——(1972c) 'The Latest Attack on Metaphysics', in M. Horkheimer *Critical Theory*, New York: Seabury.

——(1972d) 'Materialism and Metaphysics', in M. Horkheimer *Critical Theory*, New York: Seabury.

——(1974) *The Eclipse of Reason*, New York: Seabury.

——(1978a) *Dawn and Decline*, New York: Seabury.

——(1978b) 'On the Problem of Truth', in A. Arato and E. Gebhardt (eds) *The Essential Frankfurt School Reader*, Oxford: Blackwell.

——(1982) 'Egoism and the Freedom Movement: On the Anthropology of the Bourgeois Era', *Telos* 54: 10–60.

Howard, D. (1977) *The Marxian Legacy*, London: Macmillan.

Huyssen, A. (1984) 'From Counter Culture to Neo-Conservatism and Beyond: Stages of the Postmodern', *Social Science Information* 23: 147–56.

Jameson, F. (1983) 'Postmodernism and Consumer Society', in H. Foster (ed.) *The Anti-Aesthetic*, Port Townsend: Bay Press.

——(1984) 'Post-Modernism or the Cultural Logic of Late Capitalism', *New Left Review* 146: 53–92.

Jay, M. (1973) *The Dialectical Imagination: a History of the Frankfurt School and the Institute for Social Research 1920–50*, London: Heinemann.

——(1984a) *Adorno*, London: Fontana.

——(1984b) *Marxism and Totality: the Adventures of a Concept from Lukács to Habermas*, Cambridge: Polity Press.

Johnson, B. (1965) 'Durkheim's One Cause of Suicide', *American Sociological Review* 30: 875–86.

Kant, I. (1952) *The Critique of Judgement* (trans. J.C. Meredith), Oxford: Oxford University Press.

——(1953) *Prolegomena to Any Future Metaphysics that will be Able to Present Itself as a Science*, Manchester: Manchester University Press.

——(1970) *Immanuel Kant's Critique of Pure Reason* (trans. N. Kemp-Smith), London: Macmillan.

Katz, B. (1982) *Herbert Marcuse and the Art of Liberation*, London: New Left Books.

Keat, R. (1981) *The Politics of Social Theory*, Oxford: Blackwell.
Kellner, D. (1975) 'The Frankfurt School Revisited: a Critique of Martin Jay's "The Dialectical Imagination"', *New German Critique* 4: 131–52.
——(1988) 'Postmodernism and Social Theory: Some Challenges and Problems', *Theory, Culture and Society* 5: 239–69.
Kelly, M. (1982) *Modern French Marxism*, Oxford: Blackwell.
Kenny, A. (1968) *Descartes: A Study of His Philosophy*, New York: Random House.
Kilminster, R. (1979) *Praxis and Method*, London: Routledge & Kegan Paul.
Knorr-Cetina, K. (1981) *The Manufacture of Knowledge*, Oxford: Pergamon.
Kolakowski, L. (1971) 'Althusser's Marx', in R. Miliband, and J. Saville (eds) *Socialist Register 1971*, London: Merlin Press.
Koselleck, R. (1988) *Critique and Crisis: Enlightenment and the Pathogenesis of Modern Society*, Oxford: Berg.
Kroker, A. (1985) 'Baudrillard's Marx', *Theory, Culture and Society* 2: 69–83.
La Capra, D. (1972) *Emile Durkheim: Sociologist and Philosopher*, Ithica: Cornell University Press.
Larrain, J. (1979) *The Concept of Ideology*, London: Hutchinson.
Lash, S. (1985) 'Postmodernity and Desire', *Theory and Society* 14: 1–33.
——(1988) 'Discourse or Figure? Postmodernism as a "Regime of Signification"', in *Theory, Culture and Society* 5: 311–36.
Lash, S. and Urry, J. (1987) *The End of Organised Capitalism*, Cambridge: Polity Press.
Law, J. (1986) 'On the Methods of Long-Distance Control: Vessels, Navigation and the Portuguese Route to India', in J. Law (ed.) *Power, Action and Belief: a New Sociology of Knowledge?*, Sociological Review Monograph 32, London: Routledge & Kegan Paul.
Lemert, C. and Piccone, P. (1982) 'Gouldner's Theoretical Method and Reflexive Sociology', *Theory and Society* 11: 733–57.
Lenhardt, C. (1972) 'The Rise and Fall of Transcendental Anthropology', *Philosophy of the Social Sciences* 2: 231–246.
Lepenies, W. (1988) *Between Literature and Science: the Rise of Sociology*, Cambridge: Cambridge University Press.
Levine, D., Carter, E. and Gorman, E. Miller (1976) 'Simmel's Influence on American Sociology' Part 1, *American Journal of Sociology* 81: 813–845.
Lobkowicz, N. (1972) 'Interest and Objectivity', *Philosophy of the Social Sciences* 2: 193–210.
Locke, J. (1961) *Essay Concerning Human Understanding*, London: Dent.
Löwith, K. (1982) *Max Weber and Karl Marx*, London: Allen and Unwin.
Lukes, S. (1969) 'Durkheim's "Individualism and the Intellectuals"', *Political Studies* 17: 14–19.
——(1973) *Emile Durkheim: His Life and Work*, Harmondsworth: Penguin.
Lyotard, J.F. (1984a) *The Postmodern Condition*, Manchester: Manchester University Press.

——(1984b) 'Answering the Question: What is Postmodernism', in J.F. Lyotard *The Postmodern Condition*, Manchester: Manchester University Press.

——(1988) *The Differend: Phrases in Dispute*, Manchester: Manchester University Press.

McCarthy, T. (1978) *The Critical Theory of Jürgen Habermas*, London: Hutchinson.

——(1982) 'Rationality and Relativism: Habermas's "Overcoming" of Hermeneutics', in J. Thompson and D. Held *Habermas: Critical Debates*, London: Macmillan.

McHoul, A. (1982) *Telling How Texts Talk: Essays on Reading and Ethnomethodology*, London: Routledge & Kegan Paul.

McHugh, P. Raffel, S., Foss, B., and Blum, A. (1974) *On the Beginning of Social Enquiry*, London: Routledge & Kegan Paul.

MacIntyre, A. (1985) *After Virtue: a Study in Moral Theory* (2nd edn), London: Duckworth.

——(1988) *Whose Justice? Which Rationality?*, London: Duckworth.

Marcuse, H. (1966) *Eros and Civilization: a Philosophical Enquiry into Freud*, Boston: Beacon Press.

——(1968) *Negations*, Harmondsworth: Penguin.

——(1969) 'Contribution to a Phenomenology of Historical Materialism', *Telos* 4: 3–34

——(1977) *Reason and Revolution: Hegel and the Rise of Social Theory*, London: Routledge & Kegan Paul.

——(1979) *The Aesthetic Dimension: Toward a Critique of Marxist Aesthetics*, London: Macmillan.

Margolis, J. (1986) *Pragmatism Without Foundations*, Oxford: Blackwell.

Marx, K. (1968) 'The 18th Brumaire of Louis Bonaparte', in K. Marx and F. Engels *Marx and Engels Selected Works in One Volume*, London: Lawrence and Wishart.

——(1973) *Grundrisse: Foundations of the Critique of Political Economy (Rough Draft)*, Harmondsworth: Penguin.

——(1975a) *Early Writings* (ed. L. Colletti), Harmondsworth: Penguin.

——(1975b) 'Critique of Hegel's Doctrine of the State', in K. Marx *Early Writings* (ed. L. Colletti), Harmondsworth: Penguin.

——(1975c) '"Introduction" to A Contribution to the Critique of Hegel's Philosophy of Right', in K. Marx *Early Writings* (ed. L. Colletti), Harmondsworth: Penguin.

——(1975d) 'Economic and Philosophical Manuscripts', in K. Marx *Early Writings* (ed. L. Colletti), Harmondsworth: Penguin.

Meštrović, S. (1987) 'Durkheim's Concept of Anomie Considered as a Total Social Fact', *British Journal of Sociology* 38: 567–83.

Mills, C. W. (1963) 'Situated Actions and Vocabularies of Motive', in C. W. Mills *Power, Politics, People*, New York: Oxford University Press.

Mommsen, W. (1959) *Max Weber und die Deutsche Politik 1890–1920*, Tubingen: Mohr.

Mulkay, M. (1985) *The Word and the World: Explorations in the Form of Sociological Analysis*, London: Allen and Unwin.

Nietzsche, F. (1968) *Twilight of the Idols*, Harmondsworth: Penguin.

Nisbet, R. (1967) *Sociological Tradition*, London: Heinemann.

Oakes, G. (1977) 'Introduction', in G. Simmel *The Problems of the Philososphy of History*, New York: Free Press.

Ollman, B. (1976) *Alienation: Marx's Conception of Man in Capitalist Society*, Cambridge: Cambridge University Press.

O'Neill, J. (1972) *Sociology as a Skin Trade*, London: Heinemann.

Outhwaite, W. (1987) *New Philosophies of Social Science. Realism, Hermeneutics and Critical Theory*, London: Macmillan.

Parsons, T. (1960) 'Pattern Variables Revisited: a Response to Robert Dubin', *American Sociological Review* 25: 467–83.

——(1968) *The Structure of Social Action*, New York: Free Press.

——(1971) 'Value Freedom and Objectivity', in O. Stammer (ed.) *Max Weber and Sociology Today*, Oxford: Blackwell.

Passmore, J. (1966) *One Hundred Years of Philosophy*, Harmondsworth: Penguin.

Patton, P. (1978) 'Althusser's Epistemology', *Radical Philosophy* 19: 8–18.

Phillipson, M. (1976) 'Sociology, Metaphorically Speaking', *Writing Sociology* 1: 25–50.

Piccone, P. (1977) 'Beyond Identity Theory', in J. O'Neill (ed.) *On Critical Theory*, London: Heinemann.

——(1978) 'General Introduction', in A. Arato and E. Gebhardt (eds) *The Essential Frankfurt School Reader*, Oxford: Blackwell.

Plato (1974) *The Republic*, Harmondsworth: Penguin.

Pollner, M. (1987) *Mundane Reason: Reality in Everyday Life and Sociological Discourse*, Cambridge: Cambridge Universtity Press.

Pomerantz, A. (1984) 'Agreeing and Disagreeing with Assessments: Some Features of Preferred/Dispreferred Turn Shapes', in J.M. Atkinson and J. Heritage (eds) *Structures of Social Action*, Cambridge: Cambridge University Press.

Popper, K. (1962) *The Open Society and its Enemies* (two volumes), London: Routledge & Kegan Paul.

——(1976) 'Reason or Revolution?', in T. W. Adorno, H. Albert, R. Dahrendorf, J. Habermas, and H. Pilot *The Postivist Dispute in German Sociology*, London: Heinemann.

Posner, R. (1976) 'Discourse as a Means to Enlightenment', in A. Kasher (ed.) *Language in Focus: Foundations, Methods and Systems*, Dordrecht: Reidel.

Poulantzas, N. (1978) *State, Power, Socialism*, London: Verso.

Prager, J. (1981) 'Moral Integration and Political Inclusion: a Comparison of Durkheim's and Weber's Theories', *Social Forces* 59: 918–50.

Putnam, H. (1978) *Meaning and the Moral Sciences*, London: Routledge & Kegan Paul.

Rancière, J. (1974) *La leçon d' Althusser*, Paris: Gallimard.

Reid, H. (1977) 'Critical Phenomenology and the Dialectical Foundations of Social Change', *Dialectical Anthropology* 2: 107–130.

Renouvier, C. (1875) *Essais de critique générale tome 1*, Paris: Critique Philosophique.

Richter, M. (1960) 'Durkheim's Politics and Political Theory', in K. Wolff (ed.) *Emile Durkheim 1858–1917*, Columbus: Ohio University Press.

Rickert, H. (1962) *Science and History*, New York: Van Nostrand.

Ricoeur, P. (1981) *Hermeneutics and the Human Sciences*, Cambridge: Cambridge University Press.

Rorty, R. (1982) *The Consequences of Pragmatism: Essays 1972–80*, Brighton: Harvester Press.

——(1985) 'Habermas and Lyotard on Post Modernity', in R. Bernstein (ed.) *Habermas and Modernity*, Cambridge: Polity Press.

——(1989) *Contingency, Irony and Solidarity*, Cambridge: Cambridge University Press.

Rosdolsky, R. (1977) *The Making of Marx's 'Capital'*, London: Pluto Press.

Rose, G. (1978) *The Melancholy Science: an Introduction to the Thought of T. W. Adorno*, London: Macmillan.

——(1981) *Hegel Contra Sociology*, London: Athlone Press.

——(1984) *Dialectic of Nihilism*, Oxford: Blackwell.

Roth, G. and Schluchter, W. (1979) *Max Weber's Vision of History: Ethics and Methods*, Berkeley: University of California Press.

Rovatti, P. (1973) 'Critical Theory and Phenomenology', *Telos* 15: 26–40.

Runciman, W. (1972) *A Critique of Max Weber's Philosophy of Social Science*, Cambridge: Cambridge University Press.

Ryan, M. (1982) *Marxism and Deconstruction*, Baltimore: Johns Hopkins University Press.

Sandywell, B. (1975) 'Introduction: Critical Tradition', in B. Sandywell, D. Silverman, M. Roche, P. Filmer and M. Phillipson *Problems of Reflexivity and Dialectics in Sociological Enquiry*, London: Routledge & Kegan Paul.

Sandywell, B., Silverman, D., Roche, M., Filmer, P., and Phillipson, M. (1975) *Problems of Reflexivity and Dialectics in Sociological Enquiry*, London: Routledge & Kegan Paul.

Schmid, M. (1982) 'Habermas's Theory of Social Evolution', in J. Thompson and D. Held (eds) *Habermas: Critical Debates*, London: Macmillan.

Searle, J. (1967) 'How to Derive "Ought" from "Is"', in P. Foot (ed.) *Theories of Ethics*, Oxford: Oxford University Press.

Sheridan, A. (1980) 'Postscript', in M. Foucault *Power/Knowledge*, Brighton: Harvester.

Sherover-Marcuse, E. (1986) *Emancipation and Consciousness: Dogmatic and Dialectical Perspectives on the Early Marx*, Oxford: Blackwell.

Simmel, G. (1959a) 'The Problem of Sociology', in K. Wolff (ed.) *Georg Simmel 1858–1918*, Columbus: Ohio University Press.

——(1959b) 'How is Society Possible?', in K. Wolff (ed.) *Georg Simmel 1858–1918*, Columbus: Ohio University Press.

——(1959c) 'The Nature of Philosophy', in K. Wolff (ed.) *Georg Simmel 1858–1918*, Columbus: Ohio University Press.

——(1977) *The Problems of the Philosophy of History*, New York: Free Press.

——(1978) *The Philosophy of Money*, London: Routledge & Kegan Paul.

Slater, P. (1976) *Origin and Significance of the Frankfurt School*, London: Routledge & Kegan Paul.

249

Smart, B. (1983) *Foucault, Marxism and Critique*, London: Routledge & Kegan Paul.

Smith, B.H. (1988) 'Value without Truth Value', in J. Fekete (ed.) *Life After Postmodernism: Essays on Value and Culture*, London: Macmillan.

Spinoza, B. (1910) *'Ethics' and 'On the Correction of the Understanding'*, London: Dent.

Stedman-Jones, S. (1980) 'Kantian Philosophy and Sociological Methodology', *Sociology* 14: 99–111.

Stehr, N. (1986) 'Sociological Theory and Practical Reason: the Restriction of the scope of Sociological Theory', in M. Wardell and S. Turner (eds) *Sociological Theory in Transition*, Winchester, Mass.: Allen and Unwin.

Steiner, G. (1978) *Heidegger*, London: Fontana.

Strauss, L. (1953) *Natural Right and History*, Chicago: University of Chicago Press.

Strawbridge, S. (1982) 'Althusser's Theory of Ideology and Durkheim's Account of Religion: an Examination of Some Striking Parallels', *Sociological Review* 30: 125–40.

Stroud, B. (1969) 'Transcendental Arguments', in T. Penelhum and J. MacIntosh (eds) *The First Critique*, Belmont: Wadsworth.

Tenbruck, F. (1959) 'Formal Sociology', in K. Wolff (ed.) *Georg Simmel 1858–1918*, Columbus: Ohio University Press.

Therborn, G. (1977) 'The Frankfurt School', in New Left Review (eds) *Western Marxism: a Critical Reader*, London: New Left Books.

——(1978) *What does the Ruling Class do When it Rules?*, London: Verso.

Thompson, E.P. (1978) *The Poverty of Theory*, London: Merlin Press.

Thompson, J. (1981) *Critical Hermeneutics: a Study in the Thought of Paul Ricoeur and Jürgen Habermas*, Cambridge: Cambridge University Press.

——(1982) 'Universal Pragmatics', in J. Thompson and D. Held (eds) *Habermas: Critical Debates*, London: Macmillan.

Touraine, A. (1971) *The Post-Industrial Society*, New York: Random House.

Trigg, R. (1980) *Reality at Risk*, Brighton: Harvester.

Turner, B. (1981) *For Weber*, London: Routledge & Kegan Paul.

——(1986) 'Simmel, Rationalisation and the Sociology of Money', *Sociological Review* 34: 93–114.

Turner, S. and Factor, R. (1984) *Max Weber and the Dispute over Reason and Value: a Study of Philosophy, Ethics and Politics*, London: Routledge & Kegan Paul.

van den Berg, A. (1981) 'Critical Theory: Is There Still Hope?', *American Journal of Sociology* 86: 449–478.

van Reijen, W. and Veerman, D. (1988) 'An Interview With Jean-François Lyotard', *Theory, Culture and Society* 5: 277–309.

Wardell, M. and Turner, S. (eds) (1986) *Sociological Theory in Transition*, Winchester, Mass.: Allen and Unwin.

Weber, M. (1949a) 'The Meaning of Ethical Neutrality', in M. Weber *The Methodology of the Social Sciences* (trans. and ed. E. Shils and H. Finch), New York: Free Press.

——(1949b) '"Objectivity" in Social Science', in M. Weber *The Methodology of the Social Sciences* (trans. and ed. E. Shils and H. Finch), New York: Free Press.

——(1949c) 'The Logic of the Cultural Sciences', in M. Weber *The Methodology of the Social Sciences* (trans. and ed. E. Shils and H. Finch), New York: Free Press.

——(1961) *General Economic History*, New York: Collier-Macmillan.

——(1968) *Economy and Society: an Outline of Interpretive Sociology* (ed. G. Roth and C. Wittich), Berkeley: University of California Press.

——(1970a) 'Politics as a Vocation', in H. Gerth and C.W. Mills (eds) *From Max Weber*, London: Routledge & Kegan Paul.

——(1970b) 'Science as a Vocation', in H. Gerth and C.W. Mills (eds) *From Max Weber*, London: Routledge & Kegan Paul.

——(1975) 'Knies and the Problem of Irrationality', in M. Weber *Roscher and Knies: the Logical Problems of Historical Economics* (trans. and ed. G. Oakes), New York: Free Press.

——(1976) *The Protestant Ethic and the Spirit of Capitalism*, London: Allen and Unwin.

——(1978a) 'Socialism', in W. Runciman (ed.) *Max Weber: Selections in Translation*, Cambridge: Cambridge University Press

——(1978b) 'Economic Policy and the National Interest in Imperial Germany', in W. Runciman (ed.) *Max Weber: Selections in Translation*, Cambridge: Cambridge University Press.

Weingartner, R. (1959) 'Form and Content in Simmel's Philosophy of Life', in K. Wolff (ed.) *Georg Simmel 1858–1918*, Columbus: Ohio University Press.

——(1960) *Experience and Culture: the Philosophy of Georg Simmel*, Middletown, Conn.: Wesleyan University Press.

Wellmer, A. (1985a) 'Reason, Utopia and the Dialectic of Enlightenment', in R. Bernstein (ed.) *Habermas and Modernity*, Cambridge: Polity Press.

——(1985a) 'On the Dialectic of Modernism and Postmodernism', *Praxis International* 4: 337–62.

Whitebook, J. (1982) 'Saving the Subject: Modernity and the Problem of the Autonomous Individual', *Telos* 50: 79–102.

Woolgar, S. (1981) 'Interests and Explanation in the Social Study of Science', *Social Studies of Science* 11: 365–94.

——(1988) *Science: The Very Idea*, Chichester: Ellis Horwood.

Woolgar, S. (ed.) (1987) *Knowledge and Reflexivity*, London: Sage.

Woolhouse, R. (1971) *Locke's Philosophy of Science and Knowledge*, Oxford: Blackwell.

Zeitlin, I. (1968) *Ideology and the Development of Sociological Theory*, Englewood Cliffs, NJ: Prentice-Hall.

NAME INDEX

Abrams, Philip 62
Adorno, Theodore 9, 12–15, 17,
19, 55, 78, 83, 89–105, 107, 122,
130, 132, 134, 151, 204, 218;
anti-foundationalism 89, 90, 92,
95, 103, 104; and Benjamin 90,
92–3, 99, 100, 102; critical
rhetorics 92, 93, 94, 95–6, 97,
98, 103, 105; foundationalism
in 103–4; and Habermas
199–200; on Heidegger's
ontology 94–8; and Horkheimer
90, 92, 100–1; identity thinking
89–94, 97, 99, 101–2, 104–5,
198–9; ideology 95–6, 101;
negative dialectic 90–3, 105,
198–9; and Neitzsche 90, 93–4;
philosophy and 'end of
philosophy' 94–5, 97–8, 102–5;
philosophy and sociology
102–5; post-foundational
radicalism 91, 94, 103–5;
subject–object 90–2, 104; on
Wagner's aesthetics 98–102
Agger, Ben 78
Albrow, Martin 74
Althusser, Louis 9, 17–18, 135–50,
151, 152, 157, 172, 181; end
of philosophy 138–9; and
Foucault 147–9; ideology and

science 138–9, 144, 145, 151;
knowledge effect 141–6;
modernist radicalism 136–9, 146,
149–50; monism 137, 139,
140–6; postmodernism 146–50;
and Spinoza 140–6, 180; unity of
theory and practice 137
Anderson, Perry 18, 140, 162–3,
164, 166

Balibar, Etienne 139, 140, 141,
144
Barnes, Barry 211
Barthes, Roland 146
Baudrillard, Jean 5, 18, 134, 150;
nihilism 158, 161; physicalism
155–6
Bauman, Zygmunt 42, 74, 215
Beckett, Samuel 98
Bell, Daniel 3
Benjamin, Walter 9; and Adorno
90, 92–3, 99, 100, 102
Benton, Ted 136, 138, 141
Bergson, Henri 152
Berman, Marshall 27, 222n
Bloor, David 211
Blum, Alan 202
Blumenberg, Hans 22, 215–17
Brecht, Bertold 98
Brubaker, Rogers 64

252

Buck-Morss, Susan 90
Bürger, Peter 4

Callinicos, Alex 18, 141, 162–3,
  164, 166
Carnap, Rudolph 82
Chisholm, Roderick 169
Clarke, Simon 141
Collins, H.M. 211
Comte, Auguste 24, 26, 104
Connerton, Paul 79
Cutler, Antony 159

Davidson, Donald 169
Dawe, Alan, 20; origins of
  sociology 175, 177–8, 181
Deleuze, Gilles 18, 134, 150, 151,
  155, 162
Derrida, Jacques 6, 94, 96, 134,
  151, 163, 164, 186; origin and
  supplement 175
Descartes, René 20, 130, 141, 172,
  217; foundationalism 168–9,
  174–8
Dewey, John 110–11
Dews, Peter 165–6, 173
Durkheim, Emile 6, 9, 10, 11, 13,
  24–8, 36–48, 49, 62, 75, 104,
  106, 127, 131, 132, 155, 156,
  172, 174, 179, 181, 183, 185,
  189, 193; completion of
  modernity 47; 'end of
  philosophy' 37, 44–7, 225n; the
  Enlightenment 42–3, 47;
  ideology and science 37–40; and
  Kant 41, 43–4; modernist
  radicalism 37, 47–8; morality
  43–5; myth and science 41–2;
  and Renouvier 46–7;
  representations 40–1; and
  Simmel 50–3, 54; social facts
  37–8; 'unity of theory and
  practice' 37, 39–40, 45

Eagleton, Terry 162

Factor, Regis 67
Featherstone, Mike 150
Fekete, John 208, 213

Feuerbach, Ludwig 32
Fichte, Johann 107, 113
Foucault, Michel 5, 131, 134, 150,
  155, 156, 158, 161, 163, 174,
  183, 197; and Althusser 146,
  147–9, 164
Freud, Sigmund 107
Frisby, David 27, 51, 57, 58, 60

Gadamer, Hans-Georg 110, 187
Garaudy, Roger 136
Garfinkel, Harold 125
Giddens, Anthony 25, 51, 64, 67
Glass, Philip 152
Gouldner, Alvin W. 201–4, 206
Guattari, Félix 18, 155, 156, 162,
  173, 181, 187; nihilism 159, 161,
  212

Habermas, Jürgen 8, 9, 15–17, 18,
  62, 71, 72, 78, 83, 89, 106–33,
  134, 149, 163, 172, 174, 187,
  209; action 116–17; and Adorno
  199–200, 210; cognitive interests
  108, 112–14, 118, 126, 128, 170,
  186; critical theory 106, 108,
  111, 113, 117, 119, 122; end of
  philosophy 107, 122, 126, 129,
  130–3; Enlightenment 106, 109,
  114, 120–1; foundationalism 16,
  130, 131, 132, 169–70, 182, 213;
  ideology 107, 108, 121, 132;
  lifeworld and system 117–19,
  120; Lyotard on 150–1, 155;
  modernist radicalism 106, 107,
  122, 129, 130–3, 193, 198;
  modernity 106, 107, 108,
  117–22, 131–2; postmodernism
  131, 157, 162, 164–6; pragmatics
  of communication 107, 114–16,
  117, 123–16; public sphere 107,
  108–11, 114, 115–16, 117, 118,
  120, 121; rational reconstruction
  and reconstructive sciences 107,
  115, 116, 119, 122–30, 132, 164,
  170, 181, 186, 193, 198;
  transcendental arguments
  and the 'question of right'
  127–8, 132; unity of theory and

253

practice 107, 108, 110, 112, 114, 119

Hamlyn, D.W. 168, 171, 172

Harvey, David 4

Hassan, Ihab 154

Hegel, Georg Wilhelm Friedrich 27, 28, 96, 97, 107, 126, 180; estates and classes 30–1, 34; family, civil society and state 29–30, 223n; Marx's critique of 30–5

Heidegger, Martin 14, 186; Adorno's critique of 94–8, 198; reflexivity 202

Held, David 82, 113

Hesse, Mary 129

Hindess, Barry 18, 147, 150, 157, 174, 183, 187; nihilism 159–60, 161

Hirst, Paul 18, 147, 150, 157, 174, 183, 187; nihilism 159–60, 161

Honneth, Axel 154

Horkheimer, Max 9, 12–15, 17, 19, 78–89, 132, 218; and Adorno 90, 92, 100–1; 'end of philosophy' 79–80, 86–7, 88; foundationalism and anti-foundationalism 81–2, 85, 87–9; goals of critical theory 83–5; grounding of critical theory 85–6; ideology 80–1, 88; Institute for Social Research 78–9; language and rhetoric 80–1, 84–5, 86, 198; modernist radicalism 79, 85, 86; nihilism 88; totality 82–3; 'unity of theory and practice' 85, 88; validity 82–3

Howard, Dick 79, 89

Husserl, Edmund 130

Jameson, Frederick 19, 154, 158, 163; on aesthetic postmodernity 152–3

Jay, Martin 89, 91, 103, 122

Kant, Immanuel 43–4, 46, 51, 57, 61, 75, 80, 87, 96, 97, 105, 107, 113, 126, 130, 153, 170; autonomy of reason 180;

empirical knowledge 224n; transcendental arguments 127

Kellner, Douglas 150, 155, 158, 164–5

Kenny, Anthony 177

Khrushchev, Nikita 136

Kilminster, Richard 79, 81, 89

Kohlberg, Lawrence 115

Koselleck, Reinhart 35–6, 42, 109, 208

Kuhn, Thomas 185

Lacan, Jaques 144, 146

Lash, Scott 4, 154, 156–7

Lepenies, W. 42, 58, 152

Levine, Donald 77

Levy, Bernard-Henri 197

Locke, John 179

Löwith, Karl 64

Lukács, Georg 9, 54, 55, 62

Lyotard, Jean-François 5, 18, 134, 150, 152, 162, 183, 209; aesthetic postmodernity 153–4; on Habermas and modernism 150–1, 155, 165; language games 173–4; nihilism 160–1

McCarthy, Thomas 113, 128

McHoul, Alex 195

McHugh, Peter 202

MacIntyre, Alasdair 22, 207–8, 213–14, 217, 218–19

Marcuse, Herbert 77, 89, 94, 163

Margolis, Joseph 20, 169, 170, 171

Marx, Karl 6, 10, 11, 15, 24–8, 29–36, 47, 62, 63, 65, 106, 107, 109, 115, 131, 132, 140, 172, 174, 187, 189; Althusser on 136, 138–9, 147; civil society 30–5; 'end of philosophy' 33; the Enlightenment 29, 35–6; foundationalism 33, 180–1; on Hegel 30–5; ideology 31–2; modernist radicalism 31–5; postmodernism 162–3, 164; the proletariat as 'universal class' 32–3; and Simmel on alienation 54–7; 'unity of theory and practice' 33–4

Mead, George Herbert 127
Mommsen, Wolfgang 67
Mozart, Wolfgang Amadeus 105
Mulkay, Michael 203

Neitzsche, Friedrich 9, 164, 217;
  and Adorno 90, 93–4, 101

O'Neill, John 202, 204
Outhwaite, William 107

Parsons, Talcott 9, 25, 71, 73, 77
Péguy, Charles 152
Phillipson, Michael 186
Piaget, Jean 115, 127
Plato 24–5
Pollner, Melvin 21, 211; mundane
  enquiry 194–6
Pollock, Jackson 152
Popper, Karl 24
Poulantzas, Nicos 19
Putnam, Hilary 169

Quine, Willard Van Orman 169

Renouvier, Charles 26, 46–7
Rickert, Heinrich 71, 72
Ricoeur, Paul 187
Rorty, Richard 129, 169, 170, 208,
  209; irony 196–7
Rose, Gillian 18, 55, 57, 90, 94, 96,
  155, 156
Rousseau, Jean-Jacques 26, 175,
  178
Runciman, W.G. 74
Ryan, M. 163, 164

Sandywell, Barry 202–3
Sartre, Jean-Paul 136
Schluchter, Wolfgang 68
Schmid, Michael 128, 129
Schönberg, Arnold 98
Sheridan, Greg 149
Simmel, Georg 9, 11–13, 15, 19,
  27, 49–61, 77, 99, 101, 102,
  106, 134, 151, 194; and
  Durkheim 50–3; 'end of
  philosophy' 59–61; experience
  and modernity 54–8, 60, 197;

formalism 50–4, 58, 61, 226n;
ideology 53; and Marx on
alienation 54–7; modernist
radicalism 49, 52–3, 58, 60;
post-foundational radicalism
49, 75–6; realist conception of
history 58–9; synthesis 51–2,
59, 193; totality 58–61; 'unity
of theory and practice' 52–3;
and Weber 55, 61–3, 72, 74–6
Smart, Barry 163
Smith, Barbara 22; contingency
  of value 209–11, 214; egalitarian
  fallacy 195–6, 210
Spinoza, Baruch 17–18, 157,
  179–80; and Althusser 140–6
Stehr, Nico 7–8
Stockhausen, Karlheinz 152
Strauss, Leo 207
Stravinsky, Igor 98
Stroud, Barry 127, 130

Tenbruck, A. 61
Thébaud, Jean-Loup 173
Therborn, Goran 89
Thompson, E.P. 141
Thompson, John B. 124
Touraine, Alain 3
Turner, Bryan 54, 56, 58, 63, 65
Turner, Stephen 7–8, 66

Urry, John 4

Wagner, Richard 14, 98–102, 105,
  198
Wardell, Mark 7–8
Warhol, Andy 152
Weber, Max 9, 11, 12, 15, 19, 25,
  26, 49, 61–76, 77, 106, 117, 127,
  128, 134, 151, 218; action 69;
  causality 65–6, 72, 76; cognitive
  interests 71–3, 75, 76;
  development of capitalism 62–3;
  'end of philosophy' 68;
  foundationalism 74–5, 76; ideal
  type 70, 72; irony and
  modernity 62–8, 197;
  modernist radicalism 66, 68, 72;
  paradox of consequences 64–5,

67, 68, 76; post-foundational
radicalism 75–6; rationalisation
63–4, 68; relationalism 64, 65,
68; and Simmel 55, 61–3, 72,
74–6; totality 63, 65; the 'two
ethics' 66–7; 'unity of theory and
practice' 66, 68; value freedom

73–4; value relevance 71–4;
values 68–74, 206–7
Wellmer, Albrecht 165–6, 209
Whitebook, J. 3
Wittgenstein, Ludwig 82, 102,
209
Woolgar, Steve 203

SUBJECT INDEX

abstraction, in sociology 52, 54
accountability, 21, 158, 159, 161,
   192, 200–14
action-types 69, 117, 123, 182
aesthetics, Adorno on 98–102; of
   the beautiful 151; postmodernist
   4, 152–4, of the sublime 153–4
alienation 54–7, 64, 99, 138
anti-foundationalism 9, 171, 193,
   217; in Adorno 13, 14, 89, 90,
   92, 95, 103, 104; Habermas and
   169–70; in Horkheimer 13, 14,
   78, 80–2, 85, 87–9; see also post-
   foundational radicalism
archaeology of knowledge 5, 174,
   178
autonomy, foundational instance
   of 20, 179–81, 205; in Marx 33;
   in modernist radicalism 180–1;
   in philosophy 179–80; in
   postmodernism 181
avant garde 4, 120

capitalism, Weber on 62–3
causality 13, 20, 65–6, 68, 72–3, 76,
   196–8; and developmental logic
   128
civil society 15, 109; classes of
   30–1; in Hegel 29–30, 222-3n; in
   Marx 29–35, 36, 47, 174

cognitive interests 8, 13, 193,
   194, 197, 205, 206, 237n;
   in Habermas 16, 72, 108,
   112–14, 118, 126, 128, 170,
   186, 193; in Weber 71–3, 75,
   128
colonisation of the lifeworld
   117–19, 120
common sense knowlege 10, 53,
   170
communication, in Habermas 16,
   110, 111, 114–16, 117
conversation analysis 21, 125, 200,
   211
critical rhetorics 20, 152,
   198–200, 201, 203, 211, 212;
   in Adorno 14, 92–6, 97, 98, 103,
   105; in Horkheimer 14, 81, 82,
   87; see also materialist
   hermeneutic
critical theory 13, 16, 78; goals of
   83–5; grounding of 85–6; in
   Habermas 106, 108, 111, 113,
   117, 119, 122; in Horkheimer
   78–89; validity in 82–3; see also
   Frankfurt School; Institute for
   Social Research
critique of Enlightenment 15, 35–6,
   42, 109, 120–1, 207–8
cultural sciences 51, 62, 73

257

naturalism, and nihilism 159, 161
negative dialectic 14, 90–3, 105,
  106, 151, 198–9
new philosophers 197, 233n
nihilism 17, 18, 88, 92, 135, 173,
  206–7; of postmodernism 150,
  157, 158–61, 166, 193, 200, 207,
  212, 215
nostalgia 6, 8, 167, 200; in Adorno
  14; in Habermas 118

objective culture 54, 55, 57
ontology 169, 177, 196; Adorno's
  critique of 94–8
opposition, and nihilism 159,
  161
origin, foundational instance of 20,
  174–8, 205; in Descartes 175–7;
  in Marx 33; and modernist
  radicalism 174; and
  postmodernism 174–5; and
  sociology 177–8, 181
orthogonal enquiry 21, 22, 103,
  194, 200, 211, 213, 219

paradox of consequences 12,
  64–5, 67, 68, 76, 197, 204
pathologies of modernity 218; in
  Durkheim 40, 41–2; in
  Habermas 16, 108, 117–22; in
  Weber 66, 68
performativity 160–1
pessimism 64, 68, 106, 197, 218
phantasmagoria 100
phenomenology 91, 96
philosophy 3, 10, 11, 25, 29, 32–4,
  77; Adorno on 14, 98, 102, 103;
  Althusser on 139; foundationalist
  168–9; Habermas on 129–30,
  132; of history 29; Horkheimer
  on 14, 78–82, 87; Simmel on 58;
  and sociology in Durkheim 46;
  see also 'end of philosophy'
philosophy of life see vitalism
physicalism, in postmodernism
  152, 155–6, 160, 174, 208; see
  also reductionism
political economy 25, 26, 29
positivism 99, 103–4, 152, 199

post-foundational radicalism 15,
  19, 166, 191, 192–219; in
  Adorno 14, 78, 91, 94, 103, 104,
  105; critical rhetorics in 198–200;
  irony and causality in 196–8;
  judgement and value in 206–14;
  postmodernism and 152;
  reflexivity in 201–6;
  relationalism in 193–6; resources
  for 20–3; in Simmel 49, 75–6;
  thresholds in 214–19; Weber
  and 75–6; see also anti-
  foundationalism; relationalism
post-industrialism 3, 151, 155
postmodernism 3, 17, 18, 129, 136,
  150–66, 167, 219; aesthetics 4;
  Althusser and 146–50; and
  autonomy, instance of 181;
  foundationalism of 156, 171,
  185, 187, 188, 190; metaphysics
  and 150–7; and modernist
  radicalism 135, 150–2, 210, 215,
  216, 217; as nihilism 150, 157,
  158–61, 193, 200, 215; and
  origin, instance of 174–5; phase
  two 21–2, 152, 165–6, 208–9,
  214; post-foundational radicalism
  and 152; responses to 161–6
postmodernity 3–4
power/knowledge 5, 158, 163,
  174, 183, 198
pragmatics 107, 114–16, 123–6,
  183, 200, 201
pragmatism 47, 110, 129, 170, 172
proletariat, as universal class 32–3,
  109; see also working class
protestant ethic thesis 64–5
public sphere 35; Habermas on 15,
  16, 107, 108–11, 114, 115–16,
  117, 118, 120, 121

radical social theory 10, 19; as
  nostalgia 6, 167; see also
  modernist radicalism; post-
  foundational radicalism
rational reconstruction see
  reconstructive sciences
rational will, sociology as 11, 44–5,
  75